GREAT LEADER, DEAR LEADER
Demystifying North Korea Under the Kim Clan

GREAT LEADER, DEAR LEADER

Demystifying North Korea under the Kim Clan

By

BERTIL LINTNER

SILKWORM BOOKS

Great Leader, Dear Leader: Demystifying North Korea under
the Kim Clan

ISBN 974-9575-69-5

First published in 2005 by
Silkworm Books
6 Sukkasem Road, Suthep, Muang, Chiang Mai 50200
E-mail: silkworm@silkwormbooks.info
http://www.silkwormbooks.info

Front cover graphic: Umaphon Soetphannuk
Set in Stone 10 pt. by Silk Type
Printed in Thailand by O. S. Printing House

1 3 5 7 8 6 4 2

CONTENTS

Map of the Korean Peninsula vi

Author's Note vii

Introduction 1

Family Tree: The Kim Clan 12

Chapter 1: The Summit That Shook the World 13

Chapter 2: The Famine and the *Juche* Idea 33

Chapter 3: The Great and Dear Leaders 57

Chapter 4: The Army and the Party 93

Chapter 5: The Missiles and the Nukes 111

Chapter 6: The Missions 131

Chapter 7: The Chongryun 153

Chapter 8: The Camps and the Refugees 171

Chapter 9: The Future? 187

Chronology 203

Who's Who 223

Notes 231

Annotated Bibliography 259

Index 269

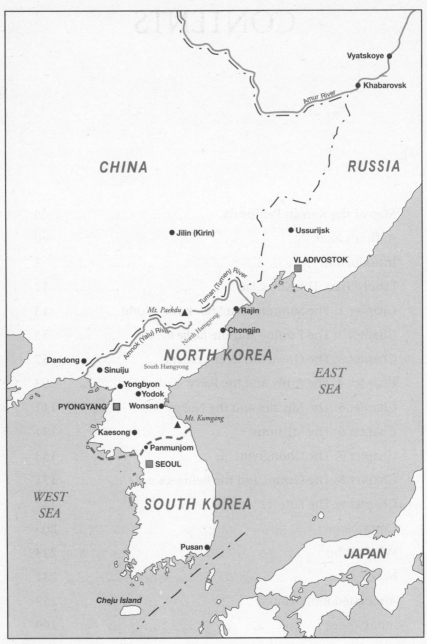

AUTHOR'S NOTE

In the fall of 2001, I was in Hong Kong researching North Korea's commercial activities in the Asia-Pacific region. The reclusive government in Pyongyang had embarked on a rather ambitious drive to increase its exports of seafood, garments, and medicines to earn foreign exchange. At first glance, it appeared that North Korea was forging a path similar to China's in the late 1970s, raising hopes that perhaps these commercial initiatives would, in the long run, lead to similar changes in the country's economy and society. The year before, the South Korean president, Kim Dae Jung, had paid his historic visit to Pyongyang, and it seemed as if his "Sunshine Policy" of rapprochement with the North was showing some results.

Returning to my hotel room from a day sifting through company registries for North Korean–owned enterprises, I turned on the TV. It was September 11. The world had changed and would probably never be the same again. I decided to broaden the scope of my research to include other aspects of the economy and politics in North Korea as well as its troubled relationship with the outside world. If the U.S. was going to wage an all-out war on terror, North Korea was likely to become a target. In January 1988, then secretary of state George Shultz placed North Korea on the list of countries supporting international terrorism following the bombing of a South Korean airliner by two North Korean agents. All 115 people on board were killed when the plane exploded in the air above the Andaman Sea on November 27, 1987. In 1983, another group of North Korean agents had detonated a bomb in Burma's capital Rangoon, killing 17 South Korean officials, including 4 cabinet ministers.

There has been little evidence of North Korean involvement in acts of terror since those bloody incidents in the 1980s, but the country nevertheless was prominently mentioned in the State Department's 1999 and 2000 reports on international terrorism. President George W. Bush's declaration of war on terror in 2001 put the leaders in Pyongyang in a precarious position and a confrontation with the U.S. seemed inevitable. Adding to the controversy was the nuclear issue. Had North Korea, as it had pledged to the international community, really scrapped its plans to develop an atomic bomb? And to what extent was it still exporting ballistic missiles and other weaponry to rogue states in the Middle East?

The outcome of my initial research was a cover story for the *Far Eastern Economic Review* titled "Another Menace: How the War on Terror Could Change North Korea," which appeared in the October 25, 2001 issue of the magazine. Then, three months later, President Bush made his now famous State of the Union speech, in which he included North Korea in the "Axis of Evil" alongside Iraq and Iran. North Korea responded with fierce, anti-American rhetoric, and began to play the nuclear card, most likely to strengthen its bargaining position with the West. In October 2002, North Korea stunned the world by saying it had the "right to possess nuclear weapons," and, in January 2003, Pyongyang withdrew from the nuclear nonproliferation treaty.

Kim Dae Jung's Sunshine Policy seemed to be giving way to a new era of tension on the Korean Peninsula, which could affect stability in the entire region, and even the rest of the world, especially if North Korea really developed nuclear weapons. Because of the significance of the North Korean issue and the far-reaching implications of what may or may not happen there, I thought it important to understand the nature of the Pyongyang regime, what kind of thinking drives its policies, and what its actions may mean for international peace and stability. In short, my ambition became to demystify North Korea, a country that is too often described in clichés such as the "Hermit Kingdom," and "the world's last Stalinist state." Journalists who had made it to Pyongyang also seemed to have little to report other than the city's wide and almost empty streets. I felt there was a real need for a more analytical look behind North Korea's own, seemingly impenetrable, Iron Curtain.

It turned out to be the biggest challenge in my twenty-five years as a journalist in Asia. Obtaining reliable information about North Korea has always been extremely difficult. The North Koreans themselves do not divulge much, and outside sources such as refugees, defectors, and U.S. and South Korean intelligence reports are more often than not politically loaded. Hazel Smith, a British professor and a senior program officer at the United Nations University in Tokyo, wrote in the March 2004 issue of the highly respected *Jane's Intelligence Review*: "Recent inquiries in the U.S. and the U.K. into alleged intelligence failures regarding the existence of Iraqi weapons of mass destruction have highlighted shortcomings in the way information is used and conclusions are drawn by Western intelligence agencies. There is a danger that the same errors could be repeated in North Korea." As an example, she mentioned reports from the North Korean famine in the mid-1990s, when foreign observers regularly cited the figure of three million dead, or more than 10 percent of the country's population. That figure was extrapolated from a 1998 survey of North Korean migrants and refugees in China, and even appeared in the reputable British medical journal *The Lancet*. The problem was that it was based on the percentage of people who were believed to have died from starvation in North Hamgyong province across the border from China. But that was the worst affected province, and not representative of the country as a whole. While conceding that there was a terrible human disaster in North Korea in the 1990s, Smith referred to the most reliable evaluation carried out by South Korean economist Suk Lee (Lee Suk), which showed that it was more likely that up to 660,000 people died from starvation and malnutrition-related diseases. However, the truth is that nobody—not even the North Korean government or the United Nations agencies—knows the real figure. As for weapons of mass destruction, it is not that difficult to calculate North Korean exports, as missiles and other equipment leave the country and then appear elsewhere. But what North Korea has in its domestic arsenal is anybody's guess.

To find answers to these and other questions, I first traveled to South Korea, where I interviewed scholars, journalists, North Korean refugees, and members of local think-tanks and human rights organizations. Another journey took me to the Russian Far East, where I interviewed people who had met both Kim Il Sung and Kim Jong Il. In order to understand why so many ethnic Koreans in Japan still support the northern regime, I went to Osaka and Kyoto, where I met current and former members of the pro-Pyongyang General Association of Korean Residents, or the Chongryun. In Hong Kong I was able to interview Ri Do Sop, then North Korea's consul general, and, in Macau, two officials from the North Korean trading firm Zokwang much to my surprise agreed to meet me. I also spent time in Washington interviewing congressional researchers and other Korea specialists.

In April 2004, I finally managed to visit North Korea, which was not easy given the fact that only a handful of journalists per year are granted visas. Although I always had an official escort, I found the officials I met surprisingly open and willing to discuss even sensitive issues such as the country's nuclear program and market reforms. While in North Korea, is was difficult not to feel deep sympathy for the ordinary people I met and saw, especially the wonderful kids at Mangyongdae Schoolchildren's Palace. This book is dedicated to them and to much less fortunate children elsewhere in North Korea with the hope that they will have a brighter and happier future.

This book is the outcome of all these interviews, meetings, and other research, and my aim is to make sense of it all in the context of international security in the post-9/11 era: Who are the rulers of this secretive nation, and where did their inspiration come from? How do they exercise power? What is the truth of the country's numerous prison camps, and who, exactly, are the people sent there? How does the regime survive economically? What about the much publicized nuclear issue? Does North Korea have the bomb? And what is the future of this country, which to many seems an anachronism in this day and age? Is it going to survive, or, if it does change or collapse, what is the most likely scenario?

I have done my best to answer all those questions, and, more precisely, endeavored to analyze the nature of the North Korean regime. Having grown up in Europe, and spent several summers in the 1970s hitchhiking through Eastern Europe, I had first-hand experience of life and society in several socialist states. But North Korea, I found, bore little or no resemblance to East Germany, Poland, Hungary or even Romania thirty years ago. It is much more tightly controlled and more disciplined. And there are no signs at all of overt dissent, unlike Eastern Europe where expressions of discontent were not uncommon before the fall of Communism in the early 1990s. The personality cult surrounding North Korea's "Great Leader," the late Kim Il Sung, and the "Dear Leader," his son Kim Jong Il, goes far beyond even that of Soviet dictator Josef Stalin more than half a century ago. Very often, official publicity about the two leaders has almost religious undertones, far removed from Marxism, which at least purports to be a science.

In order to get a better understanding of the differences between North Korea and the former socialist states of Eastern Europe, I contacted Hans Maretzki, the last East German ambassador to Pyongyang and the author of an excellent book in German about North Korea, and asked him to characterize the country's regime. His reply was more succinct than any Western observer could have put it: "A

mixture of Red Confucianism and National Socialism."
Confucianism explained the emergence of an authoritarian
elite and ruling family with the son succeeding his father as
well as the stern discipline that prevails in the country. "Red"
describes the regime's use of Marxist phraseology. But behind
the rhetoric, the state's ideology is based perhaps not on
European-style "national socialism," which equates with
Nazism, but on an extreme form of Korean nationalism.

This book does not profess to be a scholarly study of the
North Korean issue. There are many such works written by
scholars and academics whose knowledge of various aspects
of North Korean history, politics, and society are wider and
more profound than mine. To mention just a few, Don
Oberdorfer, Bruce Cumings, and Nicholas Eberstadt have
written extensively about North Korea's contemporary
history and politics; Marcus Noland has covered economic
developments; Robert Scalapino, Lee Chong Sik, Adrian Buzo,
and Suh Dae Sook have explained the emergence of
Communism in Korea, and how Kim Il Sung came to power;
Joseph Bermudez knows more about the North Korean
military than any other scholar; Aidan Foster-Carter rather
modestly calls himself "an academic turned hack," but that
has also made his in-depth knowledge of North Korea more
accessible to a wider audience; Gavan McCormack, once
sympathetic to North Korea, has also contributed much to
the understanding of the Pyongyang regime; and Helen-
Louise Hunter has written a comprehensive study of life and
society in North Korea. I have benefited from their works and
do not intend to challenge any of their views and
conclusions. This book only offers a different perspective on
the origin and evolution of the North Korean state and its
ideology. I have added a chronology to the actual text of the
book because I feel it makes it easier to see developments in
their proper context if one is aware of the sequence of events.
And for reference, I have also included a Who's Who in North
Korea, which I believe is the first of its kind.

I am grateful to a number of people who have directly and
indirectly assisted me in writing this book. I received

extraordinary help from my friend and former colleague at the *Far Eastern Economic Review*, Shim Jae Hoon, who, apart from sharing his wealth of information, introduced me to South Korean scholars and policy makers. Oh Kwi Hwan and Jeong Moontae of the *Hankyoreh* group of publications also generously helped me with contacts, information, and translations. Kevin Kim of the BBC's Seoul bureau and Paul Eckert of Reuters shared their insights with me, as did Kang Chul Hwan of the *Chosun Ilbo*, a North Korean refugee who spent ten years in the North Korean gulag before escaping to the South. In Russia, Tatiana Kirpichenko, chief of the Department of Local Research and Studies at the Far Eastern State Scientific Library in Khabarovsk, generously showed me documents from her archives and went with me to the small village of Vyatskoye, where Kim Il Sung stayed in the early 1940s—and where Kim Jong Il was really born.

Song Du Yul, South Korea's most famous exile—and, in the eyes of some, also the country's most controversial dissident—generously spent almost an entire afternoon with me in Berlin, relating his experiences from several visits to North Korea, including a long session with Kim Il Sung. Three months after my interview with Song Du Yul, he returned to South Korea for the first time in three decades. He was perhaps expecting a hero's welcome—but during his visit it was disclosed that he was indeed what his political adversaries had claimed and he had always denied: a secret, alternate politburo member of North Korea's ruling Workers' Party, and he is now being detained in South Korea on charges of subversive activities. But, in retrospect, those revelations only made my interview with him much more interesting, as his views must have reflected those of the North Korean leadership.

I am also grateful to Seo Yoon Jung for interpreting numerous interviews with North Korean refugees. Don Oberdorfer, Suh Dae Sook (or Dae-Sook Suh, as he writes his name in the West), and Joseph Bermudez answered my many questions about North Korean politics and military affairs. In Washington, Larry Niksch and Raphael Perl of the

Congressional Research Service helped me get background material on the seedier side of North Korea's overseas business ventures. Sonia Ryang, who grew up in a pro-Pyongyang Chongryun community in Japan and now teaches at Johns Hopkins University in Baltimore, helped me understand the dilemmas and the challenges of "Japan's North Koreans." Many other individual sources have to remain anonymous—especially diplomats, foreign aid workers, and government officials in Pyongyang—but they are not forgotten.

One problem in writing this book is encountered by most other authors in the field: how to romanize Korean? The Koreans have their own alphabet known as *hanggul* or *hangeul*, which literally means "Korean letters." But how to transform these into Roman script has always been problematic as there are certain sounds in Korean which have no equivalents in Western languages. To remedy the situation, the South Korean government in 2000 decided to replace the traditional way of romanizing Korean, the McCune-Reischauer System, with a new, more phonetic method. But had I followed that new system, Pyongyang would have been Pyeongyang, Mount Kumgang would have been Geumgang, and Mount Paektu would have to be written Baekdu—which would have looked strange in a North Korean context. The North Koreans have their own system of romanization, and this is a book about North, not South, Korea. I have followed a mixture of the North Korean and the McCune-Reischauer System, which I hope will make the names of places and personalities look more familiar.

There is also no consistency when it comes to writing Korean personal names. In Korea, the surname comes first, followed by a usually two-part given name. Some, but not all, prefer to hyphenate the given name to show that it is just that, while others put a comma after the surname to separate it from the given name. Thus, Kim Dae Jung can also be written Kim Dae-Jung or Kim, Dae-Jung. Koreans living in the West often put their surname last to conform with Western practice: Dae-Jung Kim. I have chosen to put the surnames first, followed by non-hyphenated given names, which is the norm in the publications I write for, the *Far Eastern Economic Review* and the *Wall Street Journal*. The only exception is the old South Korean strongman Syngman Rhee, who is commonly known by that name, not as Rhee (or Ri or Lee) Syng Man. Because so many Korean names, especially surnames, are so similar, I have also chosen to spell out the names of all Koreans in full to avoid confusion.

I hope that this book will help the reading public, as well as journalists, policy makers, and perhaps even academics, better understand the inner workings of the North Korean regime and what lies behind its policies, which often appear mercurial. North Korea may be unique in the world with its seemingly bizarre statements and actions. But it is not an enigma.

Chiang Mai, Thailand
October 2004

INTRODUCTION

Few places on earth offer a more spartan existence than Kwansan Bando, a small village at the confluence of the Han and Imjin rivers. Young and old dress in drab Mao suits and work the land by hand. The only motor vehicle plying the unpaved roads is a decrepit tractor, which chugs its way past tumbledown farm houses. At the heart of the village stands the obligatory Memorial Hall, dedicated to North Korea's founder, Kim Il Sung—the "Great Leader." He died in 1994 from a heart attack, but is still referred to as the country's "eternal president." The tiled roof is curved in the traditional Korean style, but the tall concrete obelisk in front of the hall seems out of place. Loudspeakers on high poles blare out martial music and nationalistic slogans, exhorting the people to love the fatherland and to work harder.

Remarkably, all this can be viewed through the high-powered telescopes at the Odusan Observatory on the South Korean side of the Imjin River. And in Seoul, a forty-five-minute drive away on a modern highway, young people sip Café Latte in French-style coffee houses and buy the latest designer clothes in Lotte Department Store or the trendy boutiques in the crowded back alleys off nearby Namdaemunno Avenue. Nearly everyone wears a mobile phone on a string around the neck, and, as for the Internet, South Korea is one of the most wired countries in the world. Cars and buses clog the streets, and a plethora of colorful magazines can be bought from newsstands on the sidewalks.

The capital Pyongyang with its monuments and monumental buildings is, of course, different from Kwansan Bando. But even as a showcase that projects the North Korean regime's own image of progress and prosperity, it is poles apart from the hustle and bustle of Seoul. And imagine an Asian capital that has only half-a-dozen international flights per week. Aged Russian-made Ilyushins from the national carrier, Air Koryo, fly twice weekly between Pyongyang and Beijing, and, also twice weekly, to and from Shenyang in China. Occasionally, there are additional flights to the Thai capital Bangkok and to Vladivostok or Khabarovsk in the Russian Far East.

If the two Koreas were ever to be reunited, Western experts have estimated that at least US$300 to 600 billion would be needed over a ten-year period to raise North Korean income levels to 60 percent of the South Korean average and thus prevent mass migration from North to South.[1] The World Bank believes the total cost of a Korean reunification could be as high as US$2 to 3 trillion, or about five or six times South Korea's gross domestic product. South Korean and foreign economists studying the cost of Germany's reunification calculated that the per capita GDP in North Korea is perhaps only one-tenth of that of South Korea, while the per capita GDP of East Germany was one-quarter that in West Germany.[2] Other economists have questioned these figures and suggested lower estimates, along with the fact that it is almost impossible to compare figures from capitalist South Korea with those in the socialist North, where, for instance, rents are almost nonexistent and many goods still subsidized by the government. But the consensus is the same: the South would not be able to take care of the North. The gap is just too wide today.[3] This was the main reason why former South Korean president Kim Dae Jung launched his Sunshine Policy and increased trade with the North shortly after he assumed office in February 1998. Unless the South helped North Korea develop its economy, both countries could collapse if they were reunited.

Long known for its involvement in peddling counterfeit

currency, fake cigarettes, drugs, and ballistic missiles, beginning in the 1990s North Korean business was also looking to
become more legitimate by boosting exports of seafood,
garments, and medicines. The main force behind the change
was, perhaps not surprisingly, the country's powerful
military, and the aim was to raise badly needed foreign
exchange. In June 2001, a North Korean defector described
the North Korean People's Army as the country's biggest
foreign-exchange earner. Servicemen were made to engage in
a variety of export-oriented projects including mushroom
harvesting, gold mining, medicinal-herb collection, and crab
fishing.[4]

The ruling Korean Workers' Party, or KWP, was also
reported to be operating more than forty restaurants in six
countries as a means of raising hard currency. The first North
Korean diner opened in Austria as early as March 1986, but
more followed in China, Russia, Bulgaria, and Indonesia.[5] In
2002, a restaurant called Pyongyang Ramen opened in Siem
Reap near Cambodia's famed Angkor Wat temple complex,
operated by a South Korean who is affiliated with the
Northern regime. In December the following year the same
owner opened a restaurant in the capital Phnom Penh,
serving cold noodles and other North Korean delicacies.
Called the Pyongyang Restaurant, the eatery is adorned with
neon lights, lavish gold curtains, and a karaoke machine the
size of a small car.[6] Even more imaginatively, the Tongjiang
Foreign Trade Corporation in the Chinese city of Dandong,
just across the border from North Korea, acquired in
September 2001 the exclusive right to sell North Korean
medicines in the international market—including a brand
called Cheongchun No. 1, a home-made North Korean
version of Viagra. The company's website promises that the
drug—a liquid in small bottles—will eliminate "erectile
dysfunction" and enhance "muscle power" as well as prevent
cancer.[7]

In Thailand, a North Korean–owned company, Wolmyongsan Progress Joint Venture, was for years engaged in mining
activities near the Burmese border in Kanchanaburi, west of

Bangkok, before a similar North Korean-run mining operation began in Laos in the mid-1990s. Kosun Import-Export, a North Korean-run trading company in Bangkok trades in rice, rubber, paper, tapioca and clothing. Kosun is located on the top floor of an eight-story building in a Bangkok suburb. The company is also involved in property, owning the building and renting out apartments and office space.[8]

Was North Korea following China's path towards economic modernization while maintaining the Communist Party's grip on political power? Not really. It soon became obvious that only dire straits were forcing the North Korean government to resort to commerce, not any real change of faith in the inviolability of the country's austere socialist system. North Korea was severely affected by a disruption in trading ties with former Communist allies in the late 1980s. The former Soviet Union ceased providing aid in 1987. More devastatingly, both the former Soviet Union in 1990 and China in 1992 demanded that North Korea pay standard international prices for goods, and that it pay in hard currency rather than through barter arrangements, as had previously been the case. This affected petroleum imports to the degree that they declined from 506,000 tonnes in 1989 to 30,000 tonnes in 1992.[9]

North Korea, a country that had been comparatively industrialized in the 1970s and 1980s, faced a severe crisis. Factories were forced to close because of electricity shortages. Lack of fuel for tractors and trucks, and no money to import fertilizers, caused agricultural production to decline. The outcome was famine, which the country had not experienced since the Korean War in the early 1950s. The country had to ask the United Nations and its agencies and other international organizations to provide it with emergency food aid.

Subsequently, North Korea embarked on its capitalist ventures, and even if these were caused by desperation rather than any premeditated ideological reorientation, the outcome has been a flurry of commercial activities that may change North Korea forever. The country's embassies abroad were mobilized to raise badly needed foreign exchange. This was done in the name of the diplomats themselves, or through a host of locally established trading companies, which in reality are offshoots of bigger, Pyongyang-based state trading corporations—which, in turn, are controlled by the powerful Bureau 39, the commercial wing of the KWP controlled by Kim Il Sung's son and successor, Kim Jong Il—the "Dear Leader" in official North Korean parlance.

How they raised money was immaterial. Any number of means, legal or illegal, has been employed to raise money for the state, often through the abuse of diplomatic privileges. In Bangkok, where North Korea maintains a large embassy, diplomats would import duty-free cars and sell them. In a more novel enterprise, North Koreans in Bangkok have been buying second-hand mobile telephones and sending them in diplomatic pouches to Bangladesh, where they are resold to consumers who cannot afford new ones. North Korean diplomats all over the world are involved in small business dealings which other diplomats would never dream of. They even buy duty free liquor and perfumes at airports and resell the products locally in the countries where they are based.[10] Another way of raising money is to insure a cargo consignment at a disproportionate level, and then report the goods lost. This is usually done through international insurance companies, which can do little but to pay up.[11] Fake US$100 notes, printed in North Korea, have shown up in Thailand, Cambodia, Macau, Mongolia, and India.

In a more sinister development, North Korean officials have been implicated in drug-smuggling operations in more than a dozen countries, among them Australia, India, Germany, Denmark, Norway, Finland, Nepal, Zambia, and Ethiopia.[12] While in the past the North Koreans dealt mostly in methamphetamines, recent incidents have involved heroin from Southeast Asia's Golden Triangle. In July 2002, the police in Taiwan seized 79 kilograms of high-grade heroin and arrested six suspects in a daring raid in the port city of Keelung. The investigation showed that the heroin, with a market value of US$5.63 million, was smuggled from North Korea in a fishing boat and that a Taiwanese ship had been arranged to pick up the drugs at sea and bring them into Taiwan.[13] Less than a year later, in April 2003, the Australian police intercepted a North Korean freighter off the coast of Victoria and seized 125 kilograms of heroin. Among the thirty mostly North Korean crew members arrested was a member of the KWP.[14] It is, however, uncertain if the heroin actually belonged to the North Koreans, or if they were acting as a shipping agent for traffickers in the region. The shipment to Australia seems to have involved shady businessmen in the former Portuguese enclave of Macau on the South China coast.[15]

And even in the case of more legitimate businesses, North Korea has had difficulty attracting mainstream investors. As early as 1991, the North Koreans established a "free economic and trade zone" in Rajin-Sonbong along the Tuman River near the border with China and Russia.[16] Over six hundred square kilometers were set aside for "foreign capitalists," but there have been few takers apart from ethnic Koreans from the Chongryun in Japan, who have invested because of patriotic duty rather than any expectations of quick returns. In fact, there is only one major foreign investor in the entire zone: Hong Kong entrepreneur Albert Yeung Sau Shing, who controls the Emperor Group, which has invested in gold, securities, property, and entertainment in Hong Kong and China as well as a banking venture in Cambodia.

In October 1999, Yeung opened the US$180 million Seaview Casino Hotel in Rajin-Sonbong. Although locals are banned from the establishment, it is full of gamblers from China, with the occasional visitor from Russia. The palatial casino has fifty-two slot machines and sixteen gaming tables offering everything from blackjack and baccarat to roulette. A newly built highway connects the area around the casino with China, but the surroundings are as impoverished as the rest of North Korea.[17] In Hong Kong, Yeung is best remembered for his acquittal in his dramatic trial for criminal intimidation in 1995 when all five witnesses called in by the prosecution testified that they did not remember anything. Yeung stood accused of having kept a former employee prisoner after threatening to break his leg. Even the victim himself said he could not remember what had happened.[18]

Also in 1999, Macau gambling tycoon Stanley Ho opened another casino in North Korea, but in the capital itself. Ho's US$30 million Casino Pyongyang is located in basement of the newly built luxury Yanggakdo Hotel. That casino is not big, but attracts every night a steady stream of foreign businessmen and tourists to its card tables and slot machines—and to the adjacent disco and Restaurant Macau.[19] Ho's partner at the Yanggakdo is a Macau businessman called Wong Sing-wa whose company, the Talented Dragon Investment Firm in 1990 became Pyongyang's unofficial consulate in Macau—then a Portuguese territory—with authority to issue North Korean visas. Wong, who has invested in several Macau casinos, made headlines in early 1998 when a Lisbon-based weekly, the *Independent*, protested over his presence in a delegation from Macau being received by the Portuguese president. The paper cited a Macau official as saying that Wong had "no criminal record, but we have registered information that links him to organized crime" in Macau.[20]

It soon also became clear that missiles and missile technology, rather than mushrooms, crabs, and aphrodisiacs, still made up the bulk of North Korea's exports. In December 2002, a Cambodian-registered, North Korean–owned ship was intercepted by Spanish marines, working on a U.S. tip, in the Arabian Sea—and was found to be carrying fifteen Scud missiles, fifteen conventional warheads, twenty-three tanks of nitric acid rocket propellant, and eighty-five drums of unidentified chemicals under a cargo of cement bags. The immediate destination of the shipment was Yemen, a new buyer of North Korean missiles. The North Koreans, in their own inimitable way, lashed out at the raid on its ship, calling it "an unpardonable act of piracy that wantonly encroached upon the sovereignty of the Democratic People's Republic of Korea."[21]

The ship, the North Koreans said, "was sailing for Yemen to deliver cargo in accordance with the lawful trade contract between the two countries," and the U.S. imperialists were "unrivalled barbarians and aggressors running wild to stifle the DPRK."[22] In the end, the U.S. decided to release the lethal cargo since Yemen was seen as a "friendly nation" and an ally in the war on terror. Later investigations, however, revealed that the missiles and the chemicals were ultimately delivered to Libya, which caused considerable embarrassment in Washington.[23] Other customers of North Korean missile parts and technology include Pakistan, Iran, Egypt, Syria, and Vietnam.[24]

In 2001 alone, U.S. sources asserted that North Korean missile sales totaled US$560 million, a substantial figure for a country with an estimated GDP of approximately US$17 billion. North Korean defectors believe that such sales, including the sale of other military materiel, make up as much as 40 percent of North Korea's total exports. Much of the income generated from these sales is believed to be used to acquire military hardware from abroad. What North Korea spends on arms purchases may be less in absolute terms than what South Korea does, but the much poorer North devotes 14.3 percent of GDP to its military compared to the South's 3.1 percent. And in a gesture of absolute defiance of the international community, in early 2003 North Korea asserted that it not only had "the right to possess nuclear weapons" but also admitted that it was actually developing them.[25]

A nuclear North Korea would in the eyes of many be a catastrophe. The North Korean regime has always been perceived by Western—and even Asian—politicians, diplomats, and scholars as unpredictable and inscrutable. Despite being, at least in name, a socialist state, its official publications are rife with outright metaphysics. According to one story, when in November 1996 the Dear Leader Kim Jong Il decided to inspect the situation near Panmunjom in the Demilitarized Zone between North and South Korea—the only place where the armies of the North and the South are in direct contact—a thick fog suddenly covered the area. The

Dear Leader could then come and go in the mist, observing enemy positions. When he was again at a safe distance from frontline positions, the fog lifted so he could be photographed with a group of soldiers.[26]

Such miracles never happened even in the former Soviet Union, so it is misleading to describe North Korea as the world's last Stalinist bastion. In fact, the state that Kim Il Sung created during his lifetime was not a "Workers' Paradise," as the official rhetoric went, but an old-fashioned Oriental autocracy that differed vastly from the socialist countries that emerged in Eastern Europe after World War II. For that reason, change is less likely to happen in North Korea. Its control mechanisms are absolute, and complete loyalty to the Great and Dear Leaders is expected of everyone. There is no other option to obedience than fleeing the country. There are no North Korean Andrej Sakharovs or Vaclav Havels.

The North Korean leaders are not lunatics, as they are often portrayed in the international media. They are extreme nationalists—and extremely repressive, as the country's many prison camps show. And they will stop at nothing when they have to ensure their own survival in power. Drugs, counterfeit dollars, missiles, whatever it takes. But this can be explained, if not excused, in the historical context of the emergence and development of the Democratic People's Republic of Korea.

People who criticize Kim Dae Jung's Sunshine Policy say that it assumes—wrongly in their view—that an understanding can be reached with the leaders in Pyongyang, which would then lead to closer cooperation and, hopefully, an eventual reunification of the divided peninsula. They argue that although cooperation is better than confrontation, the bitter reality is that North Korea stands and falls with the rule of the Kim clan, which they call a dynasty. And when the dynasty's end is near, they say, it could lead to economic and political instability in an already volatile part of the Asia-Pacific. How hard will it fight for its survival? Artillery barrages into South Korea? Missiles over Japan? Then, when

the Demilitarized Zone falls like the Berlin Wall, there will be
a flood of refugees leaving, not only from towns near the
South such as Kwansan Bando—whose inhabitants can just
jump into a boat and cross the Imjin River—but most
probably from throughout the country. If that crisis can be
solved, an even bigger task lies ahead: to rebuild the
economy, administration, and educational system in the
northern half of the Korean peninsula from scratch, which
would mean an enormous burden for South Korea, Japan,
and the West. Iraq at least has a fairly well-educated
population—and vast oil reserves.[27]

Others argue that this doomsday scenario is too sensational
and pessimistic. With recent economic reforms introduced in
July 2002, North Korea could change as China did in the
1980s. In the spring of 2004, Pyongyang, at least, seemed to
be more open and relaxed than ever before. A new market
had just opened in a Pyongyang suburb where locally
produced and imported goods were sold at market prices.
People were wearing more colorful clothes, and there were
more cars and bicycles in the streets. Small kiosks made from
cardboard or canvas on a wooden frame selling drinks,
snacks, and cigarettes were popping up in street corners all
over the city. These, and a host of new trading companies,
were not privately owned, but definitely operated as such.[28]

But there are also huge differences between China and
North Korea. China has always been an empire with a huge
population. North Korea is much smaller and its society
much more centrally controlled. There were several power
centers in China even before the old socialist economy was
dismantled in the 1980s. In North Korea there is only one:
the central government controlled by Kim Jong Il and his
close associates. Given its size and global as well as regional
importance, China has to listen to and cooperate with the
rest of the world. North Korea can shut itself off and ignore
international opinion.

However, in the long term it is inevitable that change will
come to North Korea as well. This could happen through
peaceful evolution—or the regime could come to a violent

end through assassinations and infighting leading to collapse and chaos. Outside intervention is also a possibility, especially after U.S. President George W. Bush's 2002 State of the Union speech. But no matter how the Korean crisis finally plays out, this long-suffering country is bound to see more misery and suffering before the situation improves. It was to explore the possibilities of minimizing the hardships, and to find a peaceful solution to the crisis on the Korean peninsula, that Kim Dae Jung undertook his historic journey to Pyongyang in June 2000.

The Kim Clan

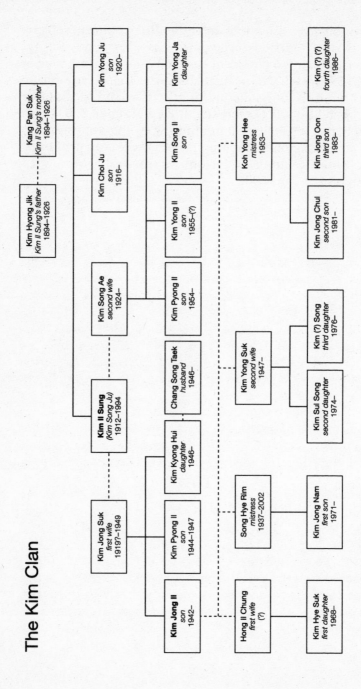

Kim Hyong Jik
Kim Il Sung's father
1894–1926

Kang Pan Suk
Kim Il Sung's mother
1894–1926

Kim Yong Ju
son
1920–

Kim Chol Ju
son
1916–

Kim Song Ae
second wife
1924–

Kim Il Sung
(Kim Song Ju)
1912–1994

Kim Jong Suk
first wife
1919?–1949

Kim Yong Ja
daughter

Kim Song Il
son

Kim Yong Il
son
1955–(?)

Kim Pyong Il
son
1954–

Chang Song Taek
husband
1946–

Kim Kyong Hui
daughter
1946–

Kim Pyong Il
son
1944–1947

Kim Jong Il
son
1942–

Koh Yong Hee
mistress
1953–

Kim Yong Suk
second wife
1947–

Song Hye Rim
mistress
1937–2002

Hong Il Chung
first wife
(?)

Kim (?) (?)
fourth daughter
1986–

Kim Jong Oon
third son
1983–

Kim Jong Chul
second son
1981–

Kim (?) Song
third daughter
1976–

Kim Sui Song
second daughter
1974–

Kim Jong Nam
first son
1971–

Kim Hye Suk
first daughter
1968–

Copyright © 2004 Asia Pacific Media Services

CHAPTER 1

THE SUMMIT THAT SHOOK THE WORLD

When his presidential jet touched down at Pyongyang on June 13, 2000, Kim Dae Jung must have had much on his mind. For the seventy-three-year-old former dissident who had survived at least one attempt on his life and several stints in South Korean prisons to become his country's president, this visit would mark the highpoint of his long struggle to improve relations between the two Koreas. But whatever Kim Dae Jung was feeling as he stepped onto the tarmac at Sunan Airport, his face bore his familiar stoic expression. Lumbering down the red carpet towards him was his host, a plump, frizzy-haired man some fifteen years his junior, who—unlike Kim Dae Jung, in his immaculate suit and necktie—wore a Mao suit at least one size too small for him. As they greeted each other, an army band played stirring martial music, while a well-drilled crowd waved paper flowers and chanted, "Kim Jong Il! Kim Jong Il!" Only then, when it had been made unequivocally clear who the host was on this historic, sunny day in June, the crowd also shouted "Kim Dae Jung! Kim Dae Jung!"[1]

A guard of honor, representing the three services of the Korean People's Armed Forces, goose-stepped in perfect formation past the two men as they shook hands. History was being made: Kim Dae Jung was the first South Korean leader to visit the North. It was also the first direct flight between Seoul and Pyongyang since the Korean War in the early

1950s. And never before had the North Korean leader Kim Jong Il himself come to the airport to welcome a visitor.

Some 600,000 North Koreans had been mobilized to greet Kim Dae Jung and his entourage of 180 advisers, businessmen, and South Korean journalists. Men in Western style trousers, white shirts, and neckties, and women in traditional Korean *hambok* dresses—called *chima jogori* in the North—lined the road and cheered as the two Kims' Lincoln Continental stretch limousine, surrounded by policemen on motorbikes and followed by a motorcade of Mercedes Benzes, drove from the airport to the city. It was all meticulously choreographed, but as the drama was being played out live on South Korean television, some started to applaud in their homes in Seoul and elsewhere. Many cried. Would it now be possible to visit long-lost relatives north of the demilitarized zone? Could it, perhaps, even be the beginning of the end of the DMZ, which had separated the Korean peninsula—and people—for half a century? Was this like the collapse of the Berlin Wall in 1991 under the pressure from another people yearning for reunification?

At 11:45 a.m., Kim Dae Jung and Kim Jong Il held their first round of talks at the Paekhwawon State Guesthouse in downtown Pyongyang. Kim Dae Jung was no doubt impressed by the event, but he maintained a straight face and a firm composure. Kim Jong Il appeared somewhat tense in the beginning, but then became more relaxed and even cracked a few jokes as the two leaders raised a toast to the summit. Kim Dae Jung, normally a teetotaler, sipped gingerly on his glass of red wine. Kim Il Jong drained his in one gulp, and went on to do most of the talking before the TV cameras. "The people of Pyongyang are impressed that you have taken the brave decision to come here," he said. "All the South Koreans including myself are impressed that you came to receive me at the airport," Kim Dae Jung replied.

The rest of the three-day visit was spent discussing family reunions and trade relations between the two Koreas. Ri Hui Ho, Kim Dae Jung's wife, visited the Changgwang Kindergarten where North Korean children—all of them well

dressed and unusually rotund and rosy-cheeked—sang
nursery rhymes and played violins. Visibly moved, the First
Lady hugged and kissed the kids. On Wednesday, Kim Dae
Jung and Kim Jong Il signed a North-South Joint Declaration
"reflecting the desire and will of all the fellow countrymen to
achieve the sacred cause of reunification and build a
prosperous country by the united efforts of the nation."
When it was time to part company on Thursday, the two
Kims also exchanged gifts. Kim Dae Jung gave Kim Jong Il
two Chindo puppy dogs named Pyonghwa ("peace") and
Tongil ("reunification"). In return, Kim Jong Il presented Kim
Dae Jung with two Pungsan puppy dogs called Uri ("we") and
Turi ("together").[2]

Not only the Koreans but the whole world watched in awe
and astonishment as the last frontier of the cold war appeared
to be melting away. Many were also taken aback by Kim Jong
Il's jovial style and mundane behavior. Was this really the
reclusive and mysterious Communist dictator who seemed to
be from another planet? The British weekly *The Economist* put
a waving Kim Jong Il on its cover with the headline
"Greetings, Earthlings!"[3]

Two days after the summit, loudspeakers in both the North
and the South, which for twenty years had been blaring out
propaganda at each other across the DMZ, fell silent. Then
followed a flurry of exchanges between the two Koreas, and
there were talks about opening rail and road links, and
perhaps even direct flights between Seoul and Pyongyang. It
was widely expected that Kim Jong Il would pay a return visit
to Seoul, and in the South Korean capital people impersonat-
ing the North Korean leader greeted pedestrians on the
streets. The feared leader of the North was gaining near-cult
status in the South.

More importantly for North Korea, South Korean investors
began to look at business opportunities north of the DMZ.
The heads of South Korea's four largest *chaebols*, or business
conglomerates—Samsung, LG, SK, and Hyundai—had
accompanied Kim Dae Jung to Pyongyang and pledged to
invest between US$500 million and US$1 billion in the

coming five to ten years. Very few South Korean companies already in operation in North Korea had actually made a profit. But many were willing to write off their losses, partly because of sentimental reasons. The chairmen of some of the biggest investors in the North—the Kohap Group, Rinnai Korea, and the controversial Rev. Moon Sun Myung's Unification Church—were refugees who had escaped to the South during the Korean War. For them, investing in the North was more an emotional homecoming than a money-making opportunity.[4]

Kim Dae Jung's Sunshine Policy was first articulated in a speech he gave at the Heritage Foundation in Washington D.C. on September 30, 1994, several years before he became president. Citing a well-known Aesop's fable on "wind and sunshine," he argued that sunshine is more effective than strong wind in making North Korea come out of its isolation.[5] In another speech delivered at the School of Oriental and African Studies in London on April 4, 1998—after he had been elected president—Kim Dae Jung was even more upbeat:

> The Republic is now able to push a North Korean policy with self-confidence arising from firm public support. I have been steadfast in advocating what I call a "sunshine policy" which seeks to lead North Korea down a path toward peace, reform and openness through reconciliation, interaction and cooperation with the South. As President, I will carry out such ideas step by step.[6]

Those steps were summarized as easy tasks first, and difficult tasks later; economy first, politics later; nongovernmental organizations first, government later; and give first, and take later.[7] This was not appeasement, Kim Dae Jung and his men argued, but a flexible approach which alone could defuse the decades-long tension on the Korean peninsula. There was only one alternative to the Sunshine Policy: continued confrontation that could even lead to war. With a little patience and endurance, active engagement would, in the long run, "thaw the frozen minds of the North Korean leadership."[8]

It seemed a reasonable policy, and North Korea's old allies, China and Russia, were also active behind the scenes to encourage Pyongyang to adopt, at the very least, the Chinese model of development. Two weeks before the summit, Kim Jong Il had traveled to China in his special train, most probably for consultations with the leaders in Beijing. And a month after the meeting between the two Kims, Russian president Vladimir Putin paid a visit to Pyongyang, the first ever to North Korea by a Russian head of state. Relations between Russia and North Korea had been cool after the Soviet Union's "betrayal" of its distant, Communist neighbor in abolishing the old barter-trade agreement between the two countries, and then establishing diplomatic relations with South Korea.[9]

For many years, the Swedish embassy had been the only Western mission in Pyongyang. Now, Spain, the Philippines, Australia, Britain, Canada, Italy, Germany, Turkey, and the Netherlands established diplomatic relations with North Korea, though few of them actually opened embassies in Pyongyang. But as tokens of support for Kim Dae Jung's Sunshine Policy, these were nevertheless important gestures. North Korea also began to attend the Asian Regional Forum, a gathering of Asian countries organized by ASEAN, the Association of Southeast Asian Nations. Vice Marshal Cho Myong Rok, number two in North Korea's powerful National Defense Commission after its chairman, Kim Jong Il, was even received at the White House—the highest ranking official from Pyongyang to be accorded such treatment.[10]

Then came what many South Koreans had been waiting for: the reunion of families separated by the Korean War. Several hundred North Koreans were allowed to travel to the south to meet long-lost relatives. Before they arrived for these emotional meetings, special rooms had been prepared with the chairs positioned close to each other and plenty of tissue paper. South Koreans also traveled north to see their mothers, fathers, and other relatives. A choir of North Korean children toured South Korea, and drew applause and more tears from their audiences. While in Pyongyang, Kim Dae Jung had said, "I sincerely hope that this visit will help deliver the seventy million people of Korea from fear of war," referring to the population of the entire peninsula.[11]

That hope now seemed almost a reality. When the Sydney Olympics opened on September 15, North and South Korean athletes arrived at the stadium aboard the same buses. They then marched together behind a "reunification flag," a single blue-on-white banner with a map of the Korean peninsula. The athletes also wore identical uniforms—dark blue jackets and beige pants—and held hands while a crowd of 110,000 people cheered them on. "It's heartwarming," said Park Pil Soon, a spokesman for the South Korean delegation. "I believe that a cooperative mood between the two sides that made the joint march possible will accelerate inter-Korean sports exchanges." Kim Un Ryong, an International Olympics Committee member from South Korea, added: "We became one body, the same race of the same blood."[12] The North and South Koreans then competed separately, but this had been an unprecedented sign of solidarity and unity among the people of the divided peninsula.

Changes were also noticed along the DMZ. After the loudspeakers had stopped their tirades, the exhibition halls on the southern side removed much of the old anti-Pyongyang propaganda material, and began to display goods from the North: liquor, beer, ginseng, and handicrafts. In 1989, Lim Dong Won, head of South Korea's National Intelligence Service, had proposed that part of the DMZ should be turned into an "Offensive-Weapons Free Zone." Tanks, mechanized infantry, troop carriers, and self-propelled artillery would be excluded and the number of troops would be subject to agreed limits.[13] Others suggested turning the DMZ into a nature reserve with a bird sanctuary. South Korea promised humanitarian aid to North Korea and deregulated the rules for private fundraising activities.

The rest of the world was taken aback by these dramatic events, and to give full backing to Kim Dae Jung's bold initiatives, the U.S. secretary of state, Madeleine Albright, flew in to Pyongyang in late October. She spent more time with Kim Jong Il than any other Western leader had done, and although she had no illusions about him, she left with the impression that "he is not a nut, but a pretty ham-handed and tough negotiator. Brinkmanship is a North Korean specialty."[14] Kim Jong Il, Albright said, was isolated but not uninformed: "He watches CNN. He has computers. While he lives in his own little world, he knows what is going on out there, even if he twists the information in his own warped way." Somewhat curiously, Kim Jong Il told Albright that he was looking at other economic models, including the Swedish one, which she found "clearly ridiculous." Sweden may be a social welfare state, but its economy is by no means state-controlled. However, it seemed evident that Kim Jong Il was searching for solutions to his country's problems. "Though publicly blaming the weather for famine, he knows that the system doesn't work," Albright concluded.

At a grand ceremony in the City Hall of Oslo, Norway on December 10, Kim Dae Jung received the most prestigious of international awards: the Nobel Peace Prize. The old dissident who had spent years in jail and under house arrest, and who, during the dictatorial regime of Park Chung Hee in the 1970s, was kidnapped in Japan by agents of South Korea's intelligence services and almost killed, joined the likes of Tibet's Dalai Lama, Burma's pro-democracy leader Aung San Suu Kyi, Calcutta's Mother Teresa, the United Nations peacekeeping forces, South African bishop Desmond Tutu, and American civil rights pioneer Martin Luther King.

Gunnar Berge, chairman of the Norwegian Nobel Committee, proudly announced that Kim Dae Jung received "the prize for his lifelong work for democracy and human rights in South Korea and East Asia in general, and for peace and reconciliation with North Korea in particular." Kim Dae Jung, Berge went on, "has had the will to break with 50 years of ingrained hostility, and to reach out a cooperative hand across what has probably been the world's most heavily guarded frontier. His has been the kind of personal and political courage which, regrettably, is all too often missing in other conflict-ridden regions."[15]

In his acceptance speech, Kim Dae Jung stated un-ambiguously that unification "can wait until such a time when both sides feel comfortable enough in becoming one again, no matter how long it takes. At first, North Korea resisted, suspecting that the Sunshine Policy was a deceitful plot to bring it down. But our genuine intent and con-sistency, together with broad support for the Sunshine Policy from around the world, including its moral leaders such as Norway, convinced North Korea that it should respond in kind. Thus, the South-North summit could be held."[16] Next to the summit itself, the solemn ceremony in Oslo was no doubt the highest recognition of the success of his Sunshine Policy. Kim Dae Jung was an international hero, who had brought his divided people together after decades of separation.

Then came the bombshell. At a National Assembly sub-committee session in Seoul on September 25, 2002, lawmaker Eom Ho Sung from the opposition Grand National Party, alleged that Hyundai Merchant Marine, a private company, had "borrowed" US$327 million from the state-run Korea Development Bank, the KDB, shortly before the Kim-Kim summit. The shipping firm later borrowed an extra US$7.5 million—and all of it, the Grand National Party claimed, was delivered to North Korea to pay for the summit.[17] Kim Dae Jung's visit to North Korea had originally been scheduled for June 12–14, and the reason for the one-day delay was supposed to be that North Korea wanted to make sure the money was in one of its overseas bank accounts. Han Kwang Ok, Kim Dae Jung's presidential secretary, had pressured a reluctant KDB chief to extend the loan, the opposition alleged.[18]

To prove his point, Eom Ho Sung cited a March 2002 report by the U.S. Congressional Research Service, which spelled out the allegation:

> The U.S. military command in Korea and the Central Intelligence Agency reportedly believe that North Korea is using for military purposes the large cash payments, over

(US)$400 million since 1998, that the Hyundai Corporation has made to the North Korean government for the right to operate a tourist project at Mount Kumgang in North Korea. (According to informed sources, Hyundai has made secret payments to North Korea, which may bring the total payments closer to $800 million.) The U.S. Central Intelligence Agency reportedly delivered a memorandum to the R.O.K. [Republic of Korea] government in February 2001 outlining U.S. suspicions.[19]

The extra US$400 million was supposed to be the amount that the South Korean government had used to "persuade" the North Koreans to agree to the summit. As the scandal unraveled, an unnamed South Korean official went public, asserting that US$200 million was sent to a Bank of China account in Hong Kong on June 12, 2000—the day before the summit. The money went from there to a bank account in the former Portuguese enclave of Macau, which reverted to Chinese rule in 1999—and that for years had served as a base for North Korean operations in the region. The Macau account belonged to Pak Ja Pyong, head of Zokwang, a North Korean company in the territory that is directly controlled by the elusive Bureau 39 of the ruling Korean Workers' Party, the official claimed.[20] For years, Zokwang has been using Macau as a base for arms deals, training of intelligence agents, and the dissemination of counterfeit US$100 bills.[21] Where the other part of the alleged US$200 million went was never revealed; whether it was paid later to the same account, or to another bank account elsewhere in the world remains unclear.

The Hyundai Company, on the other hand, was one of South Korea's most remarkable success stories. Set up in 1945 in Seoul as the modest Hyundai ("modern") Auto Repair Shop by Chung Ju Yung, who was born in deep poverty in what later became North Korea, it had grown into one of South Korea's—and Asia's—largest conglomerates. It was involved in construction, shipping and shipbuilding, and it made computer chips and cars that were exported all over the world. In order to repay his country for his good fortune, Chung established in 1977 the Asan Foundation—named after his home village in North Korea—which sponsored scholarships for research and schemes to improve health care for the underprivileged, especially in remote, rural areas.[22]

In 1992, Chung decided to enter politics and, with the help of the small Unification National Party, he ran for president. He was unsuccessful, but fared much better in forging business links with North Korea. Six years later, he became the first South Korean civilian to enter North Korea without an escort when he and his sons crossed the DMZ with five hundred head of cattle to feed the villagers of Asan. He also masterminded a tourism project at the North's scenic Mount Kumgang resort, first accessed by cruise ships from South Korea and later overland across the easternmost stretch of the DMZ. He had to pay enormous royalties to the North for that privilege, but Kim Dae Jung's government touted the project as a highlight of its Sunshine Policy, and decided to subsidize it.[23] These payments to North Korea also went through Zokwang's bank account in Macau, South Korea's opposition politicians asserted.

When Chung passed away on March 21, 2001 at the age of eighty-five, he was mourned as a national hero on both sides of the DMZ. North Korea expressed its condolences and even sent a delegation to his funeral. The patriarch who had risen from rags to riches was survived by his wife, Byun Joong Suk, six sons—Mong Joon, Mong Koo, Mong Kun, Mong Yun, Mong Hun, and Mong Il—a daughter, Kyung Hee, four brothers, a sister, and number of grandchildren.[24] Chung Mong Hun took over as chairman of Hyundai Asan, the mother company, while Mong Koo ran Hyundai Motors, and Mong Joon was in charge of Hyundai Heavy Industries.

The Chung brothers now found themselves mired in controversy over the money that supposedly went to North Korea. At first, they vehemently denied that any such pay-off had been made. Hyundai Merchant Marine admitted that it had indeed borrowed 400 billion Korean won, and then an additional 90 billion won, or altogether about US$400

million, from the KDB in 2000, but those were "operating
funds" to save the company from bankruptcy, and "not even
a penny" was sent illegally to North Korea.[25] In an interview
with the South Korean news agency Yonhap, Chung Mong
Hun stated categorically, "I wasn't involved in any alleged
diversion of the KDB loan, and the money was not sent to
North Korea. I will testify against the claims, if necessary."[26]
Mong Hun was at the time staying in a hotel in Los Angeles—
like so many others accused in the scandal, he preferred to be
away from South Korea. Hahn Hwa Kap, chairman of Kim
Dae Jung's Millennium Democratic Party, also denied the
allegation and attacked the opposition: "The Grand National
Party should stop raising groundless suspicions about the
KDB loan, which those involved said was offered to save the
giant Hyundai company from collapsing."[27]

But the controversy refused to go away, and, to the
embarrassment of the government, a former KDB governor,
Eun Nak Yong, testified at the National Assembly's hearings
into the affair—and said that the state-run bank's extension
of loans to Hyundai Merchant Marine in June 2000 was "not
a normal practice." His predecessor and bank governor at the
time of the loan, Lee Keun Young, had told him that "I had
no choice . . . I just followed the orders of my superiors." The
documents made by KDB for the loan had neither the
signature from Hyundai Merchant Marine's then president
Kim Choong Shik, nor a business address. Eun Nak Yong also
claimed that the loan was wrongly recorded as 4, not 400,
billion won.[28]

Before long, the pressure became too strong. Kim Dae Jung
was, after all, a principled man. On February 15, 2003—ten
days before he was to hand over the presidency to his
successor and long-time follower Roh Moo Hyun—the
admission finally came. Kim Dae Jung and Lim Dong Won,
now former head of South Korea's National Intelligence
Service, stated in televised speeches that the government had
indeed condoned the payment by Hyundai to North Korea
"for the sake of peace and reconciliation." A grim-faced Kim
Dae Jung went on to say, "what I have wanted the most was

to leave office at the end of my tenure on a happy note. I am extremely sorry. I feel wretched and I am in pain."[29]

It has never been clear how much the South actually had paid to the North for the summit, and the whole issue of the alleged transfer of funds to North Korea remains hugely controversial. Some South Koreans argued that even if a huge payment was made, it was worth it because tension on the peninsula had indeed eased after the historic Kim-Kim summit. Kim Dae Jung, on his part, urged the citizens and the opposition not to re-ignite the old confrontation by pushing for an investigation—but that was exactly what the Grand National Party began to demand. An independent counsel was appointed, and Kim Dae Jung's Sunshine Policy was in tatters. The whole affair took a tragic turn when Chung Mong Hun, who had returned from his self-imposed exile in Los Angeles, killed himself by jumping from the twelfth floor of Hyundai's headquarters in central Seoul on August 4, 2003. Foreign and local businessmen attended the funeral, and a large-scale mourning ceremony was held in Pyongyang, although the North Koreans did not send a delegation to Seoul, as they had done when his father died two years before. The tourist trips to Mount Kumgang were suspended to show respect for Chung Mong Hun, and condolences were expressed at the altar set up by Hyundai at the mountain resort. In a message sent to Seoul, North Korea lashed out against the investigators and the opposition: "Chung's death was not a suicide in the true sense of the word, but a murder by South Korea's independent counsel and main opposition Grand National Party."[30]

Chung's suicide coincided with escalating tension on the Korean peninsula over Pyongyang's decision to resume its nuclear program, which should have ended in October 1994, when the United States and North Korea signed an agreement in Geneva, Switzerland. Called "The Agreed Framework between the United States of America and the People's Democratic Republic of Korea," it stipulated that North Korea should replace its graphite-moderated reactors and facilities with light-water reactor power plants—and remain party to the Treaty of the Non-Proliferation of Nuclear Weapons. The United States promised to help provide those light-water plants, and to deliver five hundred thousand tons of oil annually to help North Korea overcome its energy shortages.[31]

The agreement was meant to end a major crisis over North Korea's nuclear program, which it claimed had only peaceful purposes, but which the United States and others thought was aimed at developing nuclear weapons. The nuclear facility at Yongbyon, ninety-two kilometers north of Pyongyang, was suspected of having produced sufficient plutonium to make two or three nuclear bombs.[32] At one stage, then U.S. president Bill Clinton even contemplated a surgical air strike against Yongbyon, but the crisis was defused, at least temporarily, by an unprecedented visit to Pyongyang by former U.S. president Jimmy Carter in June 1994, just a few weeks before the death of the Great Leader, Kim Il Sung. His son and successor, Kim Jong Il, continued overseeing the negotiations with the United States, and, following the Geneva agreement, a special organization, the Korean Peninsula Energy Development Organization, or KEDO, was set up to implement it.

The oil pledged by the United States was forthcoming, but the promised construction of the light-water power plants dragged on as both sides viewed each other with utmost suspicion. The United States never believed North Korea had really abandoned its plans to develop nuclear weapons, and the North Koreans never fully trusted the Americans, who, after all, had nearly forty thousand troops stationed south of the DMZ. The new president of the United States, George W. Bush, was also seen as a hawk, very different from Clinton, who had sent Albright to Pyongyang and had himself made plans to visit North Korea.

The stand-off grew more tense when U.S. assistant secretary of state, James Kelly, visited Pyongyang in mid-October 2002. According to him, the North Koreans had revealed that they were conducting a secret nuclear weapons program based on the process of uranium enrichment. Vice Foreign Minister

Kang Sok Ju, who signed the 1994 Agreed Framework on behalf of North Korea, declared that his country also possessed "more powerful weapons."[33] President Bush—who had already declared North Korea part of his "Axis of Evil"—was outraged. The oil deliveries were suspended, and Bush insisted that North Korea would have to abide by its nuclear agreements before any more crude could be delivered. Bush denounced Kim Jong Il as a "pygmy" and, in a discussion with U.S. journalist Bob Woodward, he blurted out "I loathe Kim Jong Il!" shouting and waving his finger in the air. Bush went on to declare his preference for "toppling" the North Korean regime.[34]

The North Koreans were not amused and responded by restarting the Yongbyon installations and, on January 10, 2003, withdrawing from the nuclear nonproliferation treaty. On June 9, North Korea admitted publicly for the first time that it was seeking nuclear weapons, but put the blame on the United States for the need to develop such an arsenal. According to the *Korean Central News Agency*, "We have no option but to have a nuclear deterrence if the United States keeps its hostile policy and continues its nuclear threat toward the Democratic People's Republic of Korea."[35]

Kang Sok Ju's admission to Kelly, which triggered the crisis, remains somewhat of a mystery. Was it what Albright called brinkmanship? North Korea was seeking a bilateral U.S.–North Korean nonaggression pact, and Kang Sok Ju and others might also have thought that playing the nuclear card would force the Americans into negotiating an agreement. The problem for the Americans, of course, was that the proposed bilateral pact would replace the 1953 armistice, which ended the Korean War, and would not include South Korea as a participant.[36] But that was perhaps exactly what North Korea wanted, to be recognized as the sole representative of the Korean people. Or was the admission, as Pyongyang stated, pure necessity? After all, American advances in precision-guided munitions had made it feasible to destroy the one hundred thousand artillery tubes that the North Korean military had installed in mountains north of the DMZ. Bruce Cumings, a leading U.S. Korea expert at the University of Chicago, argued, "in the absence of credible security guarantees any general sitting in Pyongyang would now move to a more reliable deterrent."[37]

Whatever the case, North Korea's announcement backfired badly. The country became even more isolated than before, and even the South Korean government, Sunshine Policy at least officially still in place, urged the North to abandon its nuclear ambitions. At the Asia-Pacific Economic Cooperation, or APEC, summit in Shanghai on October 26, 2002, President Bush, Japan's prime minister Junichiro Koizumi and President Kim Dae Jung issued a joint statement that North Korea should "dismantle this [secret] program in a prompt and verifiable manner and . . . come into full compliance with all its international [nuclear] commitments."[38]

The North Koreans did not fare much better with the Japanese. In mid-September 2002, Japanese premier Koizumi paid a historic visit to Pyongyang to ease long-standing tension between North Korea and the country's former colonial master. To the surprise of many, the North Koreans seized the opportunity to come forth with another astonishing admission. They said that their intelligence agencies had indeed abducted a number of Japanese citizens. Thirteen in all, the North Koreans said, had been taken away from 1977 to 1983, and they had been used to help train North Korean spies to pose as Japanese. Eight had died, but five were living in Pyongyang. Kim Jong Il apologized for the abductions, which he blamed on special-forces agents "carried away by a quest for glory." He promised Koizumi that they had been punished, but provided no details as to the fate of those agents.[39] But a joint declaration, signed by Kim Jong Il and Koizumi on September 17, stated, "with respect to the outstanding issues of concern related to the lives and security of the Japanese nationals, the Democratic People's Republic of Korea . . . confirmed that it would take appropriate measures so that these regretful incidents that took place under the abnormal bilateral relationship would never happen in the future."[40]

Kim Jong Il's startling revelation was most probably meant to improve relations between North Korea and Japan. But, like Kong Sok Ju's admission to Kelly that North Korea had a nuclear program, it backfired badly. The news caused an uproar in Japan, where many suspected that the North Koreans were behind a series of mysterious disappearances in the late 1970s and early 1980s. The pro-Pyongyang Koreans in Japan, the Chongryun, and several respected Japanese academics, on the other hand, had for years claimed it was nonsense. Even such an established scholar and Korea expert as Haruki Wada wrote as recently as January 2001 that "there is little credibility" to the reports of abductions by North Korea. He examined several cases, and found discrepancies in birth dates and other personal details.[41] Then, suddenly, the North Koreans provided data about all those missing persons.

The fortunate five survivors—two couples and a forty-four-year-old woman called Hitomi Soga, who had married Charles Robert Jenkins, a former soldier from the United States army who defected to the North in 1965—were even allowed to travel to Japan to visit their relatives. These were supposed to be brief family reunions, but none in the group went back to Pyongyang. North Korea claimed they had been "kidnapped" by the Japanese and demanded their return— but to no avail. For the two couples it was perhaps easier to stay on in Japan. But it must have been hard for Hitomi Soga, who received a long letter from her American husband back in Pyongyang, where he was staying with their two teenage daughters. Despite this, she decided not to return to North Korea.[42]

The backlash against the Chongryun Koreans was especially severe. The young ones attending Chongryun schools in Osaka—easily distinguished from Japanese children by their traditional Korean costumes—were spat at in the streets, and people shouted at them to "go home." Many Koreans in Japan, both old and young, deserted the Chongryun. They felt betrayed by the leaders, whom they had trusted implicitly and never thought would lie to them. The North Korean admission came as more of a shock to the

Chongryun Koreans than to the Japanese, who just had their suspicions confirmed.[43]

In the span of six months, North Korea had managed to ruin relations with Japan and alienate the rest of the world by restarting its nuclear program. Its new economic ventures also ran into unforeseen troubles. On July 1, 2002, Pyongyang surprised the world by announcing changes in economic policy. There would be "micro economic changes, macro economic changes, special economic zones, and aid-seeking."[44] Until then, citizens had been able, officially, at least as there was an acute shortage of many essential goods, to obtain rice and other commodities in exchange for state-supplied coupons. Now, money had to be used and prices were adjusted to approach those prevailing in the informal markets. Wages were to be determined by the productivity of the individual worker.[45]

Factories, which previously had got machinery and economic subsidies from the state, were told that, from now, they would have to buy their equipment. And it would not be enough to produce, let's say, two thousand teacups a week. They would have to be of acceptable standards as well. The "adjustments"—the word "reform" was avoided as that would be tantamount to admitting that the system was wrong and had to be changed—were the first real step away from central planning since the northern part of the Korean peninsula came under Communist rule in 1945.[46] Then, in August 2002, the exchange rate for the North Korean won was also adjusted to a more realistic level. Before that, it had been fixed at 2.16 per dollar, and cynics noted that Kim Jong Il was born on February 16. The new official rate was 150 to the dollar, while the black-market rate at the time remained at about 230.

These changes seemed reasonable even if they, in the beginning, led to massive price increases, and, one would assume, rampant inflation. But the world was more stunned when the official North Korean news agency announced that an agreement had been signed on September 23, 2002 to appoint Yang Bin, a thirty-nine-year-old immensely wealthy

Chinese-Dutch entrepreneur "governor" of a new Hong Kong–style "Special Administrative Region," in Sinuiju on the Amnok River, which forms the northwestern border with China.[47] Born in Nanjing west of Shanghai, Yang Bin had emigrated to the Netherlands in 1987 and acquired Dutch citizenship. He later returned to China, striking it rich as an orchid breeder and property developer.[48] Yang was reputedly the second richest man in China when he decided to do business with the North Koreans.

The idea was to move the five hundred thousand residents of Sinuiju to other parts of North Korea and replace them with two hundred thousand hand-picked "model workers" who would turn the Special Administrative Region into a capitalist paradise with free enterprise and privately owned companies and factories. A law enacted by the North Korean Supreme People's Assembly on September 12 stipulated that the new "SAR"—an abbreviation usually reserved for the former British and Portuguese enclaves of Hong Kong and Macau in China—would have an "independent legislative council, regional and district administrations, courts ranging from the supreme court to local ones, police, prosecution offices of the region and districts, and that it shall use its own emblem and flag plus those of the state."[49]

The Chinese renminbi, the U.S. dollar, and the "Korean won"—most probably the North, not South, Korean won—would be used as currency, and Korean, Chinese, and English would be the official languages of the area. But it was not to be a place to which any North Koreans could move and look for jobs. A wall would be erected around it to keep "unauthorized" people out. To finalize the unusual agreement, Yang Bin was photographed shaking hands with Kim Yong Sul, chairman of North Korea's Committee for the Promotion of External Economic Cooperation, and the news was released to the media.[50]

This new entity was going to be more autonomous, and, so Yang and the North Koreans hoped, more successful than the Rajin-Sonbong "free economic and trade zone" that was set up near the borders with Russia and China in 1991. Rajin-

Sonbong was remote and isolated. In contrast, the Sinuiju Special Administrative Region was located across the Amnok from the bustling Chinese city of Dandong, and it was thought that the best chance of success lay in an infusion of Chinese investment and infrastructural support.[51] Yang was also banking on investment from South Korea, and planned to visit Seoul to meet with president Kim Dae Jung and Korean businessmen on October 7.[52]

The problem was that the North Koreans forgot to inform the Chinese authorities about the creation of a self-governing, capitalist enclave on their doorstep. Beijing learned about the move on the same day as Pyongyang made it public, September 23.[53] Further deepening the controversy, Yang was suspected of tax evasion, stock speculation, and illegal real estate development—charges he naturally, vehemently denied.[54] Whatever had upset the Chinese, Yang was arrested in the northeastern city of Shenyang on October 4, and never made it back to North Korea—or to Seoul. After a lengthy trial, he was convicted of fraud on July 17, 2003, and sentenced to eighteen years in prison and fined the equivalent of US$277,100.[55] The Sinuiju Special Administrative Region was not officially disbanded, but the plan was never revived. It died a natural death.

North Korea seemed to be going nowhere—unless one counted its controversial nuclear plans as progress. Kim Dae Jung's Sunshine Policy had given his people and the world hope for détente and change. But three years after his historic journey to Pyongyang, tensions on the peninsula were rising once again. It was also becoming evident that rapprochement with the South, and the "adjustments" of July and August 2002 were either an enormously courageous decision by Kim Jong Il, or one of desperation.[56] They came in the wake of a disaster that had claimed hundreds of thousands of North Korean lives.

CHAPTER 2

THE FAMINE AND THE *JUCHE* IDEA

Kim Mi Ran had a story to tell, but nobody in her new home in China ever asked to hear it. A petite, twenty-five-year-old woman from North Korea's mountainous northeast, she had crossed the border to take up what she had been told was a well-paid job. She arrived to find she had been sold into marriage to an old man. It was three years until she escaped his clutches, fleeing to China's Inner Mongolia and from there on foot through the Gobi Desert to independent, and now democratic, Mongolia. In its capital, Ulaanbaatar, she contacted the South Korean embassy, and was flown to Seoul, where she arrived in December 2001. Only then, in the care of a local church group, did she start to tell of the terrible things she had seen. Like so many other refugees from the North, she had turned to Christianity to overcome her bitter experiences.

Kim Mi Ran told of how every morning, back in her hometown in North Hamgyong province, soldiers came to collect the dead bodies from houses and buried them in unmarked mass graves in the mountains. Bodies were bundled together and wrapped in plastic sheets, mainly to lessen the stench. There were no coffins, no ceremonies to honor the dead. Homeless people in rags roamed the streets aimlessly with expressionless faces. Many slept in the waiting room in the town's filthy railway station. Some died where they lay. Something had gone fundamentally wrong in Kim Il Sung's and Kim Jong Il's Workers' Paradise.[1]

Until the early 1990s, North Korea had had a fairly well-organized food distribution system, even if, as in other socialist countries, it was based on the division of the population into different social categories in order to exercise political control. In the traditional system, five strata of prominent members of the Korean Workers' Party, the KWP, were at the top of the hierarchy, followed by seven groups of ordinary citizens. Miners, defense workers, industrial workers, and fishermen received a daily ration of 900 grams of grain. Military personnel serving along the DMZ and high-ranking officers got 850 grams. Middle- and low-ranking military officers, light industrial workers, teachers, engineers, college students, and most people living in Pyongyang received 700 grams. Residents in urban centers other than Pyongyang got less than 700 grams while high-school students, disabled persons, females over the age of fifty-five, and males over sixty-one received 400 grams. Preschool children were allotted 200 to 300 grams. At the bottom of the scale were the prisoners in North Korea's many labor camps who received a mere 200 grams, hardly enough to live on. Every town had a food distribution center, where families could collect their food in exchange for coupons which they had been given at their work places.[2]

Sitting on the floor in a small apartment in a Seoul suburb, Park Yong, a short and softspoken man in his mid-twenties also from North Hamgyong, recalls that rations began to decrease in 1992: "But the real crisis began in August-September 1994, and by 1995 the food distribution system had stopped altogether. People began to grow their own vegetables, and private vendors appeared in the streets, selling food at inflated prices. Many sold their belongings, and then their homes."[3] Divorces became common and families broke up because many men, and some women, went to look for work elsewhere in North Korea, or across the border in China.

The first to die from starvation in Park Yong's village of forty households was a friend of his, a twelve-year-old classmate at school called Chul Jin. His father worked in the local town office, but was no longer given any food coupons. The local food distribution center was in any case closed, and only people with money could afford to buy grain in the "free" market. The father locked himself and his family up in their house, where they all died. At the same time, there was an outbreak of cholera in the area, which took dozens of lives every day. Those who were strong enough to climb the border mountains escaped to China. What was a trickle became a flood, and soon there were tens of thousands, perhaps hundreds of thousands, of North Koreans across the frontier, living there illegally but often sheltered by ethnic Koreans who make up nearly half of the population of Yanbian prefecture immediately north of the Tuman border river.

On July 8, 1997, the people in Park Yong's area were summoned to the town of Chongjin to commemorate the third anniversary of the death of the Great Leader, Kim Il Sung. Thousands of people were made to stand for hours in the sun in the middle of the Korean summer, which can be as hot as the winters are bitterly cold. Many were so weak that they fainted and died. But the ceremony had to go on, and people did as they were told. No one dared to raise his or her voice, or criticize the government. After the ceremony, Park Yong heard only one young man curse the authorities. But he was terribly drunk—and the police immediately dragged him away. It was rumored that he had been sent to a labor camp, but no one knew for sure because he was never seen again.

The worst-hit areas were in the remote northeast, which is inhospitable even in the best of times, but the famine was by no means confined to North Hamgyong and nearby provinces. The entire country was affected, even the regime's showcase city, the grand capital Pyongyang. According to a World Vision report from July 1997, out of 547 children under two years old surveyed in five nursery schools in the cities of Pyongyang, Wonsan, Sariwon, Haejoo, and Pyongsan, 85 percent were malnourished and 29 percent were severely malnourished.[4] In the Tosagi kindergarten in the central city of Huichon, children wore warm winter clothes in the unheated playrooms, but their sticklike limbs poked out from trouser legs and short sleeves.[5] Simple mathematics also revealed the brutal truth: the average seven-year old North Korean child was 115 centimeters tall and weighed 16 kilograms—compared to 125 centimeters and 26 kilograms for a South Korean child of the same age.[6]

Hordes of *kochebis*—"wandering swallows," the Korean term for internally displaced people—could be seen in every corner of the country looking for food and shelter. Park Yong, the young man from North Hamgyong, roamed the countryside for two years, stealing food here and there, and begging. He eventually made it across the border to China in 2001, where he found work as a day laborer offloading cement bags and boxes of beer from trucks. But he was also able to watch satellite TV for the first time in his life—and learned that North Koreans were escaping to South Korea via foreign embassies in Beijing. He left Manchuria and, together with his girlfriend, ran into the South Korean embassy in Beijing on October 27, 2002. Inside the embassy compound, the gym and a conference room had been turned into shelters for the many North Koreans who had managed to get inside the gates.

Both were later flown to South Korea together with about thirty other North Korean refugees. Park Yong had formerly been a soldier in the North Korean army, but had deserted after an argument with his officer. The fact that an army deserter could roam around the country without being caught is a clear sign that even the regime's strict control mechanisms had almost collapsed under the pressure of the famine.[7] Stories that filtered back from refugees who had made it to China, or from vendors who traveled back and forth across the border, also opened many North Koreans eyes to a different reality in the world outside.

Kim Jong Il himself referred to an "anarchical state" in one of his speeches in 1997.[8] But there was no way the authorities could forcibly block people's efforts to find food, particularly since the central government had failed to alleviate widespread hunger. In Pyongyang, peddlers carrying boxes of food were a common sight, and train passengers returning from China, or the Chinese border, were spotted carrying bags full of food, which they were going to sell in the "informal market."[9] By default, North Korea was producing its first private entrepreneurs, but as U.S. Korea expert Marcus Noland has pointed out, "the implicit marketization of the economy in the absence of any real institutions has led to an increasingly gangsterish form of apparatchik capitalism and growing social differentiation."[10]

***

By the spring of 1998, the actual famine, as measured by unusually high death rates, was more or less over. Massive international aid and somewhat improved conditions inside the country had alleviated the worst sufferings of the people. But how many actually died from starvation and related diseases? Estimates vary, and are still a matter of controversy. A study by the Johns Hopkins University's School of Public Health put the number of people who died from starvation at 2.45 million—or 10 percent of the population.[11] Other nongovernmental organizations and U.S. congressional staff, who visited North Korea during 1995 to 1998, have produced estimates of famine-related deaths in North Korea from a low 600,000 to as many as 3.5 million.[12]

The lower estimate corresponded quite well with the conclusion in South Korean economist Lee Suk's doctoral thesis at the University of Warwick in the U.K. that Hazel Smith quoted in *Jane's Intelligence Review* in March 2004, which was 660,000.[13] But even though estimates putting the number of famine-related deaths in the millions are probably exaggerated, the number was almost certainly in the hundreds of thousands. Even the North Koreans admitted, albeit indirectly, that 220,000 people, or roughly 1 percent of the pre-crisis population, had died as a result of famine, and that figure, even if an understatement, is bad enough.[14] The government in Pyongyang had to appeal to the international community for aid to feed its population. According to a farmer from Gilju-gun in North Hamgyong, "there are no trees in North Korea with their bark intact."[15]

What went wrong and why? How could a disaster of that magnitude take place in a country which in the 1970s and 1980s was seen as one of the most prosperous and industrialized in the socialist camp? A country that hundreds of thousands of ethnic Koreans in Japan saw as their "beloved homeland"? And a country that had put itself at the forefront of the struggle against "imperialism" and "colonial exploitation" and sent technical experts and military personnel to countries in Africa and the Middle East?

The trigger was the end of North Korea's special trade privileges with the socialist camp. Soviet aid was terminated in 1987, and when both Moscow and Beijing in the early 1990s demanded payment for oil and other necessities in hard currency, North Korea was unable to cope with the new situation. Besides, North Korea was never an agricultural country. Only 18 to 20 percent of its land is arable. North Korea is an industrialized nation, although its machinery has become increasingly outdated, and oil shortages have made it impossible to operate many of its factories.[16]

By 2000, industrial output—depending on the sector— stood at 10 to 30 percent of the early 1990s levels. Even jeeps, tractors, trucks, and trains stood idle because there was no petrol or diesel to run them. Road freight fell by 70 percent and rail by 60 percent. North Korea has substantial reserves of coal, which used to produce over two thirds of its energy, but many mines were closed down because of the floods as well as a shortage of spare parts for the machinery, and electricity to power equipment and lights. Twenty of North Korea's sixty-two major power plants are thermal, primarily based on coal, but the mining sector soon saw itself locked in a vicious circle. Without an increase in coal supply, sufficient energy could not be generated to drive either the mines or the machine tool sector that were needed for coal production.[17] The remaining forty-two power station in North Korea are hydroelectric, but floods and droughts reduced their output in 1996 to 38 percent of the 1990 level.[18]

And there was no hard currency in the state's coffers to buy oil—or food—from abroad.

Catastrophic floods in the summer of 1995 added to the suffering. The authorities announced that 5.4 million people were displaced, 330,000 hectares of land were destroyed, and 1.9 million tonnes of grain were lost. That was most probably an exaggeration to attract more aid, but international aid organizations nevertheless found the situation dire when they surveyed the countryside.[19] There were more floods in 1996 followed by a severe drought, and, if government figures are to be believed, cereal production declined from 7 million tons during the 1980s to a low of 3 million tonnes in 1998. It rose to nearly 4 million tonnes in 1999, and fell again to under 3 million tonnes in 2000. Even though the worst of the famine was over by then, people were still hungry.[20] North Korea needs at least 5 million tonnes of grain a year to feed its population.[21]

The health sector was also severely hit by the crisis. In principle, North Korea enjoys one of the best health infrastructures in the Third World. The country has more than eight thousand hospitals and clinics catering for 22 million people, with nearly three qualified doctors for every thousand citizens. By the late 1990s, however, the system no longer worked. Health institutions everywhere suffered from an acute shortage of essential drugs, medical equipment, vaccines, sterilizers, refrigerators, food, heating, water— everything that a hospital or a clinic needs to function normally. In 2000, the International Federation of Red Cross and Red Crescent Societies concluded that "the situation has gone from bad to worse. The country's health system depends entirely on herbal medicines which generally do not work on the acute infections and diseases associated with the economic difficulties."[22] Sick people also stayed away from hospitals, because there was no food. And the only medicine stocks at most clinics in the countryside consisted of a greenhouse, where medicinal herbs were grown.[23]

In the beginning, the North Korean authorities tried to hide the problem. But as the crisis intensified, North Korean radio began to quote accounts of Kim Il Sung's wartime exploits against the Japanese, and how he and his men endured their hardships: "When we were fighting in the mountains, we often had to do without proper food, eating such things as wild herbs, grass roots, tree bark, malted wheat, rice bran, the residue left over from brewing and so on. We ate mainly coarse food at irregular times, so we suffered from all sorts of troubles of the digestive canal."[24] According to Andrew Natsios, formerly of World Vision and now with the U.S. Agency for International Development, or USAID, who has studied the North Korean famine, "all this was intended to build patriotic fervor and direct an exhausted population's anger away from the regime's failure."[25]

Later, however, the regime came out with some comparatively realistic descriptions of the origins of the crisis. In a surprisingly candid commentary, the official party organ *Rodong Shinmun* stated on December 12, 2000: "The nineties were in fact the most difficult time for our industry. The collapse of socialism in the Soviet Union as well as in Eastern Europe, the attempts by the imperialists and reactionary forces to strangle us, one natural disaster after another . . . the 'arduous march' that we have to follow was in essence an 'arduous march' of the economy. While the imperialists were delighted to see that the Kim Chaek Integrated Iron and Steel Works, the most important in the country, was on its death bed . . . even the trains could no longer roll."[26] "The arduous march" was also a reference to the long trek that the Great Leader Kim Il Sung undertook in 1938–39 through Manchuria down to the Korean border—and a reminder of the hardships that the early revolutionaries also had to face during their struggle.

But it would be too simplistic to blame the entire North Korean crisis on machinations by the imperialists, the weather, or even just the end of socialism in the Eastern Bloc. Although Kim Il Sung was trained in the Soviet Union in the early 1940s, North Korea has its own revolutionary ideology called *juche*. According to the official version of history, Kim Il Sung is supposed to have developed it during the anti-

Japanese struggle of the 1930s. But he first used the term in a speech "before Party propagandists and agitators in December 1955."[27]

The word literally means "subject" and is usually translated as "self-reliance," but could more accurately be rendered as "self-identity."[28] On launching his new concept, Kim Il Sung declared: "What is *juche* in our Party's ideological work? What are we doing? We are not engaged in any other country's revolution, but precisely in the Korean revolution. This, the Korean revolution, constitutes *juche* in the ideological work of the party. Therefore, all ideological work must be subordinated to the interests of the Korean revolution."[29]

In another work, Kim Il Sung stated that "to establish *juche* means holding fast to the principle of solving for oneself all problems of the revolution and construction in conformity with the actual conditions of one's country and mainly by one's own efforts . . . this represents an independent stand of discarding the spirit of relying on others, on displaying the spirit of self-reliance and solving one's own affairs on one's own responsibility under all circumstances."[30]

At the very heart of the *juche* idea are the three concepts of *chaju* (political independence from other countries), *charip* (economic self-sufficiency), and *chawi* (self-defense).

In concrete terms, all this meant a potent nationalism, born of efforts to separate the country's culture and history from nearly forty years of Japanese colonialism. In terms of maintaining social order, it reflected the deep Confucian roots of Korean culture combined with a strong desire to be truly independent, rather than the teachings of traditional Marxism-Leninism.[31]By stressing the Korean aspect of the revolution, *juche* also gave North Korea a neutral position between the two rival Communist superpowers, the Soviet Union and China. Even at the height of the cold war, North Korea was never a satellite of either Moscow or Beijing. Kim Il Sung managed to solidify the North Korean nation around his ideology, but when the *juche* idea of self-reliance was extended to guide agricultural policies, it was a disaster.

Many Westerners—and others—saw this as the main

reason behind the food crisis of the 1990s. In the 1970s and 1980s, North Korea tried to achieve self-sufficiency in the production of food grains—which, given the country's harsh and mountainous terrain, proved more problematic than expected. The solution to the absence of sufficient fertile farmland, the authorities thought, was to build terraces on the hillsides. At first, this resulted in a modest increase in grain production. But, after a few years, the effects of the massive deforestation that had taken place could be felt. Erosion set in, and, coupled with the poor quality of the terraces—they were primitive, earthen structures with no rocks or concrete to support them—a heavy rain fall was all that was needed to wash the hillside crops away, and to deposit silt and sand on farmland at lower levels. North Korea ended up with no protective forest cover on its mountains, no crops—and a massive degradation of the environment.[32]

Shortages of fertilizer and farming tools even in areas where agriculture could be practiced normally further aggravated the situation. In the first year of the floods, over four hundred thousand hectares of the country's best farmland were destroyed just as the crops were due to be harvested.[33] In an almost desperate attempt to alleviate the food shortages, the authorities decided in the winter of 1996-97 to replace the country's grain-eating animals—mainly pigs and poultry—with goats, which would survive on grass and foraging. Only oxen were exempted from the new rule, because many farmers depended on them as draft animals to replace tractors and trucks for which there was no fuel. But there was no food either, so after killing and eating all their pigs and chickens, people ate the goats as well. The famine wiped out most of North Korea's animal herds, regardless of species. Even rabbits and dogs were consumed.[34] People then had to resort to eating grass, tree bark, and corn husks. But these foods were so hard to digest that, in fact, gastro-intestinal diseases became one of the main health problems in the country among those who did not actually starve.[35]

The simple solution to the failure of *juche* agriculture would have been to give it up in the same way that China disbanded its ineffective and low-producing "people's communes" in the 1980s, freed up its economy, and reached out to the outside world. Erik Cornell, who served as Sweden's chargé d'affaires in North Korea in the 1970s, and later wrote a book about the country, stated quite bluntly that *juche* could never replace international cooperation. He quotes Kenyan minister Tom Mboya, who said at a Pan-African conference that threatened to degenerate into an incantatory rite upon the theme of self-reliance: "I accept the slogan of self-reliance. The man in the bush has always been self-reliant and that is the reason why he is still in the bush."[36]

But in a Korean context, *juche* is far more complex. Grace Lee, an American scholar, describes how *juche* has even deeper roots than the bitter memories of Japan's occupation of Korea:

> Strategically located at a peninsular tip of the East Asian continent, Korea has long been a pawn of contention between its two powerful neighbors, China and Japan. From the earliest recorded history, the Korean people have fought fiercely to maintain their independence in the face of multiple invasions by Mongols, Manchurians, Han Chinese, and Japanese pirates and samurais. The sum of these invasions may qualify Korea as the most oft-invaded territory in the world. Under the Yi Dynasty, which ruled Korea from 1392 until the Japanese annexation in 1910, Korea became a highly defensive state with a foreign policy of isolation towards the outside world. When Kim Il Sung came to power in North Korea in 1945, he arguably reverted to the highly isolationist policies of pre-modern Korea.[37]

It could thus be argued that the *juche* ideology was drawn from centuries-old traditions of Korean thought. Kim Il Sung himself has acknowledged that he adopted the term and the concept from twelfth-century Korean scholars, who in turn were inspired by Confucian ideas dating back to the original state philosophy of independence as formulated by early

Korean rulers. This strong sense of nationalism among the Koreans coexisted with another tradition called *sadaechuii*, in which palace officials jockeyed for foreign support by acting as sycophants. Lee argues that Kim Il Sung's *juche* idea may represent his reaction to the slave mentality and "flunkyism" (a favorite term in Pyongyang's propaganda) of *sadaechuii*— which he could see in the South—as well as a indebtedness to the original nationalistic strain of Korean political culture: "Aside from its tremendous appeal to the deep traditional Korean antipathy toward foreign influence, *juche* serves to intensify the nationalism of the North Korean people, who are told that world civilization originated from the Korean peninsula."[38] It became, in the words of U.S. Korea scholar Bruce Cumings, "a kind of national solipsism . . . an assumption that Korea is the center of the world."[39] All eyes were on Kim Il Sung, "the supreme brain of the nation."[40]

North Korea, therefore, is not East Germany under Walter Ulbricht or Erich Honecker, or even Albania under Enver Hoxha. And it is certainly not China, a vast empire with a huge population that any central government would find it difficult to fully control. *Juche* was designed to give the citizens of the Democratic People's Republic of Korea a place in society, and a justification for the absolute rule of the *suryong*, or leader, who, of course, was Kim Il Sung himself. The division of the Korean peninsula, and the confrontation with the South and the United States, also made it imperative for the North Korean rulers to distance themselves from "capitalist" reforms and other "vermin" that would undermine the political and economic system they had created, the future of which was essential if they were not going to be absorbed by South Korea.

In a book explaining the *juche* idea, North Korean ideologues quote Kim Jong Il as saying: "Man has a physical life and also social and political integrity. The physical life is what keeps a man alive as biological organism; social and political integrity is what keeps him alive as a social being."[41] The social aspect of a man's identity is what makes him different from an animal. But he has to have "a single guiding ideology"—the *juche* idea—to become "master of his own destiny," and, most importantly, he needs "the wise guidance of the Party and the Leader" to succeed in his endeavors.[42] Society, according to "Kimilsungism"—another term for the state ideology—is an organic body in which the *suryong*, the party, and "the masses" are closely interrelated. Among these three elements, the *suryong* is the most important one, who "serves as the brain to control the body in such a way as to bring about the unity of its movements."[43]

Significantly, the 102-page North Korean book about *juche* does not once mention "Communism," nor does it quote Karl Marx, Vladimir Lenin, Mao Zedong, or any other Marxist icons. Instead, there are references to Robinson Crusoe's life on an uninhabited island, thoughts of the Greek historian Plutarch, and Charles Dickens' novels. The emphasis is on *chajusong*, a quality that enables man to take his own initiatives, be conscientious and creative—under the guidance of the *suryong*, of course. Marxism-Leninism was dropped altogether from the country's 1992 constitution.[44] Kim Jong Il in his writings about the *juche* idea refers to Marxism-Leninism, but states that his party has developed "the revolutionary theory of the working class onto a new, higher plane."[45] Portraits of the Great and Dear Leaders hang on the walls of every government office, public building, and classroom in the country. But pictures of Marx and Lenin are extremely rare. The only ones I saw in Pyongyang in April 2004 were on the walls of a building facing Kim Il Sung Square in the city center, quite unlike China in the old days, when portraits of the bearded, moustachioed, and long-nosed foreigners Marx, Engels, Lenin, and Stalin could be seen almost everywhere side by side with their own Mao Zedong.

In 1958, Kim Il Sung divided the population into three categories, again a reflection of Confucian hierarchical theory mixed with Marxist class analysis. In the ideal Confucian society there are four categories, with the degree-holding literati at the top, below which comes the large farming population, followed by the artisans and then merchants.[46] This division does not tally well with the concept of

"Confucian capitalism," which was quite popular in Asia in the 1990s and was meant to explain why East Asian economies had developed so well under authoritarian rule. To Confucius, merchants and businessmen were the lowest of the low in society. These East Asian economies had inherited from Confucius only authoritarianism, and that is, as the North Korean example clearly demonstrates, not necessarily a key to economic success.

According to Swedish chargé d'affaires Erik Cornell, Kim Il Sung combined theories taken from Confucianism's hierarchical worldview and Soviet industrialization ideology of Stalinist vintage, blending them into a unity, the specific Korean characteristics of which the North Koreans are keen to point out.[47] The first of the three categories in this "Red Confucian" society is the 25 percent of the population that makes up the trusted "core class." Their loyalty to the regime can be counted on in controlling the others, especially the 20 percent who belong to the "hostile class," descendants of old "landlords" and other "enemies of the people." The "core class" do not have to be workers, peasants, or soldiers. In keeping with his Confucian philosophy, Kim Il Sung, also emphasized the role of the intellectuals, which true Marxist-Leninists never did. Most of the members of the "core class" live in Pyongyang and other major cities, enjoying privileges such as party membership and holding administrative or military positions. In effect, they form a feudal hereditary class entitled to benefits in education, promotions, food rations, housing, and medical services.[48] The remaining 55 percent are described as a "wavering class"—people who have suspect relatives, even two or three generations back, or who for other reasons cannot be fully trusted. People from the "wavering class" would find it hard to get good government jobs, while "the hostiles" are excluded from almost everything.[49]

While traditional cornerstones of old Confucianism such as family and respect for one's parents were dismantled in Kim Il Sung's neo-Confucian North Korea, new "families" emerged—the work collective, the party, and the state—as well as a new father figure that had to be respected: the *suryong*. To hammer these concepts into the minds of the population—even the "hostiles" and the "waverers"—every worker has to study them on a daily basis. The day begins at 8:00 a.m. with a one-hour study session under the direction of a party official. Save for a rest period in the middle of the day, work then continues to 8:00 p.m. after which study sessions and self-criticism meetings are held until 10:00 p.m. Indoctrination begins at an even earlier age. A popular nursery school song expresses loyalty to the *suryong*: "Thank you Marshall Kim Il Sung for bringing us up as future pillars of society."[50] And that society is—or was until the great famine—a well-drilled army of workers and soldiers, who never questioned their leader or the policies of the party and the state. Even the parrot in Pyongyang Zoo was taught to say "Long live President Kim!"[51]

Due to the extraordinary power and importance of one man, the *juche* philosophy became inextricably embedded in the economic, political, military, and cultural aspects of life in North Korea.[52] And the "exceptionally brilliant and outstanding leader" himself became worshiped as an almost divine being. Every North Korean wears a Kim Il Sung badge, which is distributed free by schools and state organizations. Not all badges are the same as they indicate different social status. There is one for party members, another for other adults, and a third for students. But the message is nevertheless the same: loyalty to the Great Leader. Contemporary North Korean poetry also praises the *suryong* in glowing terms:

> We will follow you, dear Leader, to the limit of the Earth
> Loyally attending you 'til end of sun and moon.
> Oh, your blessing we'll convey, to this forever true,
> We'll remain forever loyal, all our faith in you.
> To our leader we pray, with all that's in our hearts,
> *To our great dearest father, long and fruitful years.*[53]

There are in North Korea no less than thirty-four thousand statues and memorials dedicated to Kim Il Sung, at least one in every town and village across the country.[54] The grandest of all towers is outside the Korean Revolutionary Museum in Pyongyang: a twenty-meter-high bronze statue that at one stage was even gold-plated. The statue was gilded in 1977 to celebrate Kim Il Sung's sixty-fifth birthday. But in what U.S. Korea specialist Helen-Louise Hunter calls "a rare admission to having exceeded acceptable limits in their idolization of Kim," the gold cover was removed a year later.[55] School children, groups of factory workers, and other visitors lower their heads in silent respect when they approach the statue in what appears to be more of a religious ritual than just paying homage to a revolutionary hero. Numerous wreaths adorn the ground in front of the statue, and it is customary for young couples to pay their respect to the statue on their wedding day. There were at least three such couples there when I visited the site on April 16, 2004, a sunny Friday.

By coincidence or not, it is located at the same spot as a shrine built during the colonial time for worship of the deified Japanese emperors.[56] The Great Leader, Kim Il Sung, was over the years elevated from being a father figure to a god-like character with unique powers and qualities. East of the Taedong River that flows through Pyongyang stands the even higher Tower of the *Juche* Idea, a 170-meter pillar, purportedly designed by the Dear Leader Kim Jong Il himself, and complete with an express elevator to the top. Made from 300 tons of granite, it is said to be the world's tallest stone tower and it offers a magnificent view of the city. To emphasize the universality of the *juche* idea, there are plaques donated by North Korea sympathizers from eighty-two countries at the bottom of the tower. But most of them seem to come from countries which at one stage or another received assistance from North Korea such as Malta and Guyana, or they represent tiny left-wing groups in Europe, Asia, and America.[57]

It was into this environment that the international aid agencies moved with their programs to help solve the food crisis in North Korea. The first request for aid was actually made in early 1991, and the World Food Program, WFP, sent a team of four officers, of whom three were seconded from the United Nations' Food and Agricultural Organization, FAO, to assess the situation. The request was peculiar because it came at a time when the country was reporting bountiful harvests, and no food shortages. The mission was also unable to establish a case for food aid.[58] Kim Il Sung was reportedly furious, as he had not authorized any such request to the international community. North Korea had reason to be deeply suspicious of the United Nations and its agencies, too. During the Korean War, the United States had fought against North Korea under the UN flag, which still flew at the "allied" command posts at the DMZ.

But as the food shortages became real, or more readily evident, aid was needed, and North Korea first turned—also somewhat curiously—to its former colonial masters, the Japanese. In early 1995, North Korea asked if it could buy a million metric tons of rice at subsidized prices from Japan. Tokyo responded by saying that the rice would only be delivered if the South Koreans agreed. At last an agreement was reached under which the South Koreans pledged to provide the North with 150,000 tonnes. This made it possible for the Japanese to send their 500,000 tonnes, half to be provided by the Japanese Red Cross and the other half to be paid for over a thirty-year period.[59]

Following the massive floods of 1995, the WFP/FAO sent another team to assess the situation and to establish a more permanent presence in Pyongyang.[60] This time, there was a real crisis. But the response from the international community was lukewarm. Few countries wanted to send aid to what was perceived as one of the most dictatorial regimes in the world. It was also extremely difficult to get accurate information out of North Korea. Was it a famine, a temporary food crisis, or a severe, long-term shortage? Even a well-respected UN agency like the United Nations Children's Fund, Unicef, initially doubted that there was a famine. It suggested that the deaths that were reported from the countryside were due not to starvation but to the failure of the public health system.[61] A relief coordinator working at the WFP's Pyongyang office at first dismissed reports of widespread famine that came from refugees who had tottered across the border to China. He suggested that they had been concocted by NGOs looking for funds, and argued that the refugees had exaggerated the situation to avoid being sent back to North Korea.[62]

The problem, obviously, was that the foreign aid workers who had set up offices in Pyongyang were, at least in the beginning, totally dependent on their North Korean minders and interpreters. Almost none spoke Korean, and trips into the countryside were initially tightly controlled and orchestrated for the benefit of the foreigners. But why would the North Koreans try to hide the famine from the same people they had asked to help them? In North Korea, there is always a huge amount of uncertainty about what is actually happening, but it is reasonable to assume that some North Koreans found their national pride hurt by reports of starvation in their country. More importantly, perhaps, the North Korean authorities wanted to control as much as possible the aid distribution themselves, so it would appear as if it was them, not foreigners, who were providing the people with food.

The foreigners could stay in their Pyongyang hotels, and bring in the aid. But they had to be kept in the dark—which was not always possible since some of the aid workers were far more professional than those who had denied the famine. One of them was Tun Myat, a British-educated Burmese, who made it clear that the WFP would not provide any more aid unless he was permitted to travel to the hardest-hit provinces in the northeast. Tun Myat's request was granted, and although the authorities did their best to keep him as isolated as possible, he was able to establish that there was a severe crisis, including massive movements of people in the countryside.[63]

Before long, substantial amounts of aid were coming in. China committed itself to sending 500,000 tonnes of grain a year from 1995 to 1998. Private relief organizations and the government in South Korea delivered hundreds of millions of dollars worth of relief materials, and even the United States provided 300,000 tonnes of grain in 1996, 500,000 tonnes in 1997, and another 500,000 tonnes in 1998.[64] WPF continued its efforts to alleviate the crisis, and so did the International Federation of the Red Cross and Red Crescent Societies, and other international organizations. Over the years, WFP's North Korea program developed into the biggest in the world, feeding millions of people. But it also became one of its most controversial. Sue Lautze of USAID argued after a visit to North Korea that totalitarian regimes seek to control the distribution of food not primarily to help their citizens, but to achieve political ends, one of which is not necessarily the equitable redistribution of food, particularly when famine threatens the survival of the regime.[65] Fiona Terry, a researcher from the well-respected international NGO Médecins sans Frontières, MSF, alleged that "by channeling [aid] through the regime responsible for the suffering, it (the WFP) has become part of the system of oppression."[66]

There were also numerous reports of diversion of aid to the army and to private hands. In 1998, MSF discontinued its relief efforts in North Korea on the grounds that the authorities denied it access to sick and malnourished children, and channeled supplies to children of the politically well-connected. The following year, the U.S.-based NGO World Concern stopped its shipments of supplies when it was discovered that food destined for an orphanage and a hospital had simply "disappeared."[67] When American CARE pulled out in 2000, its president, Peter Bell, stated that "despite a nearly four-year dialog with the North Korean government regarding the importance of access, transparency, and accountability, the operational environment in North Korea has not progressed to the point where CARE feels it is possible to implement effective rehabilitation programs."[68]

Sidiki Kaba, president of the Paris-based International Federation for Human Rights, was even more frustrated with

North Korean attitudes when he tried to discuss the human rights situation in the country: "Even when answering the questions of UN experts, [the North Koreans] denied any violation of economic and social rights in North Korea. It was like speaking to a wall."[69] Many refugees who made it to China or South Korea claimed that they had not received any aid before fleeing. Other eyewitnesses reported seeing grain in bags with international relief agency markings being sold in the open markets. It is not impossible that those bags had been recycled—ordinary North Koreans have also been seen carrying their personal belongings in bags marked "WFP"— but, at the same time, the North Korean authorities have taken pains not to let foreigners visit those markets.[70]

But the famine did create some cracks in the monolithic state. That a country whose national ideology is based on self-reliance had to ask the international community for help was an indirect admission of the failure of official policies. Despite the official rhetoric, North Korea could no longer claim to be self-reliant. The government lost face before its own citizens, even if they were too afraid to stand up and demand changes in the totalitarian system. And as aid was coming in and being distributed on a massive scale, the government's control mechanisms began to break down. The WFP set up food distribution centers all over North Korea. Its white four-wheel drives were seen in the remotest corners of the country. This, many foreign residents in Pyongyang believe, helped open up the country in a way that no one thought was possible. And local officials in the provinces discovered that foreigners were not necessarily aggressive imperialists, but were actually there to help.[71] The WFP also took the criticism seriously, and introduced more effective monitoring mechanisms to make sure the aid was not being diverted. It also managed to fend off some of the criticism by proving that several of the stories told by refugees were not true. A man claiming to have been a driver for the WFP in the northeastern port city of Chongjin, for instance, said that he had driven relief supplies right into an army camp. It was not difficult to establish that the man had not been a driver in

Chongjin at that time and that there were also other serious discrepancies in his story.[72]

But other social consequences of the famine were impossible to control. The emergence and expansion of open markets, or *jangmadang*, "farmers' markets," as they became known, effectively undermined the state-controlled economy, at least in some parts of the country. The phenomenon was actually not new. In a 1969 speech, Kim Il Sung had encouraged the establishment of farmers' markets: "Since the cooperative economy and individual sideline production are in existence under socialism, it is inevitable that the peasant market exists, and this is not such a bad thing . . . we are not yet in a position to supply everything necessary for the people's life in sufficient quantities, through state channels."[73] But the modest free-market activities that were carried out in the 1970s and 1980s paled in comparison to what happened during the famine. Roadside vendors became a common sight all over the country, and in major towns, entire marketplaces sprung up.[74] There are today about 300 to 350 such markets across North Korea, or one or two in every county and three to five in any major city.[75] In recent years, they have been renamed "consumers' markets and apart from produce from private plots—grain and vegetables that farmers have managed to hide from the authorities— basic consumer goods brought in from China are also for sale. Prices are not low, but there is almost nothing to buy in the government stores. In 2004, these markets were also becoming more permanent in line with the economic "adjustments" that were introduced two years before. Roofed market stalls are being erected where vendors previously squatted in open fields.[76]

The only major attempt to stop such free-market activities came shortly after Kim Il Sung's death in July 1994. His son and successor, Kim Jong Il, issued an edict banning them— but the backlash was so severe that he had to rescind that decision. In some parts of the country, angry people marched on local government offices in a rare display of anger with the authorities. Two years later, however, Kim Jong Il criticized the existence of the markets: "In a socialist society, even the food problem should be solved in a socialist way, and officials should not tell the people to solve it on their own. Telling the people to solve the food problem on their own only increases the number of farmers' markets and peddlers."[77]

Natsios believes that Kim Jong Il feared that the privatization of the food distribution system and the rise of the farmers' markets would make people less dependent on the party cadres for their survival. This in turn would reduce the level of state control, and—heaven forbid, Kim Jong Il must have thought—even lead to the destruction of North Korea's economic and political system, as had happened in the Soviet Union and Eastern Europe.[78] But, at the same time, the government—forced to earn hard currency—was carrying out its capitalist ventures abroad through its many trading companies in China, Hong Kong, Macau, Thailand, and Singapore. A new form of mixed and seemingly contradictory North Korean capitalism has become a reality as a result of the hardships of the 1990s. Whether they like it or not, the authorities have had to accept a certain degree of *de facto* private commerce and enterprise.

Among some ordinary North Koreans, the new consumers' markets have also led to a conspicuous increase in materialism—or, at least, conspicuous by North Korean standards. People have been buying basic necessities and earning money from selling goods. Remittances from relatives in Japan, China, and South Korea have increased the purchasing power of some citizens, and South Korean researchers have noticed that "deviant social behavior" and corruption have spread since the end of the 1980s. Even in areas near army camps, rice rationed for the military has been diverted to the farmers' markets by individual officers and soldiers.[79] The "wavering class" is expanding in North Korea, especially among the youth. In a public execution in September 1997, several leaders of the Kim Il Sung Socialist Youth League faced the firing squad, a savage indicator of just how much the regime feared youth unrest.[80]

But will this really lead to changes similar to those in China in the 1980s? Song Du Yul—the prominent dissident who was detained a few weeks after his return to South Korea in September 2003—points out that China has 1.3 billion people, while North Korea has only 22 million. North Korea is much easier to control. Korea is also a divided nation with a real or imagined threat from the capitalist South. North Korea has to justify its existence by being different, so the "pragmatism" of China's Deng Xiaoping has no equivalent here. After the collapse of Communism in Eastern Europe, and the introduction of market reforms under the continued authoritarian rule of Communist parties in China and Vietnam, Kim Il Sung stated unequivocally, "Let cowards flinch and traitors sneer. We'll keep the Red Flag flying here."[81]

Despite such rhetoric, further reforms—and it is by now clear that they are reforms and not merely "adjustments"—are very likely. Ten years after the death of the Great Leader, North Korea is facing up to certain realities, and the first steps towards a more open economy have been taken. But the pace is bound to be much slower that it was in China in the late 1970s and Vietnam in the mid-1980s. Moreover, China under Mao Zedong adopted an alien ideology, Marxism-Leninism, that Deng and others could transform into "socialism with Chinese characteristics" without betraying either their past or vision for the future. North Korea has its *juche*, which it also calls "socialism our way," an indigenous system that it would be much harder, if not impossible, to transform into something fundamentally different.[82] Marcus Noland argues similarly that North Korea's official policies "are so imbedded in the social and political fabric of the country that they may well prove more difficult to reverse than has been the case elsewhere."[83] That is the legacy of the Great and Dear Leaders, the father and son who created the Democratic People's Republic of Korea.

CHAPTER 3

THE GREAT AND DEAR LEADERS

In the winter of 1940, a small band of guerrillas slipped across the frozen border from Manchuria into the Soviet Union, somewhere west of the far eastern port city of Vladivostok. Pursued by the Japanese Imperial Army, they had fought their way north over the mountains and through the forests towards the Soviet frontier. It was December and bitterly cold, and many of the rag-tag guerrillas had not eaten for days. On the other side of the border, the Soviets verified their identities, then welcomed them with open arms. This group of guerrillas, most of them ethnic Koreans, was led by Kim Il Sung, who was only twenty-eight years old but already a legend. He had fought bravely against the Japanese, who wanted him dead rather than alive. For the first time in almost a decade, he and his men could rest and feel safe.[1]

The retreat into Soviet territory was not unusual. From the mid-1930s, guerrillas from Japanese-occupied Manchuria—both Chinese and Koreans—had frequently crossed into the Soviet Union. After 1939, when the Japanese forces intensified their counterinsurgency campaigns, the exodus of defeated guerrillas became massive.[2] For the Soviets, this presented a dilemma when, on April 13, 1941, they signed a nonaggression pact with the Japanese. The Japanese were interested in the pact to make sure they would not be attacked in the north when they turned their attention to the European colonial empires in Southeast Asia—and the Russians did not want to fight a war in the Far East when the

Germans were pushing east in Europe. In June, Germany did in fact attack the Soviet Union.[3]

According to the terms of the pact, the Soviet Union and Japan pledged to remain neutral if the other should become involved in war. That included guerrilla wars—and the Soviet Union was not supposed to support, or even shelter, anti-Japanese forces. But the guerrillas were also Communists, and the Soviets felt they could not simply push them back. Moreover, the Soviets did not trust the Japanese. The guerrillas could prove useful, if—or rather when—the pact with the Japanese broke down. Meanwhile, they could be sent back into Manchuria to collect vital intelligence for the Soviets.

For that purpose, the Soviets established two secret camps for their Korean and Chinese comrades. Many Koreans and Chinese received military and political training at a facility code-named "Camp B," located some one hundred kilometers north of Vladivostok at Nikolsk—today's Ussurijsk—where the Voroshilov and Okeanskaya army schools were located. The other, "Camp A," was even deeper inside the Soviet Union outside the village of Vyatskoye, a tiny Russian settlement perched on a forested bank of the Amur River, seventy kilometers north of the city of Khabarovsk.[4]

With utmost security and secrecy, Kim Il Sung and a few hundred of his men were brought by special trains to Khabarovsk, and from there on canvas-covered trucks to Vyatskoye and Camp A. A timber house was erected to serve as Kim Il Sung's command post, while most of his men dwelt in mud huts that extended down into the ground to keep them warm during the bitterly cold Siberian winter. The soldiers dug trenches in the surrounding forest and made shooting ranges and parade grounds, where the guerrillas could be trained in guerrilla warfare and display their military discipline. There was a field hospital, a hall for political lectures, a school for the children—and even a small grass airstrip where light planes could take off and land.[5]

Camp A at Vyatskoye was an ideal hiding place for the Korean and Chinese guerrillas. It was sufficiently far away from the frontier not to be discovered by the Japanese, but close enough for the guerrillas to carry out cross-border forays into Manchuria. These were confined to intelligence gatherings behind Japanese lines, though not fighting. In fact, Kim Il Sung complained to his Russian hosts that he was not allowed to fight the Japanese.[6] But he was made a captain of the Eighty-eighth Special Rifle Brigade of the Soviet Union's Red Army, and held command over a force of a few hundred men. The brigade also included many Chinese, and became known internally as the "United International Unit" because of its foreign composition.

Zhou Baozhong of the Second Route Army of the Chinese Communists became overall brigade commander, but he was assisted—or rather controlled—by a team of Soviet officers.[7] Kim Il Sung remained the highest-ranking Korean at Vyatskoye, and his Soviet officers evidently thought very highly of him. He was seen as a strong and energetic character with good communications skills and distinct leadership qualities.[8] But he never left his brigade, and did not return to Manchuria—or Korea—until World War II was over.[9]

Kim Il Sung had arrived in Vyatskoye together with his wife, Kim Jong Suk, one of his partisans who was in her early twenties. In the camp on February 16, 1942, she gave birth to a son. He was given a Russian name, "Yura," which is an affectionate form of "Yuri." Augustina Vardugina, a seventy-four-year-old woman from Vyatskoye, was in her teens when the Korean and Chinese guerrillas had their camp near her village. She remembers how Kim Jong Suk used to come into the village to barter military rations for chickens and eggs.[10] Holding her hand was her son, a shy little boy, who was later to become the "Dear Leader, the Great Successor of the *Juche* Idea, Marshal Kim Jong Il." A second son, called "Alexander" or "Sura" in Russian and Kim Pyong Il in Korean, was born in Vyatskoye in 1944.

The Soviet authorities had grand plans for their Korean commander in Vyatskoye. On September 4, 1945, Kim Il Sung was picked up by a few Soviet officers in Vyatskoye and flown down to Vladivostok, where he boarded a ship bound for

Wonsan on the east coast of northern Korea.[11] Kim Il Sung arrived back home on September 19—almost a month after regular Soviet forces had occupied the northern half of the peninsula, including Pyongyang.[12] His family followed shortly afterwards.

Now that Russian archives are open, and places like Vyatskoye are accessible to local and foreign researchers, it has become a lot easier to establish what the Kim family did during World War II, and where they were. But that has not prevented the North Korean propaganda machinery from painting an entirely different picture of their exploits in the early 1940s. Kim Il Sung's official biography does not even once mention his and his family's sojourn in the Soviet Union. Instead, he attended a conference in Khabarovsk from "December 1940 to mid-March 1941."[13] Admittedly, a training camp was set up in the Soviet Far East, but Kim Il Sung himself returned to Manchuria and Korea in April 1941 where he continued the struggle, "confusing and terrifying the enemy with brilliant tactics."[14]

He was operating mainly in the area northeast of Mount Paekdu, which straddles the border with Manchuria. Paekdu, an extinct volcano with a spectacular lake in the crater, is Korea's highest and most sacred mountain, and now also the cradle of the Korean revolution. It was there, in a rustic log cabin, that the official version claims that Kim Jong Il was born in 1942. A bright, new star was also born in the dark sky, a double rainbow appeared—a miracle since it was the middle of the winter—and a swallow descended from heaven to herald the birth of "a general who will rule all the world."[15] This unusual child's first toys were machine-guns and bandoleers which were lying around in the secret camp. He went through "a hail of bullets and clouds of battle smoke strapped to the back of his mother, and fell asleep fingering a rifle at his mother's breast by the side of a campfire at a bivouac."[16] When he was three-and-a-half years old, his father Kim Il Sung and his victorious guerrilla fighters—with a little help from the Soviet Army—drove out the Japanese, and liberated the northern half of the Korean peninsula.[17]

Kim Jong Il's alleged birthplace has become a place of pilgrimage and worship, complete with a conspicuously new-looking log cabin, and signs telling the visitors what was what more than half a century ago. And in the surrounding forest, people are still finding anti-Japanese slogans, supposedly carved into the trees by Kim Il Sung and his comrades during their battles against the "Eternal Japanese Enemy."[18] One of the carvings eulogizes his wife, Kim Jong Suk, "a woman commander of Mount Paekdu."[19] All this undoubtedly, proves that the entire Kim family spent their wartime years on Mount Paekdu, when they were not ambushing the Japanese.

But in 1991, Yu Song Chol, an ethnic Korean from Soviet Central Asia, wrote an incensed open letter to Kim Jong Il, which was published in a local Korean-language newspaper in Kazakhstan. He had just returned from a visit to North Korea, where he had seen the fabled log cabin in Paekdu, and, to his surprise, noticed a sign saying that this was Kim Jong Il's birthplace. He could not believe it: "I'm ashamed . . . I can still recall how you walked around Vyatskoye with your [father's] captain's cap on your head. It was there that you walked your first steps . . . how come you don't remember that?"[20]

Yu Song Chol was in a better position than most to know the truth. He was one of the highest-ranking ethnic Korean intelligence officers from the Soviet Union who were sent to work with Kim Il Sung and the Eighty-eighth Special Rifle Brigade in Vyatskoye. He followed the Soviet Red Army into Korea, and was made head of operations in the Korean People's Army's general staff in 1948, a position he served in until he returned to the Soviet Union in 1956.[21]

But the North is not alone in concocting stories. One of the most popular myths spread by the South is that the Kim Il Sung who returned to Korea in 1945 was not the real Kim Il Sung. Many North Koreans had heard about the brave guerrilla fighter years before he appeared at the victory celebration in Pyongyang on October 14, 1945. Many had expected a distinguished, somewhat elderly guerrilla fighter with a weather-beaten face—and were taken aback by his youth. O Yong Jin, a leading non-Communist who was present at the occasion, later related in his memoirs that Kim Il Sung "wore a blue suit which was a bit too small for him, and he had a haircut like a Chinese waiter. He is a fake! All the people gathered in the athletic ground felt an electrifying disgust, disappointment, discontent and anger."[22]

This man appeared to be in his early thirties, and so he must have been only in his twenties when he fought the Japanese in Manchuria in the 1930s. Could this really be the commander who, in June 1937, carried out a daring attack on the small town of Pochonbo in northern Korea? Under cover of darkness, he and 150 of his men managed to cross the Amnok border river on rafts. Storming into Pochonbo on the southern bank, they killed seven Japanese policemen and wounded many more. The town office and several other government buildings were also destroyed, and propaganda leaflets distributed. A man called Kim Il Sung then appeared in the middle of the village and delivered an impassioned speech, after which the guerrillas retreated back into their hideouts in Manchuria.[23] That attack had passed into local folklore, and Kim Il Sung became the most wanted Korean guerrilla leader in Manchuria.[24]

A rumor spread that this Kim Il Sung had assumed the name of a much older guerrilla fighter, who was supposed to have operated along the Manchurian border immediately after the Japanese annexation of Korea in 1910. That man had allegedly been killed in action against the Japanese around 1937, so this "new" Kim Il Sung must be an impostor, someone taking advantage of the fame and glory of the "older" Kim Il Sung.[25] In the South, this belief became so widespread that it even appeared in U.S. intelligence reports.[26]

It is true that Kim Il Sung changed his name in the early 1930s. He was originally called Kim Song Ju. But it was not unusual, in fact it was customary, for people in the anti-Japanese underground to assume *noms de guerre* to make it more difficult for the authorities to track them down.[27] And there is no evidence, in Japanese records or otherwise, to support the claim that there ever was another, older Kim Il Sung. In Russia, there are many people who spent years with Kim Il Sung in Vyatskoye, and they reject the "impostor theory" as pure propaganda.[28] It is more likely that many Koreans had simply expected Kim Il Sung—given his fame and, among the Japanese, notoriety—to be an older man. Everything associated with him had grown out of proportion with reality.[29]

But it is also true that he was not the only Korean guerrilla fighter in the 1930s. Despite the fabled raid on Pochonbo, he was a relatively minor leader of that era, commanding a small force of perhaps three hundred and certainly not more than one thousand men.[30] There were other guerrilla commanders who were more powerful than Kim Il Sung, such as Kim Won Bong, a leading nationalist and Communist who almost managed to unite all the splintered partisan forces in Manchuria, and Mu Chong, a close comrade-in-arms of Mao Zedong's Communists in their Yan'an base area in China's Shaanxi province. But Kim Il Sung was important because he was one of the few Korean Communists never to be captured by the Japanese.[31] More significantly, he managed to retreat into the Soviet Union, where he was trained by the Soviets to become the future leader of a Communist state in Korea.

***

The man the Soviets wanted to make "their man" in Korea was born on April 15, 1912, in Mangyongdae, a small village near Pyongyang on the banks of the Taedong River. Officially, he came from a poor peasant background, but it would be more accurate to describe his family as lower middle class. It is also extremely difficult to separate fact from fantasy and propaganda—both northern and southern—with respect to Kim Il Sung's past. However, it seems clear that his father, Kim Hyong Jik, at one stage worked as a primary school teacher, and probably also worked in a local government office. His mother, Kang Pan Sok, was the daughter of a village schoolmaster, who was also a local Protestant

minister. According to most accounts, his parents were
Christian, although this was later explained away by
propagandists as the family's "imputed intention to find a
legal cover for their alleged revolutionary activities."[32]
Following several years of gradual penetration, the Japanese
had annexed Korea in 1910, and the new colonial masters
were deeply hated by most Koreans.

Like so many others, the father may have joined an anti-
Japanese group and it is possible—as the official history
claims—that he was briefly detained for his activities. But
there is no evidence to support the claim that he was a
prominent nationalist leader, as latter day propaganda will
have it.[33] It is perhaps more significant to his life and beliefs
that he attended Sungsil School, which was established by
American missionaries in Pyongyang.[34] He and his wife raised
their son Kim Song Ju, who later become Kim Il Sung, and
his two younger brothers, Kim Chol Ju and Kim Yong Ju, to
be good and righteous children.

The family first moved to Manchuria in 1919, settling in
the small town of Pataokou on the northern side of the
Amnok River. There, Kim Hyong Jik ran a small Chinese
herbal medicine shop, and young Kim attended primary
school. Apart from a brief attempt to move back to Korea in
1925, the family remained in Manchuria. Kim Song Ju
graduated from a Chinese school, Fusong Elementary, in
Manchuria, and then attended both Chinese and Korean
schools. The fact that he had what amounts to a Chinese
education is usually omitted in official biographies, which
want to portray the Great Leader as a truly Korean patriot.[35]

The father died in 1926 at the age of thirty-two, when Kim
Song Ju was only fourteen. The mother died in 1932 at the
age of forty, leaving the three sons as orphans. By then,
however, Kim Song Ju was already in trouble with the
authorities. He had dropped out of Yuwen Middle School in
Kirin (today's Jilin), and supposedly organized the Kirin
Communist Youth League in 1927, when he was only fifteen.
More likely, this was a small underground Marxist group,
created by the local unit of the Chinese Communist Party's

youth organization.[36] Whatever the case, he was imprisoned by the Chinese authorities for several months before being released in 1930.[37]

In 1931, the Japanese moved in and seized Manchuria from the weak and fragmented Chinese republic. A vast territory, it was rich in timber, coal, iron, magnesite, oil, uranium, and gold. The following year, the Japanese proclaimed Manchuria "independent" as the State of Manchukuo (Manzhuguo in Pinyin). Pu Yi, the last emperor of China who had been deposed in a revolution in 1911, was made nominal head of state, but in real terms Manchuria became a Japanese colony just like Korea. The Japanese began to exploit its natural resources, and conducted a reign of terror over the local population.

Many Chinese—and ethnic Koreans, of whom there were a lot in Manchuria—went underground to organize armed resistance against the Japanese. One of them was Kim Song Ju, who in the early 1930s became known by his *nom de guerre*, Kim Il Sung. The Japanese were harassed, and there was some fierce fighting, but the colonial power was never seriously threatened by the activities of what it termed "red bandits."[38] Kim Il Sung's spectacular 1937 attack on Pochonbo was one of the few forays into Korea that the resistance managed to stage. In the southern half of the peninsula, however, an underground Communist movement was active, though they were not usually armed.

According to the first official North Korean version of history, Kim Il Sung had managed to unite the various factions in Manchuria when he was only twenty years of age: "Comrade Kim Il Sung, the great revolutionary leader, finally founded the Anti-Japanese People's Guerrilla Army . . . the Korean people's first Marxist-Leninist revolutionary armed force, in Antu on April 25, 1932. It was formed of progressive workers, peasants and young patriots, and centered around Korean Revolutionary Army men and the core elements of the Young Communist League and the Anti-Imperialist Youth League."[39] Two years later, in March 1934, the AJGA was transformed into the Korean People's Revolutionary

Army, establishing "a firm chain of unified command in the greatly expanded guerrilla units."[40]

In reality, the scattered Korean guerrillas in Manchuria were part of the larger Northeast Anti-Japanese United Army, which was commanded by a Chinese, Yang Jingyu, and had a majority of Chinese fighters.[41] But whatever the ethnic composition, the guerrillas suffered badly when the Japanese decided to launch a series of extensive counterinsurgency campaigns. Mao Zedong's Communists, fighting the nationalist Chinese under Chiang Kai-shek, had their famous "long march," when over one hundred thousand troops, cadres and supporters left the Jiangxi Soviet in October 1934. A year later, they arrived in Yan'an, where a new base area was set up. The anti-Japanese Machurian guerrillas were forced out on an equally hard "arduous march" in 1938–39, from Mengchiang (Jingyu) near Kirin to Changbai on the Korean border, south of Mount Paekdu. It took the guerrillas one hundred days to reach Changbai, and temperatures at times fell to forty centigrade below zero.[42] And there and then, myth and reality definitely part company. Kim Il Sung set up a base camp on Mount Paekdu and stayed there, says the official history. The Japanese pushed on, and forced him to continue north into the Soviet Union, all other sources maintain.

The exile in the Soviet Union brought a new group of Koreans into the movement. Until the late 1930s, Koreans made up a large portion of the population of the Soviet Far East. Many of them had fled across the border when the Japanese began to take over Korea in the early twentieth century. They were allowed to settle in the area, and most of them were loyal to their new host country. In 1917 many Koreans even helped establish Soviet power in the Far East and participated in the civil war on the Bolshevik side against "the Whites." But in the paranoid view of the Soviet leader Josef Stalin, they were untrustworthy "Asiatics" whom he suspected—totally without foundation—of being a potential fifth column for the Japanese.[43]

In September 1937, Stalin sent in his army and police to "purge" the area of Koreans. Some 170,000 Koreans were herded onto cattle trains, carrying with them only a few belongings. They were dumped in Uzbekistan and Kazakhstan, where many of them still remain. But when Kim Il Sung and his men arrived in the Soviet Far East, some were sent to Camp A and Camp B to liaise with the newly arrived Korean guerrillas. Many of them followed the Soviet Red Army—and Kim Il Sung—into North Korea, after the Japanese surrender in August 1945.

In that year, the Korean peninsula was divided along the 38th parallel between the Soviet-occupied North and the U.S.-occupied South, and, as the cold war gained momentum, the respective occupation forces endeavored to bring into power the political forces that suited them best. In the South, the Americans brought in Syngman Rhee, a seventy-year-old Korean patriot who had lived in the United States since 1911, and had earned a Ph.D. at Princeton University. A crusty old politician, he managed to unite several conservative and traditionalist factions, and began to prepare for an independent administration in the South.[44] His wife was Austrian, and he was staunchly anti-Communist. In other words, he was in all respects very much the opposite of the young guerrilla Kim Il Sung, who emerged as the leader of the North.

The division of the Korean peninsula was formalized on August 15, 1948, when the Republic of Korea, with Syngman Rhee as its president, was created under U.S. auspices in the South. Three weeks later, on September 9, the Soviet-controlled north became the Democratic People's Republic of Korea. Kim Il Sung was named premier of the new Communist state, but it took many years before he was able to consolidate his grip on power. To begin with, there were four distinct groups in the North Korean Communist movement: the Domestic, Yan'an, Soviet, and Guerrilla factions.[45] Some scholars have argued that these groups did not constitute actual factions within the party, but were merely made up of people of different backgrounds. Marxist-style democratic centralism would make active factionalism unacceptable in any Communist party, and the Korean one was no exception.

Whatever the case, it is clear that Korea's Communist movement was not a monolith, and that there was a high degree of rivalry between different groups within it.

The "Domestic" group consisted of Communist cadres who had been active in the underground throughout the colonial period. Led by Communist veteran Pak Hon Yong, they had their main support base among intellectuals and labor leaders in the South. The Yan'an group comprised Korean Communists who had gone to China in the 1920s and 1930s. At first, they worked with the Chinese Communists in Shanghai, who later retreated to the new base area in Yan'an. Few Korean veterans actually stayed there, but they became known as "the Yan'an faction" because of their close links with the Chinese Communist Party. Kim Tu Bong, a prominent linguist, was the most important leader of this faction.

The Soviet group, or the "Soviet Koreans" as they became known, were the Koreans from Soviet Central Asia, who had been sent to join the movement in the early 1940s. Unlike members of the other factions, few of them had lived in Korea before they arrived there in 1945. But because they spoke Russian and had good knowledge of Western culture, they were important to the Soviet occupation power in North Korea. They were also the only Koreans who had the knowledge and experience needed to build up a socialist state apparatus and a governing Communist party.[46]

The fourth, or "Guerrilla" group was Kim Il Sung and his men who had fought in Manchuria in the 1930s and then gone into exile in the Soviet Union. The problem, therefore, was that the indigenous Korean Communist Party knew very little about him. He was certainly not a party member, and he had not shared the hardships of the cadres at home under the brutal rule of the Japanese police. The KCP had been set up in April 1925, but was almost crushed a few years later. Small groups continued to operate underground until the Japanese defeat in 1945. The party was then reestablished in Seoul under Pak Hon Yong's leadership.[47]

A separate Communist party emerged in the North, and, in August 1946, it merged with the New Democratic Party—

formed by returned partisans from China—to become the North Korean Workers' Party. In November, in the South, the Communist Party also joined forces with the local New Democratic Party, and the smaller People's Party, to become the South Korean Workers' Party. It was not until June 24, 1949 that the two branches of the party merged and a unified Korean Workers' Party was formed—the party that still rules North Korea. Kim Il Sung became its first chairman.

The first challenge to Kim Il Sung's power came from the Domestic Communists, and the masses of Koreans who had fought in China and then returned to their homeland. Initially, his guerrillas were, in fact, the least influential of all groups. Their only allies were the Soviet Koreans, whom many people at home considered to be foreigners. But Kim Il Sung used the Soviet Koreans to attack the indigenous Communists—and the Soviets had all along promoted Kim Il Sung and the Soviet Korean faction to secure their own influence over the North.[48]

The Soviets dominated North Korea in the first years after the occupation, and Soviet influence behind the scenes remained strong after the proclamation of the Democratic People's Republic of Korea. Immediately after the occupation, Soviet administration was in the hands of Major General Andrei Alekseevich Romanenko, while Colonel General Terentii Fomich Shtykon, a political commissar of the Red Army's First Far Eastern Front, effectively ruled the northern half of the peninsula until 1948. N. G. Lebedev, a full-time Communist Party officer, also seriously influenced developments during 1945–48, and a colonel called A. M. Ignatiev dealt with all Korean leaders during the occupation.[49] They worked directly with Kim Il Sung, and through the Soviet Koreans, who in 1948 accounted for a quarter of the Central Committee of the then North Korean Workers' Party, and a third of the politburo members. The leader of the Soviet Koreans, Ho Kai I, or Aleksei Ivanovich Hegai, headed the Central Committee's important organizational department.[50]

In a move designed to strengthen his relatively weak internal position, Kim Il Sung, soon after his return to

Pyongyang, organized a special security unit, staffed with his own partisans. This was followed in November 1946 by a military and political school for the security services, called the Pyongyang Institute, headed by Kim Chaek, a close associate of Kim Il Sung.[51] With Soviet assistance, Kim Il Sung also built his own armed forces—and extensive political police network. The Korean People's Army was set up on February 8, 1948, seven months before "independence," and both the commander in chief of the armed forces and the minister of defense came from Kim Il Sung's group of ex-guerrillas.[52]

Kim Il Sung's special secret police, however, was the brainchild of Pang Hak Se, a Soviet Korean intelligence officer who had arrived in Pyongyang in 1946. He was immediately appointed head of the Section of the Political Defense of the State within the Security Department, North Korea's first real intelligence service.[53] Pang Hak Se was trained in the Stalinist tradition, and worked closely with Kim Il Sung as well as the Soviet authorities. And to show the other factions where real power lay, in 1949 Kim Il Sung declared himself *suryong*—supreme or Great Leader—a designation which had only been used for Stalin until that time.[54]

***

The entire power constellation—both internally in North Korea and externally in its foreign backers—changed dramatically after the outbreak of the Korean War on June 25, 1950. Despite remarkable initial battlefield successes for the Korean People's Army—they overran almost the entire peninsula within a few months—final victory eluded the Communist forces. The United States and its allies, who fought under the aegis of the UN, counterattacked, drove the North Koreans back, and bombed the North to smithereens. Conventional bombs and napalm rained down over North Korea's cities and towns, and even nuclear weapons were considered. More than two million civilians died, many from bombardment from the air. Pyongyang, and most of North as well as South Korea, lay in ruins.[55]

The destruction was immense, and North Korea would most probably have been occupied by the UN forces, had it not been for the three hundred thousand "volunteers" from China, who entered the war in November 1950. A stalemate was reached, and a new dividing line—the Demilitarized Zone—was drawn, close to the 38th parallel, but not precisely following it. The war ended not with a peace treaty, but with an armistice signed at the border village of Panmunjom on July 27, 1953.

North Korea had failed to take over the South, and the Soviet Union's lukewarm support for the war was a disappointment. On the other hand, the Communist victory in China in 1949, a year after the proclamation of the Democratic People's Republic of Korea, and the subsequent Chinese intervention in the Korean War, led to an increase in Chinese influence at the expense of Soviet power.[56] Although he owed his power to the Soviets, Kim Il Sung was said to be irritated over their constant interference in North Korea's political and military affairs. The Soviets may have thought that their Korean "puppet" would be easy to control. But they were wrong.

In late 1951, the leader of the Soviet Koreans, Ho Kai I, lost his position as secretary of the Korean Workers' Party, the KWP. According to the official version, he committed suicide on July 2, 1953, on the night before a party meeting scheduled to discuss his "mistakes." Other sources, including Russian Korea expert Andrew Lankov, believe he was murdered.[57] At the same time, Kim Il Sung moved against the Domestic group. As a guerrilla fighter with little formal education, he had always been suspicious of the left-wing intellectuals and professionals who had come from the South after the division of the Korean peninsula. In August 1953, twelve prominent members of the former South Korean Workers' Party were put on trial, accused of "sabotaging the Communist movement in the South, co-operation with the

Japanese police during the occupation, and espionage on behalf of the United States."[58]

Predictably and unremarkably in the context of a totalitarian state, the defendants "confessed" to their crimes—just like the accused at Stalin's Moscow trials of 1936–37 had done. Yi Kang Guk, a former official in the Ministry of Foreign Trade, even began his speech with "I am a running dog of American imperialism!" Yi Sung Yop, a former secretary of the Central Committee of the Workers' Party, said, "whatever punishment I am given by the [judges], I will accept with gratitude."[59] Ten, including the two Yis, were sentenced to death, while the two others received long prison terms.

Absent from the dock was the leader of the Domestic Communists, Pak Hon Yong. As one of the founders of the Korean Communist Party, he had been closely connected with Communist International, the Comintern, in the 1920s and 1930s, and he had been arrested by the Japanese. There seemed to be little doubt about his revolutionary credentials, but he was also ousted in 1953, put under house arrest, and brought to trial two years later. Accused of being a spy for the United States—from 1939!—and for conspiring with Yi Sung Yop and others to stage a coup and seize power, he was sentenced to death in December 1955. He was not executed immediately, though, because the authorities hoped to get from him more evidence that could be used in the internal political struggle. But he was most probably executed, or murdered in his cell, in the autumn of 1956.[60]

The trials of Yi Sung Yop and Pak Hon Yong were followed by sweeping arrests across the country of former cadres of the South Korean Workers' Party, and all of them were accused of "espionage" and "factionalist activity."[61] The principal mastermind behind the purges was one of the few Soviet Koreans who still had Kim Il Sung's trust, political police chief Pang Hak Se.[62] Apart from that, he also had the organizational skills and experience that were needed to carry out massive purges of a Communist movement.

In this way, the Domestic group was physically eliminated

in 1953–55, and the most prominent leaders of the Soviet faction had been purged during the Korean War. In the mid-1950s, as the Soviet Union was going through its de-Stalinization process, most remaining Soviet Koreans returned home. One of the few exceptions was Pang Hak Se, who oversaw the next round of purges—of the Yan'an veterans, who had fought in China during its civil war. The fact that Pang Hak Se held such an important position shows that there were no clear-cut divisions between the so-called factions, and that Kim Il Sung had trusted followers also outside his inner circle of former guerrilla fighters.

In the summer of 1956, Kim Il Sung—feeling secure in his position after having been reelected as chairman of the Korean Workers' Party at its Third Congress in April—undertook a long journey to the Soviet Union and nine East European countries, including East Germany, Poland, and Romania, and stopping in Mongolia on his way back. The main purpose of his trip was to get economic assistance for his first Five-Year Plan, set for 1957–61 and designed to turn North Korea into an industrialized nation. But apart from a paltry 300 million roubles from the Soviets, few were willing to support such a bold and seemingly unrealistic initiative. He returned virtually empty-handed.[63]

In August, Kim Il Sung had to submit a report from his trip to the Central Committee, and for the first time there was real opposition to his rule. The Yan'an faction, together with what remained of the Soviet faction, openly criticized his policies on a number of crucial issues. Its members were opposed to his plans to develop heavy industry, and instead advocated a less ambitious program centered on consumer and light industry. They also suggested that the North should loosen the very rigid political system that Kim Il Sung had established. Independent trade unions should be allowed. Some members were also critical of the personality cult that Kim Il Sung was building up around himself. That criticism came at a very sensitive point in the international Communist movement, as Nikita Khrushchev had publicly denounced Stalin. Kim Il Sung obviously did not want similar thoughts against a "Great Leader" to gain ground in North Korea.[64]

In the official account of the dramatic events of August 1956, the "villainous anti-Party counterrevolutionary factionalists made a frontal attack on the party. This was a ridiculous challenge by traitors of the revolution."[65] Kim Il Sung responded by launching a frontal counterattack, using his secret police, still headed by Pang Hak Se. Soviet Koreans and members of the Yan'an faction fled back to the Soviet Union and China respectively. The remaining "traitors" were purged, and the Yan'an group ceased to exist. The purges ended with the removal in 1958 of Kim Tu Bong, the leader of the Yan'an veterans who was also the first chairman of the North Korean Workers' Party and the first head of state of North Korea.[66]

The crisis was so severe that a joint Soviet-Chinese delegation led by Foreign Minister Anastas Mikoyan and Defense Minister Peng Dehuai had been dispatched to Pyongyang in September 1956. They had forced Kim Il Sung to convene a new Central Committee meeting and pardon those involved in the August incident. At first, Kim Il Sung was obliging, but in early 1957 large-scale purges of the Yan'an group began anyway; Kim Il Sung was not going to carry out policies forced upon him by foreign pressure, not even when that pressure was from his main allies in the Communist world.[67]

By the early 1960s, Kim Il Sung had consolidated his hold on power. There was no longer any opposition, or substantial factionalism, within the Korean Workers' Party. By skillfully playing off one faction against another, and through extensive use of his secret services, Kim Il Sung had turned his former guerrillas from being the weakest of the four groups into the most important one. A new generation of technocrats was also emerging, but they were loyal to Kim Il Sung as they owed their rise to prominence to him. The very few Soviet Koreans and Yan'an veterans who remained found it prudent to toe the official line. There was no point in trying to challenge Kim Il Sung's absolute grip on power.

In a move similar to China's Great Leap Forward in the late 1950s, Kim Il Sung had also launched his own *chollima* campaign to mobilize the working class to increase productivity in both agriculture and industry. The movement was named after a legendary horse that could run four hundred kilometers a day, and that was how he envisioned North Korea's path forward.[68] Although statistics from that period cannot be considered reliable, the North was making spectacular gains. Some industry had been inherited from the Japanese, but new steel works were built and the country produced chemicals, hydroelectric power, internal-combustion engines, locomotives, motorcycles, and various kinds of machine-building equipment. In the countryside, the peasantry was collectivized and new techniques were introduced to increase food production.

North Korea even managed to produce its own synthetic fiber, which played an important role in meeting the domestic demand for textiles and garments. Called "vinalon" and made from limestone and anthracite, it has been hailed as the *juche* fiber of self-reliance. It is also responsible for the chilling conformity of most North Koreans, who wake up under their vinalon quilts and have to put on their vinalon suits, caps, and canvas shoes before going to work.[69] Vinalon was actually invented in Japan in the late 1930s, but by an ethnic Korean chemist, Ri Sung Gi, who defected to the North during the Korean War. In 1956, he helped build North Korea's first vinalon factory in Hamhung, South Hamgyong province. It went into full operation on May 6, 1961 and, under the slogan "Resolving the Clothing Problem through Vinalon," North Korea soon produced tens of thousands of tons of the material.[70] When Kim Dae Jung launched his Sunshine Policy towards the North in the late 1990s, it attracted the interest of several South Korean investors as a possible "pollution-free-future-oriented new material."[71] The problem with vinalon, however, is that it is heavier than natural cotton, and wears out easily. When buying clothes made from vinalon, North Koreans generally choose larger sizes, for the material also shrinks considerably when laundered.

But it did contribute to the growth of the 1950s and 1960s. Outside observers estimated that North Korea's economy grew at 25 percent annually in the decade after the Korean War, and about 14 percent from 1965 to 1978—no mean achievement, given the almost complete destruction of the country during the 1950–53 war.[72] The first North Korean–made truck, the Sungri-*58*, was manufactured in 1958, and, in 1961, the first Pulgungi electric locomotive rolled off the assembly line in a factory that was later named after Kim Jong Thae, a South Korean underground Communist activist who was caught and executed in the South in the late 1960s. Aid was pouring in from the Soviet Union, China, and other Eastern Bloc countries, but that was not the only reason for North Korea's remarkable development in the late 1950s and 1960s. North Korea under Kim Il Sung was becoming an increasingly militarized society, where every citizen was mobilized to create a "workers' paradise." And they worked, or were worked, almost at the speed of the fabled *chollima* horse.

***

Following a turbulent decade, Kim Il Sung had emerged as the undisputed leader of North Korea, and his nation seemed to be on its way toward stability and relative prosperity—at least compared to the impoverished and chaotic South Korea, where the economy continued to flounder. Widespread political unrest and large-scale riots there had forced Syngman Rhee to leave the presidency and go into exile in 1960. It was high time to show the glory of Korea—and the role that Kim Il Sung and his family was supposed to have played in the resurrection of the Korean nation.

First, a new ideology had to be promoted. It was hardly a coincidence that Kim Il Sung had launched his *juche* idea in December 1955 during the crisis then brewing in the party. But it was not until the 1960s that *juche* was really promoted as the state ideology, and *juche* and Kim Il Sung became inseparable. Naturally, the brilliant man who formulated this concept must also have come from a long line of Korean nationalists, even though he had spent most of his life abroad in Manchuria and the Soviet Union. Again in the 1960s, official histories and biographies were completely rewritten. North Korean historians were able—they claimed—to trace Kim Il Sung's ancestry back twelve generations.

His father Kim Hyong Jik, the medicinal herb vendor in Manchuria, was now not only a nationalist, but "a professional revolutionary" who educated the "broad masses in anti-Japanese patriotic ideas" and "made preparations to wage armed struggle for national and class emancipation." Kim Il Sung's mother, Kang Pan Suk, was "an ardent revolutionary fighter who devoted her life to the struggle for independence." Kim Il Sung's grandfather, Kim Bo Hyon, and grandmother, Li Bo Ik, "were also patriots" who "fought stoutly against the aggressors." His great-grandfather, Kim Ung I, "distinguished himself in the battle in which the U.S. pirate ship *General Sherman* . . . was sunk."[73] The *General Sherman* was indeed an American ship that sailed up the Taedong River toward Pyongyang in an attempt to open up Korea to foreign trade in 1866. The Koreans resisted, killed all its crew, and burned the ship, but there are no claims other than North Korea's to suggest that a man called Kim Ung I was involved in the battle.

Kim Il Sung's shy and unobtrusive first wife, Kim Jong Suk—who had died in childbirth in Pyongyang in 1949—was turned into a heroine of the revolution, "one who served Kim Il Sung close to her body."[74] She also arranged parachute training from airplanes that somewhat inexplicably appeared in the Korean-Manchurian border mountains, and, naturally, won several shooting competitions in the secret camps in the north.[75] A museum was built for her in her hometown of Hoeryong in North Hamgyong province. Kim Il Sung also erected a monument in honor of his father at his birthplace at Ponghwari, and one for his mother at Chilgol on the outskirts of Pyongyang where she was born. A statue was even erected for Kim Il Sung's paternal uncle, Kim Hyong Gwon, at Hongwon in Hamgyong, where he was said to have been arrested by the local police in 1936.[76]

But the holiest site of all was established in the village of Mangyongdae on the banks of the Taedong River, where Kim Il Sung himself was born. Visitors are shown the simple house where he and his parents lived for a few years, the heap of stones where the children played "ships" and always chose this unusual child to be captain, and the sandpit where they wrestled and he always won because he had not only muscle but also a nimble brain. There is also the favorite tree he used to climb as a child, and simple household items are on display inside the thatched building to show the humble background of Kim Il Sung and his family. Every day, even now, the holy site receives a steady stream of visitors who file past the exhibits in reverent silence.[77]

The personality cult that the *suryong*, or Great Leader, built up around himself—and the rigid political system that he had created—was so extraordinary that even his foreign Communist comrades were dumbfounded. A Vietnamese ambassador to Pyongyang once marveled to a Western colleague at "how they falsified historical records in this country."[78] Hans Maretzki, the last East German ambassador in North Korea, found it rather amusing that German-speaking North Koreans referred to the Great Leader as "Der grosse Führer."[79] Even the Albanians, of all people, called North Korea "an unbelievably closed society."[80]

But it must be understood that North Korea's version of history was never meant to be an accurate account of events and developments on the peninsula. Rather, the North Korean propaganda machine created myths and legends to mobilize the population behind Kim Il Sung, his family, and his ideology. Portraits of the "Three Generals"—Kim Il Sung, Kim Jong Suk, and Kim Jong Il—can be seen everywhere along with paintings and tapestries depicting the alleged birthplaces of Kim Il Sung and Kim Jong Il: the humble gatekeeper's house in Mangyongdae, and the log cabin in Mount Paekdu. And, if the official propaganda is to be believed, the state that they created was rather a recreation

of an ancient Korean kingdom founded in Pyongyang—
where else?—more than five thousand years ago.

In October 1993, North Korea's Academy of Social
Sciences announced that it had found the bones of King
Tangun, who until then had been seen by most historians as
a mythical figure from ancient Korean folklore. But no,
Tangun was now a real king, born in Pyongyang, which was
proclaimed to be the "epicenter of ancient civilization."[81] His
kingdom was the "first advanced and civilized state in the
East," where "no difference existed between civil and military
officials."[82] The discovery of the bones "proved that our
nation originated in Pyongyang and that the homogeneity of
our nation was formed with Pyongyang as the centre. This
inspires a high degree of national pride and self-respect in our
people and unites the 70 million fellow countrymen of the
same blood more closely to fight for the sacred cause of
national reunification."[83] Tangun founded not only the first
Korean nation, but also a religion called *taejong*, which with
its emphasis on Korean nationalism strongly resembles the
juche idea.

A massive tomb was built at the place where the bones of
Tangun—and his heroic wife—were found. Pilgrimages are
held every year to the site, the "Holy Land of Pyongyang," in
honor of his alleged birthday on October 3.[84] While Red
Confucianism formed the basis of social order in Kim Il Sung's
North Korea, the kind of extreme nationalism that the Tangun
cult and myth emanate became the hallmark of a regime that
was fundamentally different from the socialist countries in the
Soviet bloc. A highly militarized, homogenous society, based
on unquestionable loyalty to a god king.

The streamlining of the North Korean citizenry was first
carried out under a campaign, which Kim Il Sung termed the
"Three Revolutions." Originally conceived in the late 1950s
to carry the *chollima* movement forward, the cultural and
ideological revolutions were designed to arouse enthusiasm
and creativity among "the masses" and to turn them into
selfless and patriotic citizens, loyal to the *juche* idea. The
technological revolution was aimed at modernizing

agriculture by introducing irrigation, electrification, and mechanization in a basically backward society. In the early 1970s, the movement became a nationwide mass campaign as "Three Revolution Teams" comprising twenty-five to fifty college students were sent out into the countryside to implement the government's policies. The people were taught to love their working place, their village or town, and to cultivate their dedication to public and state interests, rather then being selfish and indifferent to state directives.[85] The students stayed in farm cooperatives to help the farmers, and the state awarded outstanding students and peasants with special medals.[86]

The changes that later took place in the Eastern Bloc thus had little influence on Kim Il Sung, although he was worried that the disease would spread to his country as well. After the Berlin Wall fell in 1989, he invited one of South Korea's best-known dissidents, Song Du Yul, to Pyongyang. Song Du Yul, a South Korean who had gone to study in West Germany in the 1960s and there become involved in leftist movements and a protégé of the renowned post-Marxist social theorist and critic Jürgen Habermas, traveled to Pyongyang in 1991 where he was received by the Great Leader himself.

Song Du Yul used to be somewhat of a cult figure for South Korea's many radical students, but his reputation had suffered a severe blow when Hwang Jang Yop, the former secretary of the KWP, had defected to the South in 1997 and had revealed that Song Du Yul led a double life. Song Du Yul, Hwang Jang Yop claimed, had traveled to the North more than twenty times, and, under the alias Kim Chol Su, was appointed an alternate politburo member of the KWP shortly after his meeting with Kim Il Sung in 1991. At first, Song Du Yul vehemently denied the allegation and launched a law suit against Hwang Jang Yop for defamation. But when Song Du Yul in September 2003 at last was allowed to return to South Korea, he was interrogated by the secret services—and admitted that it was indeed true.

On October 22, Song Du Yul was arrested, accused of subversive activities and charged with fraud for filing a compensation suit against Hwang Jong Yop. Song Du Yul also admitted that it was true that he had received over US$100,000 from the Pyongyang regime, but said he spent it on "promoting Korean studies in Europe."[87] He was given a seven-year prison sentence, even though senior members of South Korea's liberal government under Roh Moo Hyun opposed legal action against him. The case divided South Korea between advocates of the Sunshine Policy, and those in favor of firmer action against the North, and anyone associated with it.

But regardless of Song Du Yul's duplicity, it was significant that Kim Il Sung would invite him to North Korea to discuss the reunification of Germany—and appoint him, a philosophy professor with German citizenship, an alternate member of the politburo, ranking twenty-third in the Northern hierarchy. During the 1960s and 1970s, Song Du Yul had been a Marxist, but later he was more influenced by the Austrian-born British philosopher Ludwig Wittgenstein. During his 1991 visit to Pyongyang, Song Du Yul gave a lecture at the Kim Il Sung University and taught North Korean students the importance of Wittgenstein's maxim that "the limits of my language mean the limits of my world." There is a lot in the world that the North Koreans cannot understand because they have never experienced it, and have no words to express many phenomena that people in the outside world take for granted.[88]

If the students understood what Song Du Yul told them is unclear as few of them asked him any questions, but Kim Il Sung turned out to be a more curious listener. Given the situation on the Korean peninsula, Song Du Yul was not surprised that Kim Il Sung would be interested in what had happened in Germany after reunification. He wanted to know what the Germans, especially the East Germans, thought about it. Kim Il Sung's conclusion, however, was that the problem in East Germany was that the country was under the control of foreign forces, hundreds of thousands of Soviet troops, without which its regime would not survive. "If the Soviet Union coughed, East Germany got seriously sick," Kim

Il Sung told Song Du Yul.[89] So when the Soviets decided to pull out, they also sealed the fate of East Germany. North Korea would not go the same way, Kim Il Sung argued, because it was truly independent, and had no foreign forces on its soil.

Under the guise of *juche* North Korea had distanced itself from both China and the Soviet Union, but, at the same time, received support from both, even when the two Communist giants fell out with each other in the late 1950s and early 1960s. In July 1961, North Korea concluded a Treaty of Friendship, Cooperation, and Mutual Assistance with the Soviet Union—and a week later, a similar agreement was reached with China.[90] But Kim Il Sung did not hide his dislike for the anti-Stalinization process of the 1950s, and relations between North Korea and the Soviet Union deteriorated markedly when Soviet leader Mikhail Gorbachev launched his policies of *glasnost* and *perestroika* in the mid-1980s.

Relations with China also had their ups and downs. China's support for North Korea in the Korean War was never forgotten, but relations soured during the Cultural Revolution in China in the 1960s when Red Guards came across the border to denounce Kim Il Sung as "a revisionist and disciple of Khrushchev."[91] Also in the 1960s a serious disagreement erupted between the two countries over the demarcation of the boundary around Mount Paekdu. An area of over a thousand square kilometers was in dispute, and the Chinese claim included the 2,744-meter summit of the holy mountain, the symbol of the Korean revolution. The North Koreans were furious. It was not until 1970 that the Chinese yielded, and relations improved.[92]

By and large, however, relations with both China and the Soviet Union, and later Russia, were—and still are—reasonable and friendly, and despite a few bilateral disputes between the two, North Korea never sided with one against the other. In many ways, Kim Il Sung managed to play off the Soviets against the Chinese, just as he had played the Soviet Koreans against the Yan'an veterans in the early 1950s.

And he always won. He got aid from both, while maintaining his independence.

Relations with South Korea were also improving. In the 1970s and 1980s an economic miracle had taken place in the South. Suddenly, the South was richer and more developed than the North. Despite its lack of natural resources—which were in the North—South Korea had built up an industry capable of producing steel and iron which was turned into ships, cars, trucks, buses, and machinery. Imports of iron ore from Australia and other countries had made the impossible possible: by the late 1970s, South Korea was emerging as a modern, industrialized nation. In the late 1980s, a political reform process also began, which turned the old dictatorship into a functioning democracy.

North Korea could not ignore these changes in the South, and a series of meetings between the Red Crosses of the two Koreas began as early as 1972, which resulted in a remarkable joint communiqué on July 4 calling for an end to propaganda and armed provocation against each other. This did not result in any significant changes in the relations between the North and the South, but then a series of secret contacts were made in the 1980s and early 1990s. Meetings between high-level representatives of the North and the South took place more than forty times in Pyongyang, Seoul, Panmunjom in the DMZ, Mount Paekdu, South Korea's Cheju Island, Singapore, and elsewhere.[93] Modest trade between the two Koreas began in the late 1980s, amounting to US$111.3 million in 1991.[94]

A thaw in relations was in the making, and the clandestine process was to have culminated in an official visit to the North in the summer of 1994 by the newly, democratically elected South Korean president Kim Young Sam. But, in the midst of the preparations for the visit, Kim Il Sung passed away on July 8. His death came unexpectedly. Despite his age—eighty two—he was strong and healthy, and less than a month before his death, received former U.S. president Jimmy Carter, who had traveled to Pyongyang to help solve the nuclear crisis that eventually led to the agreement signed in Geneva in October of that year. However, Kim Il Sung's excitement about the upcoming visit of Kim Young Sam—he personally took part in preparing the guest house for the South Korean president—was too much of an ordeal for the old man. He suffered a heart attack, and the summit never took place.

The entire nation went into a state of mourning. The TV announcer cried when he read the news. School children gathered in front of the twenty-meter bronze statue of Kim Il Sung outside the Korean Revolutionary Museum in Pyongyang, and they cried in unison. The world had never seen such an outpouring of grief at the death of a country's leader, and many outsiders brushed if off by saying that the people cried because the authorities forced them to do so. But much of the grief was probably genuine, and if someone felt compelled to cry, it was probably because all the others cried. To do nothing would have been tantamount to treachery. So everyone cried.

A year after his death, Kim Il Sung's old presidential palace was turned into a mausoleum, and a new place of pilgrimage. Visitors enter the massive building, called Kumsusan Memorial Palace, through a long culvert along some of the longest conveyor belts in the world, past a metal detector, a section where the shoes are given a cleaning, and, finally, a room where blowers make sure everyone is clean before entering the grand hall where the embalmed body of the Great Leader lies in state. And if anyone doubted that *juche* is more of a religion than an ideology, the voice in the recorders, which visitors are given when they walk into the inner sanctum of Kumsusan, refers to it as the "Temple of the *Juche* Idea."[95]

***

Many expected North Korea to change after the sudden death of Kim Il Sung. Was he not the sole leader of the country? Was its economy not showing strains, and did it not want to open up and further improve relations with the increasingly prosperous South? Had other Communist countries not already changed? Why would North Korea be different?

North Korea turned out to be vastly different. First of all, it already had an heir-apparent: Kim Il Sung's son, Kim Jong Il. His position as successor to his father had been established by the Central Committee of the Korean Workers' Party in 1974, and formalized during its Sixth Congress in 1980. Editorials in the North Korean media called for "reliable succession" so that the Korean people would not forget Kim Il Sung's "profound benevolence generation after generation."[96] Since 1991, Kim Jong Il had been supreme commander of the Korean People's Army, and, in 1992, he was made marshal. Years before the death of Kim Il Sung, Kim Jong Il was also officially referred to as the "Dear Leader" in the North Korean media, emphasizing his role as number two in the state and party hierarchy, way ahead of his father's old comrades-in-arms.

But Kim Jong Il did not immediately take over any of the titles that his father had held. He ruled the country for three years as only supreme commander, but the first step into the new Kim Jong Il era was taken on July 8, 1997, the third anniversary of Kim Il Sung's death. On that day, the Central Committee of the Korean Workers' Party and its central military commission declared that North Korea had introduced its own *Juche* calendar with 1912, the birth year of Kim Il Sung, as its initial year. His birthday, April 15, was marked as the "Day of the Sun," a public holiday.

Only when the legacy of the Great Leader had been honoured in this grand way was the time ripe for Kim Jong Il to make his moves. In October 1997 he eventually succeeded his father as general secretary of the Korean Workers' Party. Under a constitutional revision in September 1998, the Supreme People's Assembly abolished the presidency—and the late Kim Il Sung was made "Eternal President of the Democratic People's Republic of Korea."[97] At the same time, the National Defense Commission, NDC, which was originally set up in 1990, was elevated to the most powerful organ of the state. On September 5, the assembly elected Kim

Jong Il the first chairman of the reorganized NDC. The succession was complete.

The establishment of a "Communist monarchy" in North Korea amused many foreign observers. But North Korea, although officially Communist, had a ruling family theoretically dating back twelve generations, which the state's propaganda machinery had already turned into the soul of the nation. South Korean analysts—and many Western writers too—believed that the delay in Kim Jong Il's succession to his father's posts (with the exception of the presidency) was due to power struggles within the leadership in the post-Kim Il Sung era. There is, however, not much evidence to support such speculations, and most appear to have been fabricated by South Korea's intelligence agencies, or by high-level North Korean defectors, eager to impress their South Korean interrogators with their knowledge of Pyongyang palace politics.[98]

A desire to show respect for the deceased, and venerated, father is a more plausible explanation, and, as Bruce Cumings points out, "the whole point of the old [Korean] monarchy was to groom the king's first son to succeed him, just as founders of South Korea's conglomerates prepare their sons for succession, and just as the first son in Korean families inherits his father's authority and often lives with his wife under the parental roof."[99] Only a conflict within the ruling family—not interference by its subjects—could have altered the course of Kim Il Sung's succession.

The Dear Leader is the first son of a first son, but, nevertheless, he is very different from the Great Leader. Kim Jong Il never took part in any guerrilla campaigns, but, after his return from Vyatskoye in the Soviet Union, grew up in relative comfort in Pyongyang, although he was only five when he lost his younger brother—Pyong Il, who was known as "Alexander" in Vyatskoye, died in a drowning accident in Pyongyang in 1947— and seven when his mother passed away. The only really dramatic break from his sheltered life in Pyongyang occurred during the Korean War, when he had to flee to China with his younger sister, Kim Kyong Hui, who had been born after the family's return to North Korea.

Kim Jong Il attended kindergarten, primary school, and high school in Pyongyang, and there are numerous stories about how he helped his fellow students, and corrected his teachers when they were wrong. He was, from an early age, groomed to become leader of the country. In 1957, when he was fifteen, Kim Jong Il accompanied his father on a trip to Moscow. That was Kim Jong Il's first trip abroad since the family had returned from Vyatskoye. In January and February 1959, he was back in Moscow, perhaps with the intention of studying there or in some other Eastern Bloc country. But despite rumors of Kim Jong Il being sent to East Germany, and even Romania, to study, there is nothing to back up those claims.[100]

Instead, Kim Jong Il entered Kim Il Sung University in Pyongyang in September 1960, majoring in political economy and graduating in May 1964. The topic of his graduation thesis was the role of local counties in socialist construction, and an analysis of his father's theories on socialism in rural areas.[101] After graduation, Kim Jong Il went to work for the Department of Organization and Guidance of Central Committee of the Korean Workers' Party, which supervises its mass organizations, and directs the work of the party's branches in the government and the armed forces.[102] Those whose loyalty was in doubt were immediately purged and exiled to the remote northeast, or sent off to labor camps. In the late 1960s and 1970s, as a new generation of state functionaries was emerging, Kim Il Sung even purged many former comrades from his partisan days.[103]

Kim Jong Il still heads that department which remains one of the most important organs of the state. But his support base goes way beyond supervision of party branches. Kim Il Sung had placed trusted relatives in important positions. His brother, Kim Yong Ju, for instance, headed the Department of Organization and Guidance in 1954, became a member of the party's politburo in 1969, vice premier in 1974, and vice

president in 1993.[104] Following the death of Kim Jong Suk,
Kim Il Sung took a new common-law wife, Kim Song Ae,
whom he married in the early 1960s. Little is known about
her background other than that she was the secretary to Kim
Il Sung's security guards at his Pyongyang residence. But Kim
Il Sung appointed her chairperson of the Democratic
Women's Union of Korea, replacing Kim Ok Sun, wife of a
purged partisan general, Choe Kwang.[105] In 1980, Kim Song
Ae became a member of the party's Central Committee, and
later a delegate to the Supreme People's Assembly.[106]

A new generation was also emerging within the ruling
family. In 1988, Kim Jong Il's sister Kim Kyong Hui joined
the party's Central Committee, and subsequently became
director of the party's Light Industry Department in 1994.
Her husband—and Kim Jong Il's brother-in-law—Chang Song
Taek was appointed first vice director of the party's Central
Committee in 1985 and later head of its Organizational
Department. In the 1970s, Chang Song Taek had headed the
department in charge of the Three Revolutions, where his
main objective was to enhance the position of Kim Jong Il.[107]
The members of the teams that Chang Song Taek sent to
every corner of North Korea became faithful followers of the
Dear Leader and the core of his power base when he
succeeded his father in 1994.[108]

Much has been said, and written, about Kim Jong Il's
alleged lavish lifestyle, a fact he was acutely aware of when
Kim Dae Jung visited Pyongyang in June 2000. "They say I
drink a lot, but that's not true. Only a glass of wine every
now and then," Kim Jong Il told the South Korean reporters
who accompanied Kim Dae Jung to the North.[109] But it is clear
that the lifestyle of the Dear Leader is not the same as that of
the Great Leader. Kim Jong Il has fathered at least six children
by four women, both wives and mistresses. He lives in a
heavily guarded, secluded villa in downtown Pyongyang.
Kenji Fujimoto, a Japanese sushi chef, who claims to have
served Kim Jong Il for thirteen years until 2001, alleges that
he was often told to travel abroad to procure food for his
master: caviar from Iran and Uzbekistan, melons and grapes

from China, durian and papaya from Thailand and Malaysia,
Czech beer, Danish pork, and tuna and other fish from Japan.
The banquets, which the Japanese chef prepared, were
washed down with a selection from Kim Jong Il's private
cellar of ten thousand bottles of vintage wines from France
and Italy.[110]

Fujimoto's colorful tales could be dismissed as exaggerations, and it is not even clear who he is and if he really was
Kim Jong Il's chef. The Japanese media in particular likes to
relish in anything sensational about North Korea, and they
seldom let the truth stand in the way for a good story. But
another book about Kim Jong Il's personal lifestyle was
published in Russia in 2002. Ostensibly written by Konstantin
Pulikovsky, the chief representative of the Russian president
in the Far East, it is called "The Orient Express" and describes
Kim Jong Il's journey through Russia in July and August 2001.
For three weeks, Kim Jong Il traveled with his entourage in a
sixteen-carriage private train from North Korea all the way to
Moscow and St. Petersburg. According to Pulikovsky, the
train carried crates of expensive wines imported from France,
and Kim Jong Il and his men feasted on gourmet meals with
silver chopsticks while being waited upon by "beautiful lady
conductors." Live lobsters were sent in advance to stations
along the route for the North Koreans to pick up and, on a
stop in Omsk, Kim Jong Il rejected a plate of barrel-salted
pickles because they were "shoddily marinated cucumbers
from Bulgaria, not prepared in the authentic Russian style."[111]
The book prompted a diplomatic protest from North Korea.
Even some Russians criticized Pulikovsky, who had been Kim
Jong Il's host, for violating the trust of the North Koreans by
publishing the damaging account of Kim Jong Il. But there was
little or no reason for someone like Pulikovsky to exaggerate
what happened during Kim Jong Il's epic train journey, and
the book became an instant bestseller in Russia.[112]

Even more remarkable is Kim Jong Il's love for the movies.
In the 1970s, he was said to have produced six major films
and musicals, with catching, revolutionary titles such as "Fate
of a Member of Self-Defense Corps" and "True Daughter of

the Party."[113] In all, if the official propaganda is to be believed, Kim Jong Il has personally taken part in the making of 800 feature movies, 400 movies for children, and 1,000 documentaries.[114] That may be physically impossible, but such trivial concerns have never prevented the North Koreans from extolling the brilliant minds and virtues of the Great and Dear Leaders.

Kim Jong Il still wanted to know more about movie making, so in January 1978 he sent his agents to Hong Kong to kidnap a famous South Korean film actress, Choe Eun Hui. A sack was pulled over her head, and she was taken to Hong Kong's docks and bundled aboard a small boat. She was then injected with a sedative and she fainted. Eight days later, she arrived – terrified—in Pyongyang. Her husband, Shin Sang Ok, was one of South Korea's best-known film directors, and as soon as he heard of the abduction, he flew to Hong Kong. But in July of the same year, he was abducted, too.[115]

The couple spent eight years in North Korea making films—first separately without knowing that both of them were in North Korean custody, then together. Many of the productions were propaganda tales commissioned by Kim Jong Il himself, and their most famous contribution to North Korea's film industry, *Pulgasari*, became a cult movie in the North. It was about a huge iron-eating lizard, who fights with the peasants against the feudal lords—in some ways, it was an adapted North Korean version of *Godzilla* with a social conscience.[116] Although Kim Jong Il went out of his way to make the couple feel welcome and at home by praising their work and bringing them expensive clothes and Western goods, they thought of suicide.

Finally, in 1986, Shin Sang Ok and Choe Eun Hui were allowed to travel abroad, to a film festival in Austria's capital Vienna. They took the first opportunity to escape. Bursting through the doors of the U.S. embassy, they asked for asylum and were repatriated to South Korea. Kim Jong Il was furious, and thought the couple had been kidnapped by the Americans. He sent the couple a message offering to help them return to Pyongyang, which, of course, they never did.[117]

That Kim Jong Il has been able to carry out such bizarre actions goes a long way to show how immensely loyal many of his underlings have become. No one questions the Dear Leader and his orders, even if his lifestyle cannot by any stretch of the imagination be compared with that of the revolutionary heroes, the rag-tag guerrillas who fought their way through Manchuria to Siberia in the late 1930s.

CHAPTER 4

THE ARMY AND THE PARTY

The Dear Leader Kim Jong Il walked slowly along the podium, smiling and waving at tens of thousands of troops assembled in Pyongyang's Kim Il Sung Square. A flurry of balloons drifted toward the sky as a 21-gun salute echoed in the distance. The celebrations were opened by the minister of the People's Armed Forces, Vice Marshal Kim Il Chol, who praised the great commander, Kim Jong Il, for turning North Korea into "an impregnable fortress . . . if the U.S. imperialists and their followers invade the inviolable land, sea and sky of the Democratic People's Republic of Korea . . . the army and the people who hold the dignity and sovereignty of the country and nation as dear as their own lives will deal merciless blows at the invaders."[1] A black limousine carrying a huge flag with a painted image of Kim Il Sung then drove in front of elite troops goose-stepping past Kim Jong Il, his closest comrades and a few foreign guests up on the dais.

It was April 25, 2002, the official seventieth anniversary of the Korean People's Army—and less than three months after president George W. Bush made his "Axis of Evil" speech, lumping North Korea together with Iraq and Iran as the main threats against the security of the U.S. That was probably the reason why Kim Jong Il made this rare public appearance, and chose to do it on Army Day. As he was consolidating power following the death of the Great Leader in 1994, he replaced the party with the armed forces as the most important organs of the state by instituting a policy called "the military first." Now, the North Korean leadership's policy was given renewed emphasis, and the rhetoric grew fiercer. On February 8, North Korea hit back at the U.S., branding it the "empire of [the] devil."[2]

The U.S. has said time and again that it has no intention of invading North Korea, and that the situation there was different from that in Iraq. But the North Koreans were not convinced. Every North Korean schoolchild knows about the incident in 1866 when the U.S. battleship *General Sherman* sailed up the Taedong River toward Pyongyang—and the role Kim Il Sung's great-grandfather allegedly played in destroying it. A century later—in January 1968—a U.S. intelligence ship called *Pueblo* was seized by the North Korean navy off the port of Wonsan. It was on a mission to pick up electronic transmissions from North Korea, and had the capability of identifying radar locations so they could be jammed in time of war.[3] The Americans claimed it was in international waters, but even Wayne Kirkbridge, a U.S. army office who was stationed in the DMZ in the 1970s, conceded: "it is possible that due to a navigation error the *Pueblo* was inside the twelve-mile limit."[4]

The *Pueblo* carried eighty-one officers and privates and two civilian hydrographic experts. One sailor was killed and three wounded in circumstances that are not entirely clear. The crew was finally released eleven months later, but not the vessel. It sat in Wonsan harbor until it was moved to the Taedong River in Pyongyang, close to the place where the *General Sherman* was destroyed, which is commemorated with a plaque. The *Pueblo* has become a popular attraction for foreign tourists as well as locals—and a reminder of "the threat" the North Koreans perceive that the U.S. poses against them. While the U.S., Japan, and their friends and allies see North Korea as a threat, the North Korean leadership sincerely believe that they are a potential target for attacks and invasion—and it is that perception that guides not only the way in which they negotiate with outside powers but also domestic policies such as "the military first" concept. It also explains why North Korea believes it must have a huge and well-equiped army—and the right to develop a nuclear deterrent.

Somewhat ironically, however, the man at the helm of the world's most militarized society has no known military background. Still, in December 1991, Kim Jong Il was appointed supreme commander of the Korean People's Army and then, a year later, elevated to the rank of marshal. In April 1993, he was made chairman of the National Defense Commission, NDC, a position until then reserved for the president. But a constitutional amendment was enacted to enable Kim Jong Il to take up the post. The NDC had been created in May 1990 as an independent body, overseeing all military matters, including the Ministry of the People's Armed Forces, and has under Kim Jong Il become the most powerful organ in the country.[5]

When Kim Jong Il, three years after his father's death—in October 1997—added general secretary of the KWP to his various military titles, it was still the military, not the party, that mattered most to him. Significantly, North Korea celebrates the anniversaries of Kim Jong Il's appointment as supreme commander and chairman of the NDC, not as general secretary of the party.[6] Speaking at another North Korean red-letter day—Kim Jong Il's fifty-ninth birthday on February 15, 2001—NDC vice chairman, Vice Marshal Cho Myong Rok praised the Dear Leader, the "Bright Star of Paekdu," and went on to underscore that the military first politics "is a strategic political model to be constantly held fast to by the Korean Workers' Party as long as there exists imperialism on the earth . . . the people's army should not only defend the defense lines of the fatherland but also instill the revolutionary ideology and fighting spirit into the people."[7] However, this new approach to mobilizing the masses and exercising power in North Korea was most probably not prompted by a need for Kim Jong Il to consolidate his grip on the country following his father's death, but by the general, internal social instability caused by the economic crisis and the famine, which coincided with the transition of power from the Great to the Dear Leader.

Professor Suh Dae Sook at the University of Hawaii has pointed out that the very term "military first," or *songun chongchi* in Korean, is a newly coined North Korean phrase that is not found in any North or South Korean dictionaries, and which came into wide circulation only after Kim Jong Il assumed power in Pyongyang. "Military first" is also a mistranslation. The actual meaning is "to give priority to the military in politics."[8] It is a phrase to express a new kind of North Korean politics, including a new political structure, and a new leader with a new emphasis on the military throughout society.

Kim Il Sung did not use the term "military first," and by definition in almost all socialist societies the party would control the military, not vice versa. Today, the ten members of the NDC are the top elite of North Korea. They include Vice Marshals Cho Myong Rok and Kim Il Chol and other trusted colleagues of Kim Jong Il. The party serves only to give the NDC legitimacy by passing decisions it has already made, as does the country's rubber-stamp parliament, the Supreme People's Assembly.[9] Of the sixteen most senior leaders of North Korea today, three come from the Supreme People's Assembly, two from the party, one from the cabinet—and ten from the NDC.[10] The only civilian public face of the Supreme People's Assembly is the chairman of its Standing Committee, party veteran Kim Yong Nam, who often goes on trips abroad and serves as North Korea's *de facto* head of state. His brother Kim Du Nam, though, is a four-star general and once served as military secretary to Kim Il Sung, so the military is in the family.[11] The prime minister, Hong Sung Nam, holds a largely ceremonial post, and was once dismissed from his position as politburo member, as was the main foreign relations officer of the party, Kim Yong Sun.

Despite these changes in the mid-1990s, though, the party has not become irrelevant. Even if its role is not as prominent under Kim Jong Il as it was under his father's rule, the KWP still remains a potent vehicle for control over the population. It is important to remember that the political movement that Kim Il Sung built up in the late 1940s and 1950s differs considerably from the parties that once ruled the former socialist bloc. In the Soviet Union and Eastern Europe the Communist parties were vanguard institutions. In North

Korea, an estimated three to four million people are party members, or nearly 20 percent of the population.[12] In other words, it is a mass party surrounded by mass organizations for the youth, women, workers, peasants, intellectuals, and religious groups recognized by the state. In October 2001, the party even set up a special association for magicians "to contribute to the country's magic and to foster ties with magicians around the world."[13]

According to a decision taken at the Sixth Party Congress in 1980, congresses should be held every five years to coordinate the activities of the KWP and its mass organizations, but no congress has been held since then.[14] The Central Committee meets more regularly, but not actually to discuss political issues. Everybody is expected to praise and honor the policies put forth by Kim Jong Il and his closest associates. Mass mobilization, not deliberation and decision making, is the main purpose of the KWP and its affiliated organizations.

North Koreans are trained from an early age to respect the Great and Dear Leaders. Small children are members of the Young Pioneers, and spend very little time with their families. They grow up in a communal environment, where singing, dancing, athletics, and music dominate their lives.[15] Every youth over the age of fourteen is supposed to belong to the Kim Il Sung Socialist Youth League, while women join the Korean Democratic Women's League, headed by Kim Il Sung's second wife, Kim Song Ae. It is quite a sight to see thousands of North Korean school children dressed in military-style uniforms, marching in perfect formation behind the North Korean flag and shouting, "Kim Il Sung! Kim Jong Il!" When I asked a schoolboy at the Mangyongdae Schoolchildren's Palace to type something in Korean on his computer because I wanted to see what their font looked like, he immediately keyed in, "The Great Leader President Kim Il Sung will always be with us."[16]

In theory, there are two other "fraternal parties," the Chondonist Chongu Party and the Korean Social Democratic Party, but they exist in name only and do not contest elections to the Supreme People's Assembly.[17] Both parties also endorse all the policies of the KWP and promote the realization of "heaven on earth."[18] All candidates for the Supreme People's Assembly are handpicked by the top leadership, and Kim Il Sung and Kim Jong Il have never been satisfied—like many of their socialist counterparts—with 95 or 98 percent of the vote. It has always been 100 percent, which some analysts have called a curious reflection of how Korean traditions of consensus can be merged with modern totalitarian goals.[19] Achieving this remarkable national unity has been made much easier by Kim Il Sung's elimination of infighting within the party in the 1950s and to some extent into the 1960s. The different tendencies that once existed within the KWP are long gone, as are most of the veterans of Kim Il Sung's guerrilla days, through purges and natural causes.

The "new" KWP is dominated by younger cadres who rose to prominence during the Three Revolutions in the 1970s, but, ultimately of course, all power rests with Kim Jong Il and his inner circle of close relatives and advisers. Not even Enver Hoxha's Albania—let alone Mao Zedong's totalitarian but unruly China—was as centrally controlled as North Korea was under Kim Il Sung, and to a lesser but still large extent remains with Kim Jong Il at the helm. The Confucian devotion to the leaders is so profound that even North Korean refugees in the South cried at the news of Kim Il Sung's death in 1994.[20]

The almost religious adulation that the Great and Dear Leaders have spun around themselves also makes North Korea very different from other socialist states. When North Korea commemorated the seventh anniversary of Kim Il Sung's demise on July 8, 2001, the state-run *Korea Central News Agency* reported that "three mysterious birds appeared . . . It happened at sunset on July 2 in a flat on the first floor of the apartment house in Undok-dong in Hanggu district, Nampho . . . Three unknown beautiful birds perched on the window-sill of the room next to the kitchen at about 8:40 a.m. The birds remained there for one hour and forty minutes, blinking their eyes towards a portrait of the President. It was witnessed by over 100 residents in the same apartment. They were unanimous in saying that they saw the birds pay respectful homage to the President, not forgetting July."[21]

On April 15 the following year, which marked the ninetieth anniversary of Kim Il Sung's birth, the KCNA had even more astonishing miracles to report: "On the morning of April 15 the wind stopped blowing in Mangyongdae where President Kim Il Sung was born and the temperature around his old home and its surrounding area was 16.2° C, recording the highest temperature (for April 15) since the meteorological observation began." In the run-up to the big day, "11 swan-like birds circled a statue of Kim Il Sung ten times and 90 white azaleas bloomed, stirring up deep emotion among the people."[22] When Kim Jong Il turned sixty two months earlier, the KCNA claimed that it had snowed for sixty days and dumped exactly sixty centimeters of snow on his alleged birthplace in Mount Paekdu.[23]

The country led by these two men with their extraordinary powers and personalities—Kim Il Sung may be dead, but his spirit is still alive and he is, after all, president in all eternity—maintains the fifth largest armed forces in the world after China, the United States, Russia and India. Some 1,173,000 men are in active service in the army, navy, and air force.[24] Foreign estimates put North Korea's defense spending at 25 percent of GDP, and with the national income shrinking since the economic crisis began in the mid-1990s, military expenditure is eating into the civil budget.[25] But the armed forces have to come first. Military service is compulsory, and can be as long as ten years. Only university students are exempted from service as long as they are studying, and then they are recruited to special duties based on their area of expertise. Graduates of medical colleges, for instance, are commissioned as medical officers.[26]

Top officers, such as government officials, live in an exclusive area of Pyongyang known as the Executive Apartments. The complex is surrounded by a high concrete wall and guarded by soldiers with automatic rifles. The apartments are furnished with luxury goods that are beyond the reach of most ordinary North Koreans including color televisions, refrigerators, and imported Japanese air conditioners.[27] This is the privileged elite that Kim Jong Il can count on for loyalty and support. The famine never affected them, and they are shielded from the sight of other citizens, who never get to peek inside the walls of their complex in Pyongyang.

In addition to the regular forces, 7.45 million Korean men and women—or 30 percent of the population between the ages of fifteen and sixty—belong to paramilitary reserve forces such as the Workers'-Peasants' Red Guard, the Red Youth Guard, the Paramilitary Training Unit, and the People's Guard troops.[28] They are lightly armed, but can be called upon in an emergency. More specifically, these units serve as training centers for millions of North Koreans, whom the regime wants to integrate into its highly militarized and strictly controlled society.

The core, however, of all the military units, and the backbone of Kim Jong Il's support base, is the Special Operations Force. It is a huge unit, about ninety thousand strong, which makes it one of the largest special forces in the world. But all its personnel are still carefully selected. The majority are drawn from politically reliable families—mostly the "core class"—and have usually served at least four years in the regular forces before being recruited.[29] In the words of U.S. North Korea specialist Joseph Bermudez, the new recruit "is typically educated, indoctrinated and motivated by the strict and regimented society of his country. His view of the world has been regulated since birth by the state-controlled information and educational systems."[30]

Kim Jong Il frequently visits North Korea's many military bases to remind his men of his presence and to provide "on-the-spot guidance," to use a favorite phrase of the country's propaganda machinery. On these visits, he is always accompanied by other, high-ranking military officers such as Vice Marshals Cho Myong Rok, Kim Il Chol, and Pak Gi So, and four-star general Pak Chae Gyong, deputy director of the General Political Bureau of the armed forces, and one of the fastest rising officers in the North Korean army. Many of these officers are much older than Kim Jong Il, but there is no question that he is in charge, being the son of the Great Leader they all respect.

Many Special Operations personnel are based just north of the DMZ, where they are involved in very secretive work. On November 15, 1974, a nine-man patrol from the South Korean army observed a vapor rising from the ground, more than a kilometer south of their part of the DMZ. As soon as they started digging, they were fired on by North Korean snipers on the other side. The South Korean patrol had stumbled on a tunnel that North Korean engineers were building under the DMZ. It was constructed with reinforced concrete, and had electric lines and lighting, weapons storage areas, sleeping quarters, and a narrow gauge railway with carts.[31] In March 1975, a second tunnel was discovered near Chorwon, one hundred kilometers northeast of Seoul. It was two meters high and two meters wide, and capable of providing passage for thirty thousand fully armed men plus their weapons per hour. A third tunnel was found on October 17, 1978, near the "truce village" of Panmunjom. It ran 73 meters below ground, and was big enough for a full division of North Korean troops to move through it every hour. Later, on March 4, 1990, a fourth tunnel was discovered extending a kilometer south of the Military Demarcation Line and 135 meters below the surface near Yanggu in Kangwon province on the eastern side of the peninsula.

It is possible that there are many more tunnels that the South Koreans have not discovered, and some South Koreans suspect the North Koreans are still digging tunnels under the DMZ, despite the easing of tension resulting from Kim Dae Jung's Sunshine Policy after the June 2000 Kim-Kim summit in Pyongyang. These are military secrets not known to ordinary soldiers in the North Korean army. People involved in clandestine projects like the digging of the tunnels are trusted, but despite their loyalty, and the loyalty displayed by most ordinary citizens, control mechanisms are strong and the North Koreans must be some of the most supervised people in the world today. If many of the control mechanisms broke down during the famine, they now appear to have been restored. Another famine, followed by social chaos, could break out again. The World Food Program estimates that they would need to feed 6.5 million, or 28 percent of the population. 3.2 million people are getting food from the WFP, while bilateral donors such as China and South Korea are feeding a few million more.[32] In other words, many North Koreans go hungry, but there are no signs of civil unrest. Even at the height of the famine, fear of the authorities remained as strong as ever. There were some disturbances, but never any uprising with starving, angry people storming government offices and warehouses, which would have been the case in most other countries under similar circumstances. Instead, those who did not want to live under the Kim Jong Il regime escaped to China.

The KWP's powerful Organization and Guidance Department—headed by Kim Jong Il with his brother-in-law Chang Song Taek as his deputy—oversees the activities of government employees and members of the party, and the State Security Department functions both as an intelligence agency abroad and a secret police at home. Its duty is to identify and eliminate "anti-state criminals," to maintain surveillance of North Koreans who have returned from abroad, and to monitor national borders and international entry points.

The department is believed to have fifty thousand agents, all dedicated Kim Jong Il loyalists, and its local branches cover the entire country, even in the smallest municipalities. It is most likely under the direct control of Kim Jong Il, as no successor to the former head of the department, Lee Jin Soo, was selected when he died in 1987.[33] The clearest indication of Kim Jong Il's power over the department is that it was placed under the NDC following a constitutional amendment in 1988.[34] North Korea also has a Ministry of Public Security, which too is responsible for political surveillance. It is believed to have 130,000 agents maintaining checkpoints to inspect buses, trucks, and trains—and to perform "normal" police and civil defense duties.[35] "Serious" political cases, however, are usually deferred to the State Security Department, which controls the Prison Camps Bureau that maintains North Korea's many detention centers for real and imagined "enemies of the fatherland."[36] Control is also exercised through a system called "five households," which is designed to keep the populace under constant surveillance. Under this system, each of the five households is expected to inform on its neighbors, and to attend self-criticism sessions regularly where everybody is compelled to criticize him- or herself, and others.[37] In high-rise apartment blocks in Pyongyang, there is an informant on each floor, and on every fifth floor an informant who supervises the other informants. The chief informant, who is located in the basement, checks all of them.[38]

Furthermore, a special investigation department—called the Research Department for External Intelligence until the 1990s—is responsible for the collection of intelligence abroad. It is headquartered in Pyongyang, but has sections in the Americas, Europe, Africa, Asia—and in Japan: the pro-Pyongyang association of Korean residents, the Chongryun. At least until the 1990s, it was known to have secret offices in Moscow, Beijing, Berlin, Guangzhou, Macau, Singapore and Hong Kong.[39] Overall intelligence and security policy is coordinated by the National Intelligence Committee—which, not surprisingly, is headed by Kim Jong Il.

The primary objective of all these agencies is to protect Kim Jong Il and his inner circle of power holders, and to ensure their hold on the populace. Kim Il Sung appointed trusted relatives to important positions in the party and the state—and Kim Jong Il has not acted any differently. Apart from relying on support from his sister, light industry department head Kim Kyong Hui, and her husband, the immensely influential Chang Song Taek, he has placed the brothers of his brother-in-law in important positions in the power structure. The eldest brother, Chang Song U, commands one of the army units that defends Pyongyang, and the middle brother, Chang Song Kil, is political commissar of another unit in the capital.[40]

The transition from the Great to the Dear Leader went smoothly precisely because there was no other possible successor or opposition to Kim Jong Il and his inner circle of relatives and close associates. South Korean sources have speculated that there is, or was, a rivalry between Kim Jong Il and his younger half brother, Kim Pyong Il, who is the son of Kim Il Sung's second wife, Kim Song Ae. His long stints abroad as ambassador—first to Bulgaria, then to Finland and Poland—are the basis for these speculations.[41] But Kim Pyong Il is much younger than Kim Jong Il—he was born in 1954— and is not in a position to challenge the Dear Leader. Nor is he known to have any following in the armed forces or even the party. Very little is known about Kim Il Sung's and Kim Song Ae's three other children, two sons and a daughter, and it is highly unlikely that any of them would act against the wishes of their older half brother. They are respected because they are the children of the Great Leader, but they are not contenders for power over the state.

What is likely, however, is that there is a different mindset—but not necessarily a conflict—between older conservatives and younger cadre who want to see at least some economic changes. It is impossible to find out what is going on behind the scenes in Pyongyang, and even foreigners who have lived there for years can do little more than guess what might be happening. A widely held notion in Pyongyang is that there might have been a slight power vacuum after the death of Kim Il Sung in 1994, or at least some uncertainty as to who was going to call the shots. According to this theory, Kim Jong Il could not count on nearly the same respect as his father enjoyed from army veterans. But they needed him, because he was Kim Il Sung's son and they needed someone to hold the legacy of the Great Leader in trust. Likewise, Kim Jong Il needed the old guard to protect his own position. Significantly, all the members of the NDC are at least ten years older than Kim Jong Il. Gradually, however, Kim Jong Il has managed to consolidate power in his own right.[42] In 2002, English language texts began to refer to Kim Jong Il as the "Great Leader," while his father became the "Respected Leader, President Kim Il Sung." But in Korean Kim Il Sung is still the *suryong*. There is no other *suryong* but he.

In the absence of any reliable inside information, it is only possible to speculate. But the way in which North Korea has developed since the death of Kim Il Sung lends credence to this theory. This would also explain why Kim Jong Il did not immediately take over all his father's duties. People who subscribe to this theory also argue that it was only when Kim Jong Il felt he was firmly in the saddle that he dared to experiment with economic reform. But, at the same time, he still needs the army for his own protection, and that can only be achieved by making sure they remain a highly privileged group in society. Hence the "military first" policy. More critical voices would argue that desperation, not political courage, was the reason why North Korea decided to ease old price and wage controls and permit some more market-oriented enterprise.

It is equally difficult to determine the actual role of the country's First Family. The North Koreans themselves detest the use of the word "dynasty," and even foreign residents in Pyongyang say it is too simplistic to look at the country's power structure in terms of dynastic tendencies. But if it is not a dynasty, it is at least a very powerful clan and Kim Jong Il appears to be promoting a third generations of Kims, who are being groomed to continue ruling North Korea once he is gone from the scene. Kim Jong Il's first wife is believed to be Hong Il Chun, whom he married in 1966. She was later appointed vice minister of education and a delegate to the Supreme People's Assembly. They are supposed to have had a daughter, Kim Hye Suk, who is now in her mid-thirties.[43] Kim Jong Il then took a mistress, Song Hye Rim, who was five years older than he and an actress of the Korean Art Film Studio. She bore him a son, Kim Jong Nam, in 1971. In order for him not to grow up alone, Song Hye Rim's niece, Lee Nam Ok, was called into Kim Jong Il's heavily guarded residence in Pyongyang. She was only thirteen when she went to live with Kim Jong Nam, a lonely child who was not allowed to go out and play with other children.

An interview Lee Nam Ok gave much later—in February 1998—to the Japanese magazine *Tokyo Bungei Shunju* is one of the few available accounts of the Kim family's private life. She describes Kim Jong Nam as "totally submissive to his father" and says that he "never criticized what Kim Jong Il decided for him." Lee Nam Ok's own life in the Kim residence was that of "a princess who was not allowed to go out of her castle, which was far removed from the realities of the lives of ordinary North Korean people."[44] The only times they went around Pyongyang was in a chauffeur-driven Mercedes Benz. Teachers came to the residence, and it was only later they went to a normal school—in Geneva in the 1980s. That was a happy time for the two teenagers. Both of them became fluent in French, and learned to live in an open, capitalist society.

Naturally, there were also contradictions between what they had been told in North Korea and what they learned in Switzerland. Kim Jong Nam, however, wanted to believe in what he had been told back home in Pyongyang, and remained immensely loyal to his father and his country. When something happened and North Korea was blamed for it, Kim Jong Nam always denied the accusations, believing the official version of any untoward incident. Lee Nam Ok defected to the West in 1992, and is now believed to be living in Cambodia with her French husband.

Kim Jong Nam, though, has remained loyal to his father and soon found a job with the State Security Department. He was also put in charge of one of Kim Jong Il's favorite projects: the Korea Computer Center in Pyongyang, which was set up in 1990 and employs more than eight hundred people. In 1995, the center was rebuilt with state-of-the-art equipment, much of which was obtained in Japan through the Chongryun.[45] Kim Jong Il's fascination with computers is well-known, and his eldest son clearly shares that interest. Kim Jong Nam's rise to prominence led many to believe that he would be the next ruler of North Korea.

But in May 2001, he was caught at Tokyo's Narita airport traveling on a passport he had bought from the Dominican Republic. He had arrived with a small group of children to visit Tokyo Disneyland, but now they were all expelled. The incident caused a major diplomatic embarrassment for North Korea, which led to speculations that he would perhaps not succeed his father. His mother, Song Hye Rim, also left North Korea and died in exile in Moscow in 2002. Her sister Song Hae Rang—Lee Nam Ok's mother—defected to the West in 1996, where she now lives at an undisclosed location. Song Hae Rang did not go unpunished for that action. Her son, Lee Il Man, who had fled to the West at the age of twenty-one in 1982 and later made it to South Korea, was gunned down in Seoul in 1997, most probably by Northern agents.[46]

North Korea pundits have therefore begun to look at some of Kim Jong Nam's younger half brothers for a possible successor to keep the Kim family in power. Kim Jong Il married again in 1974 to Kim Yong Suk, the daughter of a high-ranking military official. But she had only two daughters and no sons, so he took a new mistress, Koh Yong Hee, a dancer in the state-sponsored Mansudae Art Troupe. Koh Yong Hee was born in Japan, but came with her parents to North Korea in the early 1960s, when many ethnic Koreans emigrated to what they saw as their real "fatherland." They have two sons and a daughter, and the elder son, Kim Jong Chul, was soon identified as a possible alternative to Kim Jong Nam. Born in 1981, he has also studied at an international school in Switzerland and, despite his tender age, is a key official in the KWP's Department of Agitation and Propaganda.[47]

Speculation that he is the new heir apparent began in February 2003, when a North Korean magazine published a report based on a document from the Korean People's Army entitled "The Respected Mother is the Most Faithful and Loyal Subject to the Dear Leader Comrade Supreme Commander."[48] The mother was not named, but was generally assumed to be Koh Yong Hee and the respect with which she was mentioned in the article resembled the campaign elevating Kim Jong Il's mother, Kim Jong Suk, to the pantheon of revolutionary heroes preceding his ascension to power.

Then, all of a sudden, Koh Yong Hee's younger son, Kim Jong Oon—two years Kim Jong Chul's junior—appeared in discussions about the succession. According to Kim Jong Il's former Japanese sushi chef, who spent a lot of time with the family, Kim Jong Oon "resembles his father in every way, including his physical frame."[49] Like his brother, he is Swiss-educated, and speculations about a role for him as the future leader of North Korea began when South Korean intelligence claimed to have intercepted communications indicating that Kim Jong Il favors the younger son, whom he sees as stronger, more political savvy, and more masculine than his older brother.[50]

But all these speculations are based on Western or South Korean perceptions of the North Korean power structure. If the North Koreans follow their established Confucian pattern, the eldest son of the eldest son of the eldest son, Kim Jong Nam, would still be the favorite. It is highly unlikely that the incident at Tokyo airport in May 2001 has had any severe impact on how Kim Jong Il views his sons and what is expected of them. And there is nothing to indicate that he has left his central position as head of the Korea Computer Center, which many believe is part of North Korea's cyber warfare machine, and thus a mainly military facility.[51] It also directs Pyongyang's worldwide clandestine intelligence-gathering efforts, a very important task that would not be left in the hands of someone who is not fully trusted by Kim Jong Il. Kim Jong Nam is reported to spend a lot of time in China—and Macau, where he goes to gamble—but that does not mean that he is out of favor. Pyon Jin Il, editor of the *Korea Report* in Tokyo, also believes that Kim Jong Nam is the most likely successor: "North Korea is a feudalistic country. Under feudalism the eldest brother is the heir of the father."[52]

Kim Jong Il may have many more years to contemplate his succession, and no outsiders can know what he has in mind. But it is becoming increasingly clear that he has used his decade in power to consolidate his and his family's leading role in society, politics, and the military. He has also promoted other loyalists within the army. The latest promotion occurred on the occasion of the anniversary of Kim Il Sung's ninetieth birthday in 2002, when fifty-five senior commanders were given higher positions. One of them was Chang Song U, who was promoted from general to vice marshal.[53]

It is these loyal officers that comprise the pillar of support for Kim Jong Il. His "military first" policy has provided the ruling elite with a sense of security that the party could not do in the times of severe economic crisis.[54] Typically, when Kim Jong Il visited China in January 2001 to inspect the Shanghai stock exchange and the high-tech industrial complex in Shanghai's sister city Pudong, he did not bring with him economic experts or government ministers responsible for economic development, but high-ranking military officers. Among them were four-star generals Pak Chae Gyong and Hyon Chol Hae, another deputy director of the General Political Bureau of the Korean People's Army. They may know everything about the *juche* idea and have a good grasp of military affairs, but they know nothing about how to run a stock exchange or a privately owned enterprise. As Prof. Suh Dae Sook argues, "they assume that [a] strong and prosperous country is built by the labor of soldiers, and therefore, the generals need to know more about economic development than the party officials or government bureaucrats in charge of the economy."[55]

In fact, for many years, North Korea's industrial development has been mainly geared up to producing military hardware—including missiles and missile technology for export. North Korea is now one of the world's leading manufacturers of all types of ballistic missiles, and they are of such high quality that the country has never had any difficulty finding foreign customers for their deadly hardware.

CHAPTER 5

THE MISSILES AND THE NUKES

They seemed to be just another Asian couple who had moved to Eastern Europe to take advantage of business opportunities in the former socialist bloc. They drove a big Mercedes and lived in a luxury apartment in a posh part of Bratislava, the Slovak capital, where they counted among their neighbors the city's mayor and a cabinet minister. But Kim Kum Jin and Ri Sun Hui were no ordinary businesspeople. They were North Koreans arranging the sale of millions of dollars of missile components to the Middle East, primarily Egypt.

By the time Slovakia's secret service realized in August 2002 what was going on and raided the North Koreans' apartment, the couple had vanished. They left behind not only their Mercedes but also a trove of invoices and other documents, which provided the Slovak secret service—and its new allies, Western countries—with a rare inside look at North Korea's missile and military technology business.[1] From their base in Bratislava, the North Koreans had imported dual purpose goods from China and Russia, and shipped them to a variety of delivery addresses in Egypt.

Taken separately, there was nothing particularly suspicious about the goods they were ordering. But put together, there was a clear pattern: Egypt was developing a new, more powerful missile than the old Scuds it has had for years. And, if any proof was needed, all the invoices for the different shipments went to the same company: Kader Factory for Developed Industries, a military complex in Cairo that belongs to the Arab Organization for Industrialization, AOI, and is funded by the Egyptian government. Situated in Cairo's Nasser City, the sprawling complex is surrounded by high walls, armed guards and signs saying: "Approaching and photos are prohibited."[2]

Kim Kum Jin, formerly economic counselor at the North Korean embassy in Cairo, first visited Slovakia in 1999 together with Sin Tong Suk, the head of the North Korean intelligence service's section for secret operations in Eastern Europe, to look into the possibility of establishing a trading base there. The choice of Slovakia was no accident. The country is centrally located between Western Europe with its excellent communications, and the states of the former Soviet Union, where necessary raw materials and equipment could be obtained.

Moreover, since 1982, the North Koreans have had their own bank in Austria's capital Vienna, just up the Danube River from Bratislava. Called the Golden Star Bank, it is 100 percent owned by the Korea Daesong Bank, a state enterprise headquartered in Pyongyang. Daesong comes under the jurisdiction of Bureau 39, a shadowy wing of the Korean Workers' Party which was set up to generate hard currency for the North Korean government.

For more than two decades, the Austrian police have kept a close eye on the Golden Star Bank, but there is no law that forbids the North Koreans from operating a nonretail financial institution in the country. Nevertheless, the Austrian police intelligence department stated in a 1997 report: "This bank [Golden Star] has been mentioned repeatedly in connection with everything from money laundering and distribution of fake currency notes to the illegal trade in radioactive material."[3]

The latter was exactly what Kim Kum Jin and Ri Sun Hui were going to do in Slovakia. They moved into their new apartment in Bratislava in November 2000, and in March 2001 set up a company called New World Trading Slovakia. According to the Slovak Companies Registry, it was engaged in "retail and wholesale trade, advertising, promotion activities, and market surveys."[4] In reality, the company belonged to a secret North Korean commercial network spanning Europe, the Middle East, China, Thailand, and Singapore, which was supplying Middle Eastern countries with missile components and other, highly specialized military equipment. Kim Kum Jin and Ri Sun Hui were in fact part of North Korea's multi-million dollar missile business, one of the country's most important schemes to earn foreign exchange.[5] As can be expected, only high-level and very loyal officials are allowed to be engaged in this business, but Kim Kum Jin and Ri Sun Hui must have been exceptionally trusted as they were allowed to live and work alone in a country where there was no North Korean embassy. But, as is the case with all North Koreans living abroad, some close family members had to remain at home. The couple had two sons, both in their early twenties, and they were left behind in Pyongyang.[6]

Kim Kum Jin's and Ri Sun Hui's operation in Bratislava was impressive. Bills of lading, packing lists, and invoices seized in their apartment showed that between 2000 and mid-2001, they ordered more than US$10 million worth of chemicals, trucks, vehicle parts including "military standard" tires, measurement devices, pumps, and high-speed photographic equipment. And these were items that Kader could not obtain on its own. In April 1999, the Clinton administration had imposed trade sanctions on Kader and two other AOI companies for "having engaged in missile technology proliferation activities."[7] Clearly, a middleman was needed if Kader wanted to obtain restricted or controlled items—and that middleman was New World Trading in Bratislava.

In December 2000, a shipment of Hydroxy Terminated Polybutadiene, HTPB, was sent to Cairo from Xingang, a small port north of Shanghai in China. HTPB, a binder in solid propellant—or missile fuel—is restricted under the Missile Technology Control Regime, or MTCR, and controlled under the Wassenaar Arrangement, which was signed in September 1995 by twenty-eight states to establish a multilateral control system for the export of conventional weapons and related dual-use goods and technology. Although New World Trading Slovakia invoiced Kader for HTPB, the shipping documents from China declared it as "liquid polybutadiene rubber" on a list which also contained a number of other nonrestricted items.

Gradually, the shipments became even more convoluted. In June 2001, 8,100 kg of Dioctylazelate, a low-temperature plasticizer, which can be used to seal swimming pools—and as binder in solid propellant—was delivered. According to the bill of lading, it was shipped from China to an obscure company in Cairo called Omar Fahmy. But New World Trading in Slovakia sent its US$182,250 invoice for the shipment to Kader. At about the same time, aluminium powder microne 10-22 (microne 14-21 can be used in solid rocket fuel) was sent to another Cairo company, Ibrahim Ali, but billed to Kader, which was also invoiced for a shipment 10 metric tons of ammonium nitrate from China. Kim Kum Jin and Ri Sun Hui used three companies in China to procure these dual-use items, New World Trading, the Crocus Group, and Golden Star Trading. All three companies shared the same address, a nondescript hotel room in Beijing's Chaoyang District.

An attempt to order Dynemar HX-752—a propellant bonding agent restricted under the MTCR—was thwarted by the Singapore-company from which it was ordered. The company faxed New World Trading in Bratislava saying that the item it needed was "restricted by the US government," and that an end-user certificate was needed.[8] But in other cases such certificates seem to have been issued with ease. When Kim Kum Jin went on to shop for a high-speed HSV-1000 camera, he was able to produce an end user certificate from the "Helwan Factory"—another AOI subsidiary—saying that it was going to be used to "take pictures of production lines . . . for the production of pipes." That production line must have had very fast workers, as an HSV-1000 takes five hundred to one thousand pictures per second. It is normally used to take pictures of missiles and other fast-moving objects.

A purchase in May 2001 of ten chassis for MAZ-543 Russian-made multi-axle vehicles was approved by Egypt's Ministry of Housing, bought in Minsk, Belarus, shipped from the Ukrainian port of Odessa to a company called the Arab Contractor Osman Ahmed Osman & Co—and billed to Kader. The end user certificate indicated construction, not military purposes, but a separate invoice for special tires for the vehicles specifies "special tires of military standard."[9] The MAZ-543 can be employed as a heavy truck for cranes, but in military terms it is a transporter for conventional missile launchers. Kader produces missile launchers but not the vehicles for them. Among other items that Kim Kum Jin ordered for Kader was several million dollars worth of Inertial Measurement Units, devices critical to guidance systems in missiles and aircraft.

Kim Kum Jin and Ri Sun Hui managed to get away, but there are many more teams in various capitals across the world making money for the North Korean state and circumventing international rules to provide countries with missile components and technology. But North Korea's main market for missiles has always been the Middle East, with Egypt being the oldest and closest partner. North Korea first helped Egypt in the war with Israel in October 1973 by providing some pilots. In return for that assistance, Egypt transferred a small number of its Soviet-supplied FROG-7B TELs and rockets to North Korea, which had already started a ballistic missile program. As early as 1965—and with the Korean War still in fresh memory—Kim Il Sung established the Hamhung Military Academy to conduct research into missile technology. In a speech before the academy, Kim Il Sung stated:

> If war breaks out, the U.S. and Japan will also be involved. In order to prevent their involvement, we have to be able to produce rockets which fly as far as Japan. Therefore it is the mandate of the Military Academy to develop mid and long-range missiles.[10]

In the early 1980s, Egypt provided North Korea with Soviet-made Scud B missiles, which can carry a 450-pound warhead 180 miles or more. None of these missiles was test-fired, but they were used as models for reverse-engineering in a string of new factories which were built near the Chinese border in the north, far away from the DMZ and prying South Korean and U.S. eyes. The first North Korean–made replica was finished in 1984 and called the Hwasong 5.[11] Throughout the Hwasong program, North Korea cooperated closely with Egypt, and part of the deal was that the North Koreans would set up a production capability for Scud-type missiles in Egypt. North Korea also realized that there was money to be made from its new invention. At an early stage, Iran expressed an interest in buying missiles, which it needed for its long and bloody war with Iraq, from North Korea. In June 1987, the two countries concluded a US$500 million arms agreement, which included about one hundred Hwasong 5s. In Iran, the missile was given a new name: the Shehab 1.[12]

Most of the engineering was done by the North Koreans themselves with some assistance from the Egyptians. There is nothing to indicate that the then Soviet Union and other Communist states were involved in North Korea's missile development, although China provided technical training to North Korean engineers as well as high-quality machine tools.[13] As skills and techniques improved, North Korea began to develop more advanced missiles. The Hwasong 5 was followed by the Hwasong 6, which could be armed with chemical and cluster warheads. It was also sold to Iran as the Shehab 2. In March 1993, North Korea test fired a new missile called Rodong, which could carry either a 1,200 kilogram warhead 1,300 kilometers, or a 1,000 kilogram warhead as far as 1,500 kilometers—or enough to be able to reach major cities and U.S. bases in Japan.[14] A twenty-one-member delegation headed by Brig.-Gen. Hossein Mantequei, the Iranian Revolutionary Guard commander in charge of Teheran's missile force, had arrived in Pyongyang to observe the test.[15] They were satisfied, and as many as 150 Rodongs were sold to Iran, where the missile was renamed the Shehab 3.

New customers were also found in the Middle East. Not only were Syria and Libya among them, but even the conservative United Arab Emirates bought twenty-five Hwasong 5 missiles as well as artillery pieces and multiple rocket launchers in 1989. The UAE, however, was not pleased with the quality of the Hwasongs, and they were left to rust in a remote warehouse.[16] Outside the Middle East, Pakistan— like Egypt, not a socialist state but an ally of the U.S.— emerged as North Korea's foremost trading partner for military hardware. And the alliance with Pakistan brought a new and even more dangerous technology to North Korea: nuclear power. Pakistan initially approached North Korea to buy conventional weaponry in the early 1970s, when tension was escalating with India over East Pakistan's attempts to break away. On September 18, 1971 the first shipment of North Korean weapons arrived in Karachi, but East Pakistan managed to break away anyway—with help from India—and form independent Bangladesh in December.

The following year, North Korea and Pakistan established diplomatic relations, and North Korea sold artillery, multiple rocket launchers, ammunition, and a variety of spare parts to Pakistan.[17] Relations were especially warm when Zulfikar Ali Bhutto was president of Pakistan, but he was overthrown by the country's military in 1977 and subsequently executed. His successor, Muhammad Zia ul-Haq, was less enthusiastic about the friendship with Pyongyang, and relations did not improve until Zulfikar Ali Bhutto's daughter, Benazir Bhutto, became prime minister in 1988. She was determined to develop a missile capability for Pakistan, and sent a delegation to Pyongyang to examine the new Rodong. In December 1993, after being ousted and then reelected as prime minister, Benazir Bhutto herself traveled to Pyongyang, and a joint Pakistani–North Korean ballistic missile project was established.

North Korea agreed to provide Pakistan with major components for the Rodong, and, on April 6, 1998, Pakistan conducted its first test of its version of the missile, which was called the Ghauri. It had been developed at the Khan

Research Laboratories in Kahuta by North Korean experts from the Changgwang Sinyong Corporation, which is also known by the inconspicuous name the Korea Mining Development Trading Bureau.[18] In return, Pakistan provided North Korea with access to Western technology and systems which Pyongyang could not obtain through "normal" channels. With North Korean assistance, Pakistan was able to narrow the gap in its arms race with India, and India had to respond by further strengthening its defenses. Thus, North Korea helped escalate tension in a region far away from its own borders.

For years Pakistan denied that its cooperation with North Korea included nuclear technology. But in late 2002, a U.S. official stated quite bluntly that North Korea was using uranium enrichment technology with "'Made in Pakistan' stamped all over it."[19] The equipment included, at the very least, gas centrifuges used to create weapons-grade uranium.[20] In October 2003, *The Economist* quoted Pakistan critics as saying that the country had "sold nuclear know-how to North Korea in exchange for missile technology so that Pakistan can deliver its nuclear warheads."[21]

The question of the collaboration between North Korea and Pakistan in missile and nuclear programs was highlighted in a chilling manner on June 7, 1998, when Kim Sa Nae, the wife of Kang Thae Yun, a senior North Korean diplomat in Pakistan, was shot dead in the capital Islamabad. Kang Thae Yun left Pakistan under mysterious circumstances within a month of his wife's murder and his whereabouts are unknown. Officially, Kang Thae Yun was "economic counselor" at the North Korean embassy in Islamabad, but press reports at the time stated that he was, in fact, the local representative of the Changgwang Sinyong Corporation.[22] The plot thickened when it was discovered that Kang Thae Yun and his wife were close to Dr. Abdul Qadeer Khan, the director of the Ghauri program at the Khan Research Laboratories. Dr. Khan was considered the father of Pakistan's nuclear bomb—and the murder took place just a week after Pakistan's first nuclear tests.[23]

What was the motive? Was there any connection between the murder and the six tests that Pakistan carried out at Chagai Hills in Baluchistan on May 28–30, 1998? According to diplomats who were based in Islamabad at the time, there was. Agents from the U.S. Central Intelligence Agency, CIA, had begun to cultivate a friendship with Kim Sa Nae. One of them was a Korean speaker, and it was obvious that the Americans were trying to get information about Pakistan's clandestine nuclear program, and the extent to which North Korea was benefiting from it. The relationship between Kim Sa Nae and the American CIA operative caught the attention of Pakistan's own intelligence service, the Inter-Services Intelligence, which tipped off the North Korean ambassador in Islamabad. Two North Korean agents were assigned to deal with "the problem" and entered the home of Kang Thae Yun and Kim Sa Nae shortly after midnight on June 7. The agents fired repeatedly at Kim Sa Nae. She died on the spot. The Pakistani authorities later described the incident as "an accident, not a murder."[24]

Eventually, Pakistan had to admit that it had assisted North Korea in obtaining nuclear technology. On January 23, 2004, Pakistan's president, Gen. Pervez Musharraf, acknowledged that scientists from his country had sold nuclear designs to other nations probably "for personal financial gain." He denied, however, that the Pakistani government knew of any sales at the time. This claim was disputed by several sources. A senior European diplomat said that "it stretches credulity that proliferation on this scale can occur without senior officials in the government knowing about it."[25] The transfer of nuclear technology and hardware was also part of an official deal. North Korea got nuclear know-how in return for providing Pakistan with ballistic missile technology.[26]

Dr. Khan himself was summoned for questioning and it transpired that he had provided not only North Korea with nuclear technology but also Iran and Libya. Khan confessed to having visited North Korea on numerous occasions, and brought with him centrifuges and centrifuge parts. The

Pakistani government claimed that no transfers of nuclear know-how or equipment took place after 1999. U.S. intelligence sources, however, are convinced the transfers continued at least until 2002.[27] Nevertheless, the United States chose not to confront Musharraf, an important ally in the war on terror, and praised him for "breaking up what appears to have been one of the world's largest nuclear proliferation networks."[28]

***

That Pakistan had been obtaining missile technology from North Korea was an open secret, but its role in North Korea's nuclear program was much more disturbing—because Pyongyang was not supposed to have any such program. It was supposed to have shut down its old nuclear installations in Yongbyon and elsewhere under the agreement signed with the United States in Geneva on October 21, 1994. So what was really happening?

North Korea's obsession with nuclear power—and weapons—goes back to the U.S. atomic bombing of Hiroshima and Nagasaki in 1945. This was reinforced by the stories told by Koreans returning from Japan in the late 1940s—many of whom had been in Hiroshima and Nagasaki at the time of the bombing—and it grew even stronger during the Korean War, when the U.S. contemplated launching nuclear strikes against the North.[29] On December 9, 1950, the commander of the U.S. forces, Gen. Douglas MacArthur, even submitted a list of targets for which he said he needed twenty-six atomic bombs to halt the advance of the North Korean army and its Chinese allies.[30] In the end, that did not happen, but it instilled fear in the North Koreans, who saw the nuclear bomb as the ultimate "doomsday" weapon. Since then, North Korea has wanted to possess it as a means of countering what it perceives as a military threat from the U.S. and thus ensuring the continued existence of the regime in Pyong-yang. The Dear Leader, and the Great Leader before him, has also always perceived nuclear weapons as an important aspect of greatness.[31] In 1998, the high-ranking defector Hwang Jang Yop described the reason behind North Korea's nuclear strategy:

> For one thing, they [the North Koreans] will use them [nuclear weapons] if South Korea starts a war. For another, they intend to devastate Japan to prevent the United States from participating. Would it still participate, even after Japan is devastated? That is how they think.[32]

Kim Il Sung must have sighed with relief when his ally, China, exploded its first nuclear device on October 16, 1964. The following year a basic research reactor provided by the Soviet Union became operational at Yongbyon, north of Pyongyang, and the nuclear program had begun. The center at Yongbyon was set up with Soviet assistance and, apart from the research reactor, included a radiochemical laboratory, a K-60,000 cobalt installation, and a B-25 betatron, a sophisticated apparatus for accelerating electrons in a circular path by magnetic induction.[33] North Korea was taking its first steps towards developing its own nuclear power. The Soviets provided all the blueprints, and soon Yongbyon was a sprawling complex of circular buildings housing the reactor storage facilities and a special laundry to decontaminate protective clothing and undergarments for the scientists and the workers, and a boiler plant generating 40 tons of steam per hour.[34] U.S. satellite images of the reactor showed no attached power lines, which would have been the case if it was meant for electric power generation.[35]

In the 1960s and 1970s, more than three hundred North Korean nuclear scientists were trained at the Moscow Engineering Physics Institute, the Bauman Higher Technical School, and the Moscow Energy Institute. Some North Koreans even worked at the nuclear scientific research complexes in the cities of Dubna and Obninsk.[36] This training in the Soviet Union came to an end when the Communist state collapsed in 1991, but East German and Russian nuclear and missile scientists were working in North Korea throughout the 1990s, most probably in a private capacity.[37] In December 1992, Russian security minister Victor Barannikov reported in a speech before the Russian parliament that his men had blocked the departure of sixty-four Russian missile specialists to "a third country" which had hired them to build military-purpose missile installations capable of delivering nuclear weapons. Barannikov did not specify what country it was, but Russian journalists managed to find some of the missile specialists and learned, not surprisingly, that it was North Korea. In an even more bizarre attempt to obtain know-how from its former ally, two North Korean intelligence agents were arrested near Vladivostok in 1994 when they were trying to sell eight kilograms of heroin to raise money to acquire Russian military secrets. In particular, they were interested in buying technologies related to the dismantlement of nuclear reactors at one of the shipyards in the Russian Far East.[38]

Now, any assistance—private or otherwise—from the former Soviet bloc appears to have stopped. Instead, with the old Soviet archives available to independent researchers and journalists, more information is being revealed about the Soviet involvement with North Korea's nuclear program. In December 1985, at Pyongyang's initiative, the Soviet Union and North Korea signed an agreement on cooperation in the construction of a nuclear power plant in the North. But North Korea guaranteed that nuclear materials, nuclear equipment, and installations imported from the Soviet Union would neither be diverted for the production of nuclear weapons nor facilitate the attainment of any other military goal. The installations would also be kept under the control of the International Atomic Energy Agency, IAEA.[39]

But that was a promise that North Korea did not intend to keep. IAEA inspectors, who came to North Korea, soon came to suspect that plutonium from the Yongbyon reactor had been diverted during secret, unsupervised refueling operations.[40] In 1985, North Korea had actually signed the nuclear nonproliferation treaty, but in late 1992, the IAEA found evidence that it had reprocessed more plutonium than the mere eighty grams it had disclosed to the agency. In February the following year, the IAEA called for a special inspection of two concealed suspected waste sites at Yangbyon—a request that was rejected. And in May 1994— just before the first nuclear crisis was resolved and North Korea promised to freeze its program in exchange for oil and light-water reactors—another requested inspection of eight thousand fuel rods, which had been removed from the research reactor in Yangbyon, was rejected.[41] Obviously the North Koreans were up to something extremely secret, which the Geneva agreement was not going to stop.

In 1994, the Russian media broke the news that the former Soviet intelligence service, the KGB, had compiled a report in 1990 asserting that "According to available data, development of the first nuclear device has been completed at the Democratic People's Republic of Korea nuclear research center in Yangbyon." The North Korean government, the report went on, had decided not to test the device in order to avoid international detection.[42] Other Russian sources, however, remain skeptical, arguing, "The present scientific and technical level and the technological equipment of nuclear facilities in the Democratic People's Republic of Korea do not allow North Korean specialists to create a nuclear explosive device applicable for field tests, even less so to model a cold test of a plutonium-type military-purpose charge under laboratory conditions."[43] But that does not mean that North Korea is not striving to obtain nuclear weapons.

Much of the research is now carried out at the city of Pyonsong, fifty kilometers from Pyongyang, where several hundred scientists are working on nuclear issues. Several of the computers as well as other electronic equipment were made in Japan, most probably supplied by the pro-Pyongyang Korean community there, the Chongryun. Besides the research institutes—and the reactor and other facilities in Yangbyon—North Korea also has its own uranium mines in Pakchon and Pyongsan as well as two uranium enrichment plants.[44] And the suspicion that North Korea does not have purely peaceful intentions for its nuclear program has grown stronger due to the secrecy surrounding the program, and the multiple designations given to each facility—a cover designation, official designation, and sometimes an honorific name.[45] The Yangbyon research center, for instance, was called a "furniture factory," or "Object 9559."[46] Furthermore, many nuclear installations, like other North Korean facilities earnestly working for defense purposes, are hidden inside mountains where no foreigners are allowed.[47]

But it is known that the Korean Workers' Party has all along provided guidance to the country's nuclear ambitions through the Atomic Energy Committee, which is believed to be subordinate to the powerful Department of Organization and Guidance headed by Kim Jong Il and his inner circle of henchmen in the National Defense Commission.[48] And dramatic changes in the international environment—especially in the former Soviet bloc—in the 1990s most probably prompted Kim Jong Il to ignore the 1994 agreement with the U.S. and to speed up his secret nuclear weapons program, now with technical support from Pakistan. Or with equipment obtained in a manner similar to what Kim Kum Jin and Ri Sun Hui did in Bratislava.

Kim Jong Il and other North Korean leaders feel abandoned and betrayed by their former allies, China and Russia, which have both established diplomatic relations with South Korea and chosen to develop market-oriented economies. However, keeping the nuclear program secret defeats its purpose as a deterrent—which could be the reason why Vice Foreign Minister Kang Sok Ju made his startling statement to U.S. Assistant Secretary of State James Kelly in October 2002, which led to a second crisis over North Korea's nuclear program, and North Korea's withdrawal from the nonproliferation treaty. But was it a bluff or a threat? Do the North Koreans really possess nuclear weapons, and if they do, do they have the capability to launch them?

In January 1994, the U.S. Department of Energy reported that, depending on the technology applied, as little as four kilograms of plutonium would be sufficient to produce a nuclear weapon. With the eleven to thirteen kilograms of weapons-grade plutonium that North Korea is estimated to have extracted prior to signing the 1994 agreement with the U.S., the country could theoretically have between one and three nuclear devices.[49] And, if it is true that North Korea has acquired fissile material from Pakistan—and possibly illegally from Russia—it would further increase the country's nuclear weapons inventory. Apart from extracting plutonium, North Korea has been pursuing a uranium enrichment program with the assistance of Pakistan.[50] It was enriched uranium that Kang Sok Ju mentioned during his meeting with James Kelly.

In a little-seen interview with a small leftist weekly in Sweden in October 2003, the newly appointed North Korean ambassador in Stockholm, Jon In Chan, stated quite clearly that his country already has nuclear weapons: "Our defense includes a nuclear deterrent."[51] If the ambassador was boasting or telling the truth is hard to say, but even if North Korea has not yet managed to produce a fully fledged nuclear device, it is certainly conducting research to develop one. In January 2004 a U.S. delegation led by Charles (Jack) Prichard, a former U.S. special envoy to North Korea, led a delegation to Pyongyang—and were allowed to visit Yongbyon. They were able to confirm that the eight-thousand fuel rods had indeed been removed from the reactor's pool, which had long been suspected. They were also shown two glass jars, one said to contain 150 grams of plutonium oxalate powder and the other with 200 grams of plutonium metal. Siegfried Hecker, a scientist from Los Alamos National Laboratory who accompanied Prichard later stated that although he was not able to definitely confirm that it was the real thing, "all observations I was able to make are consistent with the sample being plutonium metal."[52] His North Korean hosts had asked him if he now was convinced that they had a nuclear deterrent, but all that Hecker could confirm was that they had most probably managed to produce plutonium metal. He was not able to confirm that the North Koreans had the ability to design and build a nuclear device, or that they had the required delivery systems. But it was clear the North Koreans wanted to show him and the other visiting Americans that they were engaged in advanced nuclear research.

It is also evident that North Korea has been improving its missile technology, which it would need to deliver the bombs, which they may have, or may not yet have, produced. In 1998, a new generation of North Korean missiles was born with the three-stage Taepodong 1, which it test-fired over Japan on August 31 from the Musudan-ni launch facility on the coast of North Hamgyong province. The Japanese were outraged and saw it as a grave provocation, but the North Koreans stated that the purpose was only to place their first satellite—the Kwangmyongsong-1—into orbit to beam down hymns in praise of Kim Il Sung.[53]

Whatever the case, the missile flew 1,090 kilometers from the launch site in North Korea into the Pacific Ocean east of the main Japanese island of Honshu.[54] Since then, a Taepodong 2 with a range of 6,700 kilometers has been developed, which has brought U.S. bases in Okinawa, Alaska, and Hawaii within the potential range of North Korean missiles. The North Koreans are working on a third Taepodong, which will be capable of delivering a 500- to 1,000-kg warhead at a distance of 10,000 to 12,000 kilometers—anywhere in the U.S.[55] But the development of a fully workable and reliable nuclear warhead for the Taepodong family would require a significant level of design sophistication, which the North Koreans have yet to develop.

What North Korea most certainly possesses at the moment, though, are chemical and biological weapons—and they can be just as devastating as nuclear devices. Refugees and defectors from the North have testified that the country produces altogether twenty different chemical agents for military use, but is focused on the production of mustard, phosgene, sarin, and the V-agents, potent poisons which can wipe out entire communities. The main chemical weapons factories are said to be at Kanggye and Sakju in the northern mountains, where mortars and artillery rounds are filled with chemicals. A maze of tunnels have been dug into the mountains to avoid detection from the air and tests are also often conducted underground, or on small islands off North Korea's west coast.[56] Current estimates of the inventory by Western and South Korean military analysts suggest that North Korea has between 2,500 and 5,000 tonnes of chemical weapons of several kinds, and that they can be loaded in the warheads of ballistic missiles.[57]

While several of the chemical agents were shipped from the former Soviet Union and China, North Korea's biological weapons program is entirely home grown. Research began in the early 1960s and has focused on about a dozen different strains of bacteria.[58] Biological agents in North Korea's arsenal are reported to include the bacteria that cause anthrax, cholera, botulism, haemorrhagic fever, plague, smallpox, typhoid, and yellow fever.[59] Again, these are tested on the islands off the west coast.[60]

There are numerous reports concerning possible North Korean chemical weapons proliferation activities with Egypt, Iran, Libya, and Syria, though none has been independently verified.[61] But North Korea's exports of ballistic missiles continues, and as long as the country does not produce much else that other countries want to buy, sales are likely to increase despite international criticism. Attempts to force it to halt its nuclear program and rejoin the nonproliferation treaty have also failed miserably. Rightly or wrongly, North Korea feels threatened—and it is responding in its own way to recent events elsewhere in the world. If the North Koreans were outraged that Bush had included them in his Axis of Evil speech, the invasion of Iraq the following year prompted them to reemphasize Kim Jong Il's "military first" policy even more forcefully than at the spectacular army parade in April 2002. On March 29, 2003, the official party organ *Rodong Sinmun* wrote in a commentary that North Korea "would have already met the same miserable fate as Iraq's, had it accepted the demand raised by the imperialists for 'nuclear inspection' and disarmament." The paper stressed that North Korea "will not make any slightest concession or compromise" and that it would increase defense capacity as the country's "number one lifeline."[62]

And that may have to include nuclear arms and other weapons of mass destruction, as North Korea's conventional forces—even if they are more than a million strong and prioritized under the "military first" policy—are reeling under the economic crisis. The North Korean army may be much bigger than South Korea's in terms of numbers, but it is not nearly as well equipped. Most of its tanks are decades old, and there is an acute shortage of spare parts. And even if the army is given preference for patrol rations, it is not enough to keep it on the move. Soldiers even have to grow vegetables and raise pigs to feed themselves. The North Korean navy is small and only 40 of its 420 combat vessels are believed to be fully operational. Its air force is old, obsolete, and almost dysfunctional, while South Korea's is one of the most modern in Asia. Fuel shortages mean that pilots are limited to less than ten hours of flight training per year, compared with the two hundred to three hundred flight hours that U.S. and South Korean pilots receive.[63]

North Korea believes it really needs a nuclear deterrent to survive, while wanting to show everybody that it will not bend under pressure, and that it will defy any forms of control.[64] But North Korea may also be playing the nuclear card to extract concessions and benefits from the rest of the world. After all, Pyongyang got a fairly good deal in 1994 although it did not live up to its part of the agreement. It may be hard for North Korea to get any substantial concessions from the U.S. after the breach of the Geneva agreement, but Japan may be different. North Korea has repeatedly asked Japan to pay compensation for its colonial rule of Korea—and Japan is extremely sensitive to North Korea's nuclear and missile capabilities. In 1999, Hwang Won Tak, adviser to then president Kim Dae Jung, indicated that North Korea may demand hard currency and food from Japan in return for not test-firing missiles.[65] In early 2003—as the crisis was gaining momentum—North Korea launched two missiles into the sea between the Korean peninsula and

Japan. In October, North Korea test-fired another missile in the same direction. All of them were short-range missiles, but the tests nevertheless caused alarm in Japan. South Korea would be even more willing to give aid to the North in exchange for some kind of concession on the nuclear issue.

But the danger is that North Korea will continue playing its cards the way it deems fit and ignore warnings from the rest of the world. And there is a real concern, at least in Washington, that it may be willing to sell nuclear technology, or devices, in the same way as it has been exporting ballistic missiles. In 2003 concerns were raised over Iran's plans to build a nuclear reactor with technology transfers from Pakistan's Khan Industries, and most probably with the North Koreans helping the Iranians with their delivery systems—which indicate a less than peaceful purpose for the program.[66] Unless North Korea's tentative market reforms work and the economy improves significantly, there will be crafty agents such as Kim Kum Jin and Ri Sun Hui peddling whatever they can to raise money for the regime in Pyongyang.

CHAPTER 6

THE MISSIONS

No one could possibly have predicted the drama that was set to unfold when Interpol and local police raided an office in Cambodia's capital Phnom Penh in March 1996. They were searching for counterfeit dollar bills, which had been discovered in neighboring Thailand and traced to the Cambodia. An Asian man in the office fled—and sought refuge in the North Korean embassy a few blocks away. The police waited outside, and, after a few days, a Mercedes with blacked-out windows and diplomatic license plates left the embassy compound and sped out of Phnom Penh. A police team decided to follow it as it drove toward the Vietnamese border. The Mercedes tried to evade the police, but the chase continued all the way down to Bavet, the last Cambodian checkpoint before Vietnam. There it stayed for almost two days and its occupants "ate, slept, shat and pissed" in the car.[1]

Eventually a deal was struck. The North Korean diplomats in the car were given immunity and allowed to return to Phnom Penh. But the counterfeiter had to be handed over to the police. He had a North Korean diplomatic passport under the name "Kim Il Suu"—but turned out to be Yoshimi Tanaka, a wanted member of the Japanese Red Army Faction, one of Japan's most feared terrorist group. As a twenty-one-year-old student Tanaka along with eight other members of the Red Army Faction had hijacked a Japanese airliner to Pyongyang. Apart from his North Korean passport, US$

40,000 in fake US$100 bills was also seized from Tanaka. He was extradited to Thailand a few days later.[2] In 2000, he was sent back to Japan, where he was charged with hijacking and other violent acts.

This rather bizarre incident epitomized three important aspects of North Korea's foreign policy: the use of its diplomatic missions abroad for illegal activities, its links to certain terrorist groups, and its rather curious relationship with the royal family of Cambodia. Kim Il Sung and Cambodia's ruling prince Sihanouk first met in 1961 at a meeting with the Non-Aligned Movement in Belgrade, Yugoslavia, and, four years later, Sihanouk was invited to visit Pyongyang. A personal friendship developed between the Cambodian ruler and the North Korean, supposedly Stalinist, leader. When Sihanouk was ousted by his own military, led by General Lon Nol, in a coup in March 1970, the prince was offered sanctuary in North Korea. Sihanouk's government in exile was located in Beijing, but, in 1974, Kim Il Sung had a new home built for Sihanouk about an hour's drive north of Pyongyang. A battalion of North Korean troops worked full-time on it for almost a year, and, when it was finished, only specially selected guards were allowed anywhere near the sixty-room, palatial residence.[3]

Overlooking the scenic Chhang Sou On Lake and surrounded by mountains, the Korean-style building even had its own indoor movie theater. Like Kim Jong Il, Sihanouk loved movies. He had both directed and acted in his own romantic feature movies, and a few more were made in North Korea with Cambodian actors strutting their stuff against the backdrop of the Korean mountains. French wines and gourmet food were flown in via China, and Sihanouk and his entourage were treated as royals would have been in any country that respects monarchy.[4] Perhaps that was the reason for the friendship: Kim Il Sung had created his own ruling family, and wanted to be in the company of "real" royal households. Sihanouk, on his part, admired Kim Il Sung's leadership style. "[He] has a relationship with his people that every other leader in the world would envy," Sihanouk stated.

When asked how that compared with his own relationship with the Cambodian people, the prince was blunt: "It just doesn't compare. Kim [Il Sung] is so much closer."[5]

Sihanouk returned to Cambodia after the Lon Nol regime was overthrown in April 1975 and his Communist allies, the Khmer Rouge, came to power. That was a serious mistake, even if Sihanouk had all along been the figurehead of the anti-Lon Nol resistance. The Khmer Rouge put him under virtual house arrest in his palace in Phnom Penh—and turned the entire country into a virtual prison where hard labor, mass executions, and an almost total isolation from the outside world followed years of civil war and destruction. Eventually the Vietnamese invaded Cambodia, and drove the Khmer Rouge from power in Phnom Penh in January 1979. Sihanouk escaped to China before the Vietnamese marched into the capital—and returned to his grand residence in North Korea.

Despite intense pressure from Moscow, Kim Il Sung refused to recognize the new, pro-Soviet Communist regime that the Vietnamese installed in Phnom Penh. During a meeting between Kim Il Sung and Sihanouk on April 10, 1986 in Pyongyang, the Great Leader reassured the prince that North Korea would continue to regard Sihanouk as head of state of Cambodia. North Korea was under no circumstances going to give in to Soviet pressure to do otherwise. In official dispatches from the North Korean news agency the deposed Cambodian ruler was referred to as "His Royal Highness Samdech Norodom Sihanouk," and he continued to enjoy Kim Il Sung's hospitality.[6] Back home in the jungles of Cambodia, a coalition supported by China and the West battled on against the government in Phnom Penh which was backed by Vietnam and the Soviet Union.

Eventually the United Nations intervened and a peace agreement was signed in October 1991. All the warring parties agreed to take part in free, UN-supervised elections—and, in November, Sihanouk triumphantly returned to Phnom Penh. With Sihanouk came the North Koreans, both as personal bodyguards for the prince and as diplomats, who took up residence in a huge, new embassy near the Independence Monument in downtown Phnom Penh. In 1993, Sihanouk, still with his North Korean bodyguards, was officially installed as King of Cambodia, and he did not forget to repay the North Koreans for their support during his many years in exile.

North Korean trading companies set up shop in Phnom Penh, and a Cambodian shipping registry was established to provide North Korean vessels with a flag of convenience.[7] Several of the North Koreans—and special agents such as Yoshimi Tanaka—operated under deep cover. The firm Tanaka worked for was headed by a man whose passport identified him as Ng Leong Huat, an ethnic Chinese citizen of Malaysia. But he managed to escape back to North Korea—and a copy of his passport, which the Cambodian police managed to obtain from the immigration authorities, led to further investigations. The real Ng Leong Huat was discovered in his hometown—Kuala Kedah in Malaysia. A few years before this incident he had lost his passport, or it had been stolen. Anyhow, it ended up in the hands of a North Korean gang, who did not change the photograph as is usually done when someone is reusing a stolen passport. In fact, the passport was not tampered with in any way. Instead, a North Korean lookalike was found, and his appearance may also have been altered with plastic surgery. The new Ng Leong Huat also learned to speak Malay and Mandarin.[8]

The importance of Cambodia as a base for North Korea's commercial operations in Southeast Asia began to decline following the Tanaka affair. After the seizure of the Cambodian-registered North Korean vessel off the coast of Yemen in December 2002, the Cambodian shipping registry also came under scrutiny by international law enforcement agencies. The Cambodian government had actually canceled its contract with the privately owned, royalist-controlled Cambodian Shipping Corporation in July 2002 after a series of embarrassing maritime incidents, including a massive haul of cocaine off the West African coast from another Cambodian-registered—but not North Korean-owned—vessel in June of that year. A new shipping registry was set up, controlled, somewhat ironically, by the Cosmos Group, a company based in South Korea.[9]

The Tanaka affair was also the last concrete evidence of North Korean involvement with international terrorists, or, at least, a former terrorist. In the 1970s, many idealistic revolutionaries, especially in the Third World, admired North Korea because of its independent stance between the Soviet Union and China, and North Korea perceived it as its mission to support revolutionary movements in power, or fighting to gain power, in Asia, Africa, and Latin America. In the 1970s and 1980s, there were ten known training facilities in North Korea for militants from the Third World. During the same period, North Korea maintained training facilities, at one time or another, in Algeria, Angola, Chile, Cuba, Guyana, Lebanon, Libya, Zimbabwe, Mozambique, then South Yemen, Peru, Somalia, and Uganda.[10]

In August 1970, a delegation from the Palestine Liberation Organization, PLO, traveled to Pyongyang, where they were greeted by Kim Il Sung himself. A month later, George Habbash, leader of the Popular Front for the Liberation of Palestine, PFLP, also went to Pyongyang and was promised assistance from North Korea. During that trip, links were established between the PFLP and Japanese Red Army radical, which led to a bloody attack carried out by a team of Japanese guerrillas at Lod airport in Israel in 1972. Twenty-six people were killed, including sixteen Puerto Ricans on a pilgrimage to the Holy Land.[11] Several hundred Palestinians were trained at three locations near Pyongyang, the most important of which was Wonhung-ri. Weapons from North Korea reached the PLO and PFLP through Syria.[12] Palestinians—and members of the Japanese Red Army—were also trained in what was then the People's Democratic Republic of Yemen, or South Yemen, which merged with North Yemen in 1990. Special Purpose Corps instructors from North Korea taught them to use explosives, bombs, and booby traps, and how to organize kidnappings and assassinations.[13]

In Africa, North Korean instructors helped train the forces of independent Mozambique's army, and those of Robert

Mugabe's Zimbabwe African National Union, both before and after the settlement in 1980 which brought him to power. It was North Koreans who trained the newly established Fifth and Sixth Brigades of the Zimbabwean army, which in 1983 were deployed to the southern Matabeleland, home of Mugabe's political rival, Joshua Nkomo. During the six-month campaign the Fifth Brigade distinguished itself for its brutality and atrocities against civilians. The last North Korean instructors under the command of Maj-Gen. Sin Hyon Dok, left Zimbabwe in March 1986.[14]

During its first decade of existence, North Korea showed little or no interest in America. But with the success of the Cuban revolution in 1959, and the subsequent emergence of revolutionary movements all over Latin America, North Korea saw an excellent opportunity to strike at the U.S. in its own backyard. North Korea extended support to *Ejercito Revolucionario del Pueblo*—the People's Revolutionary Army—and the Montoneros in Argentina, the Bolivian Communist Party, the Chilean Communist Party, the Sandinistas in Nicaragua, the *Movimiento de Action Revolucionaria*, MAR, or the Revolutionary Action Movement of Mexico, and the *Fuerzas Armadas Revolucionarias de Colombia*, FARC, or the Armed Revolutionary Forces of Colombia.

Some of the guerrillas were trained in North Korea, others by North Korean instructors in Cuba—and in Guyana, with which North Korea signed a secret military assistance agreement in the mid-1970s. Six thousand tons of North Korean arms and ammunition were shipped to Guyana from 1979 to 1983, and relations with its anti-American prime minister, Forbes Burnham, were excellent. Guyana, whose official language is English, also proved to be an excellent place for the training of North Korean intelligence operatives. In the late 1970s, there were an estimated one hundred North Koreans studying English in Guyana.[15]

In Mexico, support for the MAR continued throughout the 1980s, and several of its militants were trained in guerrilla warfare at Wonhung-ri. But one of the most intriguing aspects of Pyongyang's interest in Mexico came to light in

January 1983, when at least four North Korean "shrimping trawlers" were discovered in the Gulf of California. One of the ships was seized by the Mexican authorities for "fishing illegally in the gulf," but American intelligence sources believed it—and the other ships, which were all bristling with antennas—was involved in an intelligence operation aimed at the U.S. In May of the same year, another North Korean ship attempted to establish a listening post on the small island of San Ildefonso in the gulf.[16]

But none of the North Korean operations in Latin America—or the groups trained by the North Koreans, with perhaps the exception of FARC—turned out to be especially effective. One of the few revolutionary movements in the continent that grew to pose a real threat to its government, the Maoist Shining Path in Peru, even stayed clear of North Korea, which it considered a "revisionist" state. In April 1987, Shining Path guerrillas seized the courtyard of the North Korean trade office in Lima, and exploded a bomb at the front door. The attack could have been in retaliation for a North Korean sale of assault rifles to the Peruvian government.[17]

***

North Korea's links with the world's leftist revolutionaries and the interrelationship of all these groups was inadvertently disclosed in 1977 in, of all places, Sweden in northern Europe. The Special Branch of the Swedish police discovered a plot to kidnap the country's former labor minister, Anna-Greta Leijon. The plot was being hatched by a German, Norbert Kröcher, who was going to demand 2 million dollars in ransom, along with the release of several members of the Baader-Meinhof gang imprisoned in West Germany. The Swedish minister was targeted because she had been behind the deportation of surviving members of "Commando Holger Meins" and a couple of Japanese terrorists. In 1975, six members of the Baader-Meinhof gang from the "Commando Holger Meins" had occupied the West German embassy in Stockholm, and blown it up. One of the terrorists, Ulrich Wessel, was killed in the explosion, but the survivors were extradited to West Germany, where one more, Siegfried Hausner, died from his wounds.

The plot failed, however, and the Swedish police apprehended not only Kröcher, but also another nine suspects. Among them was an Englishman, Alan Hunter, and a Mexican, Armando Carillo, whom the Mexican authorities identified as a "professional killer" and a "bank robber," and who had spent 18 months in a guerrilla training camp in North Korea. Kröcher was handed over to the West German authorities, who gave him a ten-year jail sentence. Hunter was sent back to Britain, and Carillo and the others were extradited to Cuba, where they most probably remain.[18] The link, albeit indirect, between North Korea, Cuba, the Baader-Meinhof gang, and at least one Mexican revolutionary pointed to a unholy alliance between Pyongyang and Latin American as well as European terrorist networks.

Otherwise, North Korea's only political toehold in Europe was in the small, Mediterranean island state of Malta. Following the election victory of labor leader Dom Mintoff in 1971, a special relationship was established between his new government and the regime in Pyongyang. During Mintoff's premiership, North Korea even signed a secret military assistance agreement with Malta, and the 14,000-tonne North Korean cargo ship *Doo Man Gang-Ho* docked in Malta's capital Valetta to unload a massive shipment of small arms, mortars, and anti-aircraft guns, along with four Special Purpose Corps advisors—far more than Malta's tiny army could possibly need. It is believed that most of the weaponry was transferred to members of the Italian Red Brigades, and Britain's Provisional Irish Republican Army.[19]

And, like Guyana, Malta is an English-speaking country, so North Korean agents were also sent there for language training. In July 2003, a Maltese daily, *Malta Today*, claimed that Kim Jong Il himself spent a holiday on the island, including not only English study but also piano lessons, all the time guarded by Mintoff's North Korean–trained riot squad, the Special Mobile Unit.[20] No records of the alleged visit exist in Malta's diplomatic records, but when *Malta Today* quizzed the foreign minister under Mintoff's regime, Alex Sciberras, about the alleged visit, he did not deny it, only telling the journalists not to waste his time asking such questions. Whatever the truth, North Korea's influence in Malta began to wane when Mintoff resigned as prime minister in 1984, and it may have come to a definitive end when the labor government lost the 1987 election.

***

North Korea's own involvement in violent activities was not confined to infiltrating South Korea—which it did in January 1968, when a group of its commandos managed to enter the heart of Seoul and attack the presidential palace, the Blue House, almost killing president Park Chung Hee—but included actions well beyond the Korean peninsula. In the most spectacular operation, carried out in September–October 1983, a small "direct action" team was dispatched to Burma to assassinate the new South Korean president, Chun Doo Hwan. The leader of the hit squad, major Zin Mo, was assisted by two demolition specialists, captains Kim Chi O and Kang Min Chul. They managed to get into Burma aboard a North Korean ship called *Tong Gon Ae Guk-ho*, which was ostensibly carrying construction materials to Egypt via Rangoon. On September 22, the three team members—disguised as sailors from the ship—went ashore, and contacted the North Korean embassy. On October 9, a powerful bomb ripped through the Martyrs' Mausoleum in Rangoon, erected to honor Burma's independence hero, Aung San, who was assassinated in 1947. It killed eighteen visiting South Korean officials, including Deputy Prime Minister So Suk Chun and three other government ministers.[21]

That night, Zin Mo was arrested by a Burmese security squad—missing one eye and an arm which he had lost when he detonated a grenade in an attempt to kill himself. Kim Chi O and Kang Min Chul were arrested two days later, and, on November 4, the Burmese authorities officially announced

that the North Koreans were behind the bomb blast. The
North Korean embassy in Rangoon was closed down, and its
diplomats escorted to the city's airport, where they boarded a
plane bound for Pyongyang. Kim Chi O was hanged in 1985,
but Kang Min Chul's life was spared because he cooperated
with the prosecution. He still languishes in Rangoon's
notorious Insein Jail in one of the city's northern suburbs.[22]

The next major North Korean terrorist attack took place on
November 29, 1987, and also involved Burma—but this time
up in the sky over the Andaman Sea. On that day, a bomb
exploded aboard Korean Airlines flight 858, a Boeing 707 en
route from Baghdad to Seoul via Abu Dhabi and Bangkok
with 104 passengers and 11 crew members aboard. There
were no survivors. A few days later, two North Koreans—an
older man and a very attractive, twenty-five-year-old
woman—were arrested in Bahrain. During the interrogation,
both of them swallowed cyanide capsules, which they had
concealed in cigarette filters. The man, Kim Sung Il, died
immediately, but the woman, Kim Hyun Hee, got her capsule
stuck in her throat, and was resuscitated by a Bahraini
policewoman. On December 15, Kim Hyun Hee and the body
of Kim Sung Il were flown to Seoul.[23]

In South Korea, Kim Hyun Hee confessed everything. She
and her much older minder had boarded the plane in
Baghdad, placed a time bomb in the overhead compartment,
and got off in Abu Dhabi, from where they were going to fly
via Bahrain in a round-about way to Europe. She was
sentenced to death, but was never executed. On the contrary,
she was granted a special amnesty and became something of
a celebrity in South Korea. Her book about her life in North
Korea and her experiences as a special agent for Pyongyang's
secret services, *The Tears of My Soul*, was an instant bestseller,
dedicated to "the families of the victims of Flight 858. All the
proceeds will be donated to them."[24]

The book was most probably ghost-written by her South
Korean minders and interrogators but, if the details are true,
it is nevertheless an astonishing document about the way in
which North Korea selects and trains its agents, and also

about the motive behind the bombing. When Kim Hyun Hee first heard that they had succeeded in blowing up the plane— years before she wrote her book—she felt no remorse: "I was relieved to know for certain that we had accomplished our mission and been faithful to Kim Il Sung and Kim Jong Il. I was sure now that the 1988 Olympics would not take place in Seoul and that I had been part of an important step toward Korean reunification."[25]

That the 1988 Olympics were going to be held in South Korea was seen by Pyongyang as a blow to its prestige—but so, too, was the bombing of flight 858. The North Korean government denied any involvement in the outrage, claiming that it has been staged by the South Korean government to discredit Pyongyang. The rest of the world was not convinced, and in January 1988, the U.S. placed North Korea on its list of nations supporting international terrorism.[26]

Perhaps as a result of the international outcry over the bombing, no further attempt to disrupt the Olympics was made. Instead, North Korea organized its own "World Festival of Youth and Students" in Pyongyang in July 1989. It was the first time North Korea allowed large numbers of foreigners into the country, and more than twenty thousand visitors from all over the world flocked to the North Korean capital. Most of the residents of Pyongyang had been evacuated before the arrival of the foreigners, but those who remained were able to get their first taste of information from the outside world. A major scandal for the regime occurred at Pyongyang's May Day Stadium as a group of foreigners began to chant anti-dictatorial slogans before an audience of a hundred thousand people, including Kim Il Sung and Kim Jong Il. The security forces intervened, but word spread throughout Pyongyang about the unprecedented expression of disdain in public for North Korea's political system and leadership.[27] But the perpetrators were all foreigners, not North Koreans.

Among Kim Hyun Hee's other revelations, one especially caught the attention of international intelligence agencies. She mentioned that she and another young North Korean woman were sent to the then Portuguese enclave of Macau opposite Hong Kong "to practise our Cantonese and improve our abilities to impersonate Chinese nationals."[28] In Macau, they also learned how to live in a capitalist society. They had an apartment and a bank account. They paid bills, went to the supermarket and visited night clubs—skills which would prove useful when they were later posted abroad, posing as Cantonese-speaking Chinese from Hong Kong or Macau.

North Korea's presence in Macau dates back to the aftermath of the Carnation Revolution in Portugal in 1974, when the old fascist dictatorship was overthrown and the new, left-leaning leaders recognized the government in Pyongyang. Since that time, Zokwang Trading—one of the oldest North Korean trading companies abroad—has carried out some of North Korea's most nefarious activities from its obscure office on the fifth floor of a nondescript concrete building on a quiet back street, Avenida de Sidonio Pais. The company does not even have a sign outside, and when I met two of its officials in Macau in September 2001, they claimed that they were only "exporting sweaters and other knit-wear to Canada and France, and selling ginseng locally."[29] But millions of dollars have been processed there and transferred through Zokwang's bank accounts in Macau. In June 1994, the head of Zokwang and four other North Koreans were arrested in Macau for depositing US$250,000 in counterfeit US$100 bills. But nothing came of the investigation and, in 1999, more counterfeit dollars were discovered in Macau.[30] Again, no action was taken.

The forgeries are so excellent that they have been called "supernotes." The first series of counterfeit bills was so good that they forced the U.S. to issue redesigned currency in 1996.[31] But even the new ones have been copied in North Korea. In March 2003, it was reported that the Pyongyang authorities had acquired state-of-the-art equipment from Europe that can detect counterfeit bills. They would not be used to help stop bad bills being passed in North Korea, but to control and improve the quality of their own fakes.[32]

In 2002, Kim Jong Il's son, Kim Jong Nam, was spotted in

a casino in Macau using some of those counterfeit dollars.[33] Kim Jong Nam is said to be a frequent visitor to Macau, which has a small North Korean community centered around Zokwang Trading—and including local businessmen such as Wong Sing-wa of the Talented Dragon Investment Firm. At any one time, there are usually forty North Korean citizens stationed in Macau. Apart from peddling counterfeit currency, they buy electronic equipment and send it on to Pyongyang. In the past, the North Korean airline, Air Koryo, maintained a weekly flight from Bangkok to Pyongyang with a stop over in Macau. The flights, now monthly, carry few passengers—but plenty of cargo. The arms business is also an important activity carried out by the North Koreans in Macau. In 1986, a Western banker in the enclave was approached by a North Korean who wanted to deposit several million dollars in cash from arms sales to Iran.[34] And, of course, Hyundai's secret payments to North Korea for its tourist trips to the Mount Kumgang resort—as well as part of the alleged payoff for the June 2000 summit in Pyongyang— were supposed to have been sent to Zokwang's bank accounts in Macau.

The training of North Korean intelligence operatives in Macau may be continuing, but the operatives in recent years have become businessmen rather than terrorists blowing up airplanes. In fact, everything suggests that North Korea in the late 1980s shifted the focus of its overseas operations from forging alliances with revolutionary organizations and governments to making money for the state. After all, the regime has to survive, and, even veteran terrorists like Yoshimi Tanaka were sent abroad to make money. Since Kim Jong Il's ascension to power, the money-making aspect of North Korea's foreign operations has become more important than trying to export revolution and the *juche* idea.

However, the idea of using smuggling operations to finance North Korea's diplomatic missions abroad—and to raise money for the regime in Pyongyang—was first suggested in the mid-1970s by Kim Jong Il's brother-in-law, Chang Song Taek, who was only thirty years old at the time but already extremely powerful.[35] Older diplomats may have questioned the wisdom of jeopardizing their country's relations with the rest of the world by engaging in outright illegal activities, but no one dared to oppose such a prominent member of the First Family.

Before long, a major smuggling scandal occurred where it was least expected—in the Scandinavian countries, which had made a real effort to develop good relations with North Korea and could not be accused of engaging in conspiracies aimed at discrediting the regime in Pyongyang.[36] For some time, the police in Sweden, Denmark, Norway, and Finland had noticed that North Korean diplomats were bringing in large quantities of duty-free liquor and selling it on the black market. Initially, the police tried to handle the problem quietly to avoid publicity. But it became impossible to keep it secret when it was discovered that the North Koreans in Copenhagen were also involved in selling hashish. During the weekend of October 16–17, 1976, it was publicly announced that North Korean diplomats had been expelled from both Denmark and Norway. A few days later, all the North Korean diplomats in Finland were expelled for violating their diplomatic status.

In Sweden, police investigations continued, and, in the end, a compromise was reached: all the North Korean diplomats who had engaged in smuggling went back to Pyongyang voluntarily. Diplomatic relations between Sweden and North Korea were salvaged and, for years, the Swedish embassy was the only Western diplomatic mission in Pyongyang. Erik Cornell, the Swedish chargé d'affaires in Pyongyang who worked out the deal, later wrote that the affair revealed the North Korean's "monumental lack of any awareness of the world around them and of standard diplomatic practice . . . foreign emissaries [in Pyongyang] were not seen as representatives of sovereign states; rather, their arrival was seen as a sign of respect and submission."[37] Before accepting Cornell's compromise proposal, the North Koreans expressed only anger and outrage at the action taken by the police in the Scandinavian countries. Cornell also noted that his East European colleagues in Pyongyang could barely suppress their joy at North Korea being taught a lesson—and that they had not been obliged to do it.[38]

It was a lesson that was quickly forgotten. Since the Scandinavian smuggling crisis of 1976, international law enforcement agencies have linked North Korean officials to nearly fifty incidents of drug trafficking in at least sixteen countries on all continents. And it no longer involves only hashish.[39] In January 1977, Venezuelan law enforcement officials arrested three North Korean diplomats and seized 174 kilograms of opium. Four months later, Indian police detained Kim Il Soo, secretary to the North Korean ambassador in New Delhi, for attempting to import 15 kilograms of marijuana. In October 1985, a North Korean diplomat was arrested in East Germany and deported to Pyongyang for attempting to smuggle 150 kilograms of heroin and 150 kilograms of morphine into the country.

The seizures continued into the 1990s. In December 1991, Japanese authorities arrested three North Korean intelligence officers for possession of 13.3 kilograms of heroin, which the police suspected was smuggled into Japan aboard a North Korean merchant ship, the *Mangyongpong-Ho*. In January 1995, Chinese officials in Shanghai arrested two North Koreans and seized 6 kilograms of opium. One of the North Koreans carried a diplomatic passport and was identified as an executive of Zokwang Trading in Macau. In July of the same year, the police in Zambia arrested a North Korean diplomat and seized 2.4 kilograms of cocaine. In January 1998, Russian law enforcement officials at Moscow's Sheremetevo International Airport arrested two North Korean diplomats and seized 35 kilograms of cocaine, which they had brought from Mexico. In October of the same year, German police in Berlin arrested a North Korean deputy ambassador and seized heroin. In February 2000, Japanese police seized 250 kilograms of methamphetamines, which had been smuggled in from North Korea.[40] And then came the big heroin seizures in Taiwan and Australia in July 2002 and April 2003 respectively.[41]

Despite the overwhelming evidence of the involvement of North Korean officials in the drug trade, the Vienna-based United Nations International Narcotics Control Board, INCB, claimed in May 2003 that there was no proof of a "state-sponsored trade." The INCB secretary, Herbert Schaepe, blamed the involvement in the drug trade of North Korean officials on "corruption within the system. That doesn't mean that was accepted necessarily at the highest ranks of the country."[42] Schaepe went to on say that the UN narcotics agency had visited North Korea twice, and was shown 63 hectares of poppy cultivation that he was told was for licit drugs. North Korea had also sent officials to the INCB headquarters in Vienna, and Schaepe proudly announced that Pyongyang is looking at signing international drug control treaties.

The UN's denial was perhaps not surprising. For years, UN drug agencies have also praised, and partly financed, the military government of Burma's supposed drug eradication efforts, while most independent analysts assert that the export of drugs is also an important source of income for the regime in Rangoon. Burma remains one of the world's leading producers of opium and heroin, with estimates of opium production varying between eight hundred and one thousand tons annually.[43] But it has signed several international and regional treaties, and sent officials for training in Vienna as well. Burma and North Korea may be the only two Asian countries where the drug business remains a state affair.

In North Korea, drugs are being sold by government officials, whereas in Burma the trade is carried out by a former rebel group, the United Wa State Army, UWSA, which has a cease-fire agreement with the government in Rangoon. Significantly, the heroin that was seized in Taiwan and Australia was of the Double-UO-Globe Brand, the most infamous heroin brand produced in laboratories controlled or protected by the UWSA, another recipient of UN largesse.[44] Diplomatic relations between North Korea and Burma were never restored after the 1983 Rangoon bombing, but a clandestine military cooperation program was reestablished in 1999. In that year, Burma bought about a dozen 130 mm M-46 field guns from North Korea, and since 2002 between fifteen and twenty North Korean technicians have been stationed at a Burmese naval base near Rangoon, believed to be helping Burma to equip some of their naval vessels with surface-to-surface missiles.[45] Military-ruled Burma is just as cash-strapped as North Korea, and Western narcotics officials suspected a barter deal—weapons for drugs—although that has never been proven.

Apart from contraband liquor, illicit drugs, and counterfeit US$100 bills, North Korean diplomats have also been implicated in the smuggling of bootleg CDs, fake antiques, and illegal elephant tusks and rhinoceros horns from Africa. In 1997, Chang Myong Sik, a counselor at Pyongyang's embassy in Lusaka, Zambia, was arrested at Harare airport in neighboring Zimbabwe with thirty-three pieces of raw ivory in his luggage.[46] Two years later, a North Korean diplomat's wife stationed in Nigeria and traveling from Lagos to Beijing was stopped at Moscow airport with eighty-five elephant tusks, amounting to over half a ton of ivory.[47] Official North Korean involvement in ivory trafficking has been so extensive that in 1999 the secretariat of the Convention on the International Trade in Endangered Species even sent an official diplomatic protest to the North Korean embassy in Switzerland.[48]

In 2000, low estimates by Western intelligence sources of revenue from all these illegal activities—and not including missile sales—were about US$150–200 million, of which 75–85 percent was believed to have come from narcotics. This was equivalent to a quarter of the country's total legal exports, which stood at US$730 million. More critical reports have put the revenue for illegal activities at US$500 million, or even more.[49] The INCB's explanation for this illegal activity—that it is the fault of "low-ranking" party members and is out of state control—would have been easier to swallow if North Korea did not have arguably the most tightly controlled society on earth. Government officials may at times operate independently and their departments may be largely autonomous. But it is inconceivable that higher authorities would be unaware of these activities and, since they do not take any action against those involved in illegal trading, there is also at the very least tacit approval from above.

***

Whether legal or illegal, the basis for North Korea's overseas business activities is its many diplomatic missions and trading companies abroad. Because of the country's economic crisis, the embassies have been instructed to start earning enough hard currency to pay their operating cost—and remit some home to Pyongyang.[50] The pressure from Pyongyang to raise money has become even stronger as the number of North Korean missions abroad is declining. In 1999–2000, there were fifty-four North Korean embassies and consulates abroad, down from sixty-eight in 1997.[51] With fewer diplomatic missions—and increased surveillance of those remaining by law enforcement agencies in the host countries—the North Koreans are turning to establishing joint-venture companies with local partners mainly in countries and territories in East and Southeast Asia. There are at least half a dozen such companies in Thailand, and about ten each in Singapore and Hong Kong, often disguised as "import-export firms" and "electronics companies."[52] What they have in common is that they are all answerable to Bureau 39 of the Korean Workers' Party.

Housed in a heavily guarded, six-story building close to Kim Jong Il's personal office in central Pyongyang, Bureau 39 has been described as the Dear Leader's own slush fund which is used mainly to dole out cash and gifts to key military men and party officials to ensure their allegiance to the regime.[53] It is uncertain when Bureau 39 was set up—or, rather, when the money-making arm of the KWP got that curious name—but its activities date back to 1974, when Kim Jong Il was named to the KWP politburo.[54] Its most important overt branch, the Daesong Economic Group, controls the Golden Star Bank in Vienna, Zokwang Trading in Macau, and other enterprises in Japan and East and Southeast Asia. Bureau 39 does not necessarily keep its funds in the Golden Star Bank in Vienna, but uses a wide range of offshore bank accounts—and a well-known local bank in Macau.[55] Golden Star's "mother bank," the Korea Daesong Bank in Pyongyang, has normal correspondent relations with banks in Japan, Britain, Germany, Switzerland, India, France, Singapore, and Sweden.[56]

In the beginning, Bureau 39 dealt mainly in agricultural produce and precious metals, but as North Korea's food crisis began to worsen, it turned increasingly to contraband trade as well as the export of pine mushrooms, seafood, and ginseng.[57] In recent years, it also appears that Hong Kong, rather than Macau, has emerged as its most important base in East Asia. As long as Hong Kong was British, the North Koreans were kept at bay. But since it reverted to Chinese rule in 1997, the North Koreans have at long last been allowed to open a consulate in Hong Kong in February 2001. Its first consul general, Ri To Sop, speaks fluent English, is open and approachable, and tried hard to get local Hong Kong companies to invest in North Korea.[58]

The opening of the consulate was followed by the establishment of several new, North Korean–controlled trading and shipping companies. They are there to buy electronic devices which are readily available in Hong Kong's specialist stores at very competitive prices. But when North Korea asked for permission for Air Koryo to use the territory's new Chek Lap Kok airport, the authorities turned down the request. The North Korean airline's old Tupolev Tu-154 aircraft were just too noisy.[59]

Concerns about increasing North Korean involvement in illegal activities were real, but they received a severe blow when South Korea's intelligence agencies in May 2003 "leaked" a report to the country's national news agency, *Yonhap*, saying that a personal confidant of Kim Jong Il, and the alleged head of North Korea's drug-smuggling operations,

Kil Jae Gyong, had defected to the West along with Han Myong Chol, vice president of Zokwang Trading.[60] Kil Jae Gyong was indeed among the diplomats who left Sweden in disgrace in 1976, and he had in 1998 been caught in Vladivostok with US$30,000 in counterfeit dollar bills trying to buy Russian caviar. The problem, however, is that he had died of illness in June 2000, and was buried in the Patriotic Martyrs' Cemetery in Sinmiri, Pyongyang. Han Myong Chol had not defected either; he turned out to still be in his office in Macau.[61] *Yonhap* was forced to publish a letter of apology for disseminating the completely inaccurate report, which was picked up by a number of Western publications, including the *Washington Times* and some other newspapers in the U.S.[62]

At about the same time, another astonishing piece of news appeared in the international media, claiming that the U.S. and "at least" ten other countries had assisted in the defection of twenty top North Korean officials, including Kyong Won Ha—allegedly the father of the country's nuclear program—and other key nuclear scientists. They had managed to escape via China, ferried by diplomatic cars from the Beijing embassy of the tiny, twenty-one square kilometer island republic of Nauru in the Pacific to some safe house, and then ended up in the West, the reports said.[63] U.S. State Department spokesman Richard Boucher responded that it was "great reading, but untrue. I'm enjoying this . . . it was a great story. I hate to [refute] it."[64]

Telling fact from fiction is equally difficult when it comes to allegations of actual drug production inside North Korea. For centuries, small quantities of opium poppies have been grown in the mountains of northern Korea and along the coast of the peninsula, but the cultivation and processing of the drug became more systematic during the Japanese colonial era. Especially active in promoting poppy cultivation in Korea was the Tokyo-based Taisho Pharmaceutical Company, which bought opium from local cultivators and turned it into morphine. But repeated smuggling scandals involving Taisho officials prompted the Japanese governor general of Korea to cancel the company's concession in 1928. Hence the cultivation of opium poppies and the production of morphine and also heroin were placed under the jurisdiction of the state-controlled Monopoly Bureau.

In the 1930s, Korea's production of narcotics expanded rapidly. At the time the Monopoly was established, Korea produced 808 kilograms of raw opium on 415 hectares of land. This increased to 5,564 kilograms on 1,054 hectares in 1931, 14,059 kilograms on 2,241 hectares in 1933, peaking at 50,725 kilograms on 8,464 hectares in 1941. However, very little of the opium produced in Korea actually remained there. Over 90 percent of the Japanese colony's output was exported to Manchuria and China, earning substantial revenues for the Japanese authorities.[65]

Opium production probably never ceased in northern Korea, and current estimates by U.S. sources put the area under poppy cultivation at 4,000 hectares in the early 1990s and 7,000 hectares for 1995. Current production is believed to be below these figures because of heavy rains in the mid-1990s which affected all crops, including poppies, but no one knows for certain as there are no reliable satellite images showing the poppy fields and no ground surveys have been made by independent researchers.[66]

But it seems clear that, at least since 1996, some North Koreans have turned more aggressively into the production of methamphetamines—or importing methamphetamines from China and reexporting the drug to third countries.[67] According to congressional researchers in the U.S., North Korea's drug business is also under the elusive Bureau 39, and drugs are exported through China and Russia to Asia and Europe via government trading companies, diplomatic pouches, and concealed in legitimate commercial cargo.[68]

And it is all meant for export, as drug use is not common in North Korea. In March 2002, Kim Jong Il even announced that drug users, if found, would be executed by shooting: "I will subject all those who sell or use illegal drugs to a firing squad, and have ordered that Chinese drug traders be beaten with sticks."[69] In October 2003, the official *Korean Central*

News Agency reported that a Japanese national, Yoshiaka Sawada, had been arrested trying to bribe a North Korean into buying drugs from "a third country"—obviously China—and smuggle them into Japan on board the North Korean ship *Mangyongbong-92*, which sails regularly between Wonsan in North Korea and the Japanese port of Niigata.[70] Thus, the North Koreans would be blamed for bringing in the shipment. Clearly, North Korea wanted to make it known that it is firm on the issue of drug abuse—and that the traffickers, if there are any, are actually Chinese or Japanese.

The main destination for drugs smuggled through and from North Korea is without doubt Japan, which does not have a huge population of heroin or cannabis users, but where the abuse of amphetamines and methamphetamines has been widespread since the end of World War II. The country has an estimated six hundred thousand amphetamine and methamphetamine addicts and 2.18 million casual users.[71] Between 1999 and 2001 Japanese authorities seized 1,113 kilograms of amphetamine-type substances smuggled in from North Korea, and sold to Japanese criminal gangs. This makes up 34 percent of Japan's total seizures of the drug. China, the main source, accounted for 38 percent.[72]

Japan is not just a major market for methamphetamines from North Korea. It is also the home of one of its most important overt support bases abroad: the ethnic Korean community in the Chongryun. And with the shift in North Korea's emphasis away from sponsoring revolutionary organizations towards making money and obtaining carefully selected goods for its defense industries, the Chongryun is, of course, far more useful for Pyongyang than the idealistic militants of the Japanese Red Army.

CHAPTER 7

THE CHONGRYUN

From a distance, there is nothing particularly suspicious about the eight-story, gray concrete building on a quiet side street in Chiyoda district, downtown Tokyo. But the high wall around it with surveillance cameras monitoring movements in and out of the automatic, sliding gates—and the riot police and barriers on the street outside—reveal that this is not an ordinary office block. For years, this has been the headquarters of the General Association of Korean Residents in Japan, or Chongryun, which groups together ethnic Koreans in Japan who remain so loyal to Pyongyang that they consider themselves to be overseas nationals of North Korea.

Known as *Chosen Soren* in Japanese, and *Chochongryon* in South Korea, it holds seats in North Korea's Supreme People's Assembly, and its headquarters, which—in the absence of diplomatic relations between Japan and North Korea—serves as Pyongyang's de-facto mission in Tokyo. When, on November 29, 2001, for the first time ever the Japanese police entered the building in connection with an embezzlement case involving Chongryun functionaries, the organization's official organ branded the raid "a flagrant infringement upon the sovereignty of the Democratic People's Republic of Korea."[1]

The police barriers outside the Tokyo headquarters were reinforced after Kim Jong Il's astonishing admission to Japanese prime minister Junichiro Koizumi, who was visiting

Pyongyang in September 2002, that several Japanese citizens, who had disappeared mysteriously in the late 1970s and 1980s, had indeed been abducted to North Korea. The Chongryun's leaders had always dismissed the allegation as slander and anti–North Korean propaganda, but now they found themselves with the almost impossible task of explaining their position to the Japanese public. The Chongryun's chairman, So Man Sul, immediately issued a statement: "We hope the abduction problem will be resolved in a sincere way between the two nations."[2]

He may have expected that his conciliatory stand would help ease the grief and anguish people felt about the abductions, but it had exactly the opposite effect. Angry crowds gathered outside the Chongryun's Tokyo head-quarters, and other offices, shouting abuse. Known Japanese Koreans were assaulted in the streets, and the Chongryun's offices received a flood of angry phone calls and emails.[3] Although the Chongryun was not implicated in the abducti-ons, their support for North Korea was real, and it was widely believed that the kidnappings would not have been possible had there not been a large, well-organized pro-Pyongyang community of Koreans in Japan. The North Korean agents must have had help from local people where the abductions took place, especially to whisk the captives away so cleanly. And where did the North Korean agents get their information about the identity and movements of young Japanese deemed suitable to train North Korean agents? All the thirteen Japanese, both boys and girls, were in their teens or early twenties when they "disappeared" more than twenty years ago.[4]

The public storm over the abductions brought to the fore a number of other accusations against the Chongryun. For years, Japanese Korean individuals, and companies run by Japanese Koreans, had been sending huge amounts of money to North Korea. Some went to relatives, but large donations to the North Korean state were not uncommon. Moreover, Japanese Koreans affiliated with the Chongryun were said to have bought sophisticated computer equipment, computer parts, machine tools, and other technology necessary for ballistic missile and nuclear programs, and shipped the kit to North Korea.[5]

The Chongryun responded by condemning the physical attacks as "criminal acts punishable by law," and by emphasizing the organization's social and educational activities. It runs 143 Korean-language schools, ranging from elementary schools all over Japan to a university in Tokyo. It has its own daily newspaper, *Chosun Sinbo*, football teams, youth leagues, a women's union, an art institute, bookshops, credit institutes, a movie company, and a music recording studio as well as a host of import-export companies. It even provides match-making services for younger members.[6] The Chongryun plays an important role in upholding a Korean identity within Japan's 650,000-strong Korean community, and many Japanese Koreans spend almost their entire lives in the organization's schools and social clubs. They form a semi-autonomous community in Japan, and every summer thousands of Japanese Korean schoolchildren visit North Korea to learn more about their "homeland."

But with the powerful Chongryun on the defensive, the Japanese police began to check the cargo transported to North Korea from Japan aboard the ship the schoolchildren use for their excursions: the 9,393-tonne *Mangyongbong-92*, which plies the route between Niigata in Japan and the North Korean port of Wonsan every two weeks. Owned by the North, and accommodating two hundred passengers, it can also carry up to one thousand tonnes of cargo.[7]

Japanese authorities also put pressure on the privately owned Ashikaga Bank to suspend remittances to North Korea. Ashikaga Bank was one of the few Japanese banks through which such remittances were possible and was the bank through which the Chongryun primarily operated. During the first nuclear crisis in 1993–94, the U.S. government strongly urged the Japanese to stop those remittances, and, eventually, in 2002 that window was closed.[8] For several decades, most of the money flowing to North Korea has come from Japanese pinball, or *pachinko*. Many of Japan's eighteen thousand *pachinko* parlors were and still are run by ethnic Koreans.[9] It is a huge industry, which employs 318,000 people and attracts 28 million players, who pour hundreds of millions of dollars a year into the machines.[10]

The ethnic Korean dominance of Japan's lucrative *pachinko* industry is only one of many inadvertent legacies of Japan's rule over Korea from 1910 to 1945. During the colonial era, hundreds of thousands of Koreans were brought to Japan to work in factories, primarily in Osaka and Kobe. When World War II broke out, even more Koreans were brought to replace Japanese workers as the war took Japan's own labor force to the battlefields of China and Southeast Asia. By the end of the war and the time of Japan's withdrawal from Korea, there were 2.4 million Koreans in Japan. Nearly all of them, or 97 percent, came from the southern part of the Korean peninsula, or the island of Cheju between Korea and Japan.[11]

By 1950, rapid repatriation had reduced the number to half a million. Denied Japanese citizenship, and excluded from Japanese society, most of them were poor day laborers in Osaka, Kobe, Nagoya, Tokyo, and other cities. The second generation was slightly better off, but few, if any, could find employment opportunities in major Japanese companies. Some went into private business: first *pachinko*, and then Korean barbecue restaurants, which became popular among the Japanese. Only the third or fourth generation has managed to break into the Japanese labor market, and some of the best educated work as computer specialists, translators, or salesmen for big enterprises. It is now also easier for Koreans in Japan to become Japanese citizens, but, despite improvements, discrimination still prevails, and many Korean residents are still considered "foreigners," even though they have lived in Japan for generations.

Seen in an historical context, it is therefore not surprising that many Koreans in Japan have sided with the North. In the 1950s, South Korea was under the repressive rule of Syngman Rhee. It was poor, and, in effect, occupied by the United States. The bureaucracy was filled with "collaborators" from colonial times, and there was not much for an impoverished Korean in Osaka to be proud of. In the North, however, a new, truly independent Korean nation seemed to be emerging, a Korea that did not hesitate to lash out against the Japanese and the Americans, and where the economy was making impressive headway.

In the beginning, most Korean leftists and nationalists in Japan were active in the Democratic Front of Koreans, Minjon in its Korean abbreviation, or in the Japanese Communist Party. But that relationship began to change when, in February 1955, the North Korean foreign minister issued a statement declaring that his government was prepared to establish normal relations with Japan. Under such circumstances, if the Koreans were to continue struggling against the Japanese government, they would become an obstacle to the normalization of ties between Tokyo and Pyongyang. The JCP, on the other hand, argued that the Koreans were an ethnic minority in Japan and as such they should be fighting for a revolution, not be Korean nationalists. The interests of the Koreans and the JCP became incompatible, and the inevitable happened. The Koreans broke with the Japanese Communist Party, dissolved the affiliated Minjon, and, on May 25, 1955, formed the Chaeilbon Chosunin Chong Ryonhaphoe, Chongryun for short, or, in English, the General Association of Korean Residents in Japan.[12]

Its first chairman, a labor activist called Han Duk Su, declared that the aim of the new organization was "safeguarding the fatherland first, putting off the international joint struggle for the time being."[13] The Chongryun defined its agenda in no uncertain terms:

1. We shall organize all Korean compatriots in Japan around the Democratic People's Republic of Korea.
2. We shall fight for the peaceful reunification of the fatherland.
3. We shall institutionalize our own education among the Korean children in Japan.

4. We shall safeguard firmly our honor as overseas nationals of the Democratic People's Republic of Korea.[14]

In the mid-1950s, Japanese authorities estimated that about 90 percent of Koreans in Japan were behind the Chongryun and thus supported Pyongyang.[15] Although mostly southerners, they became known as "North Koreans," based on their ideological choice, not the birthplace of their families. Their hatred of the regime in Seoul had deepened when, in the late 1940s, the authorities quelled a peasant uprising on Cheju Island—where many of them came from— killing up to fifty thousand people, or 20 percent of the population.[16] The smaller, pro-Seoul Mindan, or the Association of Korean Residents in Japan, had a much weaker profile, and was itself divided between supporters and opponents of the South Korean regime.

Han Duk Su himself came from North Kyongsang province in the southeast of the peninsula. He went to study in Japan in 1927, when he was twenty, but he was poor and had to work while attending college. At one point he was arrested and sentenced to two years in prison with a three-year stay of execution by the Japanese police on the charge of having organized a labor dispute among fellow Korean workers. Throughout the 1940s, Han Duk Su continued to fight for the rights of the Koreans in Japan and never wavered in his loyalty to Kim Il Sung. In 1967, he was even "elected" deputy to the Supreme People's Assembly, and Kim Il Sung personally received him every time he went to Pyongyang.[17]

The many schools that the Chongryun established—in the beginning with substantial help from Pyongyang—used the same text books as in North Korea. Portraits of Kim Il Sung and Kim Jong Il adorned the wall above the blackboard, and the children were taught that "we have nothing to envy in the whole world."[18] Older Koreans referred to their own youth as "the time when our respected and beloved Marshal Kim Il Sung was fighting the Japanese in Paekdu Mountains."[19] But, above all, the Chongryun Koreans were grateful to Kim Il Sung: "Thanks to the love and care of the Great

Leader, we are living here in Japan without having to worry about anything. He and the government of the Democratic People's Republic of Korea protect us, the overseas nationals in Japan."[20] Kim Il Sung had rescued them "from being reduced to a mere ethnic minority in Japan. We are not inferior or passive; we have our own fatherland; we are overseas nationals of our glorious fatherland."[21]

At the close of the 1950s, however, many decided to return to Korea—the North, of course. The voyage back to their beloved homeland was facilitated under an agreement signed between the Red Cross Societies of Japan and North Korea in 1959. Full of enthusiasm, they flocked to Niigata, singing and shouting slogans. The returnees stayed in Red Cross tents before they went on board and, while they were waiting for the journey "home," they planted 305 willow trees along a one-mile stretch northeast of Niigata's railroad station and a few hundred meters from the Shinano River. Known as the Willow Tree Road, it is still there, a monument to the repatriation of the Koreans.

As the first ship was ready to leave, the pier was packed with well-wishers shouting "Long Live!" After a blast of the horn, the ship sailed away, bound for North Korea.[22] When it approached the North Korean coast after a fifteen-hour journey from Niigata, Kim Yong Gil, a famous Korean opera singer from Japan, got up on the bridge. He turned to the promised land and launched into an impromptu but powerful rendition of *O Sole Mio*, causing emotions to swell among his fellow passengers.[23] From December 1959 to 1967, about ninety thousand Koreans—and almost two thousand Japanese women married to Korean men—went to North Korea. It was a one-way journey. Once in North Korea, there were no arrangements for anyone wishing to return to Japan.[24]

Occasional letters and audio tapes filtered back to relatives in Japan, and it was clear that life had not turned out as expected in North Korea. But many Chongryun Koreans chose not to believe the horror stories they heard, remaining blindly loyal to Pyongyang. For many, it was also a question of identity: who were they if not overseas nationals of the Democratic People's Republic of Korea? Incongruous as it may seem in modern, industrialized Japan, beginning in the 1970s, *juche* became a symbol of that identity, occupying a central place in all the Chongryun's cadre education programs.

Sonia Ryang, a Korean scholar from Japan who grew up in a Chongryun community in Tokyo, remembers how participants at the organization's rallies used to chant: "Let us mold and remold ourselves in the great *juche* style!" and "Let us become revolutionaries in whose veins flows pure *juche*-type blood!" Adherence to the *juche* idea may have kept the downtrodden Koreans in Japan together as a community in an often hostile environment, and given them a sense of belonging to a greater and proud Korean nation. But it was never clear to Ryang, and presumably other Koreans in Japan, exactly what the substance of "*juche* style," or "*juche*-type blood," was. Rather, they were often employed as synonyms for loyalty to Kim Il Sung.[25]

The Japanese government tolerated the activities of the Chongryun, as long as it did not get mixed up in Japanese leftist politics. Somewhat paradoxically, the Chongryun leader, Han Duk Su, instead cultivated close links with the conservative, ruling Liberal Democratic Party—perhaps because that was where the power lay.[26] And, as his importance grew—and the Chongryun consolidated its grip over a significant segment of the Korean population in Japan—he moved into a grand home in a quiet residential area of Tokyo. Guards watched Han Duk Su's residence around the clock, and he had several luxury cars and personal bodyguards to accompany him wherever he went.[27] His lifestyle could hardly be described as proletarian, and was in sharp contrast to that of the often-impoverished members of the Chongryun, who were expected to donate a large share of their meager salaries to the organization.

Things began to change as relations between South Korea and Japan soured when on August 15, 1974, a young man ran down the aisle of Seoul's National Theater. Somehow, he had managed to get through the security checks at the entrance with his .38 caliber pistol. He fired his gun repeatedly against a couple sitting in the front row—the president of South Korea, Park Chung Hee, and his wife, Yook Young Soo. The president survived, but his wife slumped to the floor, bleeding profusely. She died within hours, as did a high-school girl who was part of the chorus singing at the occasion—the twenty-ninth anniversary of Japan's surrender and the liberation of Korea.[28]

The gunman was soon apprehended. He turned out to be a twenty-two-year-old Korean from Osaka and a Chongryun member, Mun Se Kwang. He had flown into Seoul a week before the celebration in the National Theater with a gun he had stolen from a Japanese police station and concealed in a radio before the flight. His motive was quite simple: having sold out to the Americans and the Japanese, Park Chung Hee was a traitor to the Korean nation and had to be eliminated. Who was he to celebrate the liberation of Korea? But Park Chung Hee outlived the young assassin from Osaka. On December 20, Mun Se Kwang was convicted and hanged in Seoul.

There is nothing to indicate that the Chongryun as an organization was involved in the murderous attack, but the South Korean government demanded an apology from Japan, and that the Chongryun be disbanded. Given the sensitivity of the Korean issue in Japan—the relationship between the former colonial power and its downtrodden former subjects, now stateless residents, has always been a delicate issue—it was hardly surprising that the Japanese government was not prepared to take such drastic action against the Chongryun, even if surveillance of the organization increased after the attempt on Park Chung Hee's life.

But it was an entirely different matter with respect to the flow of money—and technology—to North Korea from Japan. For years, the Japanese authorities had turned a blind eye to remittances to North Korea, but a massive "gift-sending campaign" that the Chongryun waged in 1972 to commemorate Kim Il Sung's sixtieth birthday—a milestone in the life of a Korean as it signified the completion of five twelve-year cycles—could not be ignored. A total of fifty-nine hundred tonnes of gifts were shipped to North Korea, including food, decorative items, electrical appliances, medical instruments, construction material, and cars.[29] Wealthier Japanese Koreans traveled to Pyongyang, and paid up to US$20,000 to have their picture taken together with the Great Leader.[30]

The Chongryun's support for North Korea again came under scrutiny in the mid-1990s, when the Soviet Union had collapsed and aid from China had all but dried up. Somehow, North Korea still seemed to have substantial reserves of foreign hard currency, and not all of it could be traced to the commercial activities of its embassies abroad. Japan's interest in the links between Chongryun and Pyongyang grew considerably after the North on August 31, 1998 fired its Taepondong-1 missile over Japan and into the Pacific Ocean. Where did that sophisticated technology come from?

The *pachinko* industry was the first to be investigated. In 1994, the Japanese police testified in the country's parliament, the Diet, that between US$650 and 850 million was being sent to Pyongyang annually, much of it derived from *pachinko*.[31] In the early 1990s, as much as US$2 billion a year in remittances, cash gifts, and investment was flowing from Japan to North Korea, according to then foreign minister Tsutomu Hata.[32] Nicholas Eberstadt, a leading Korea expert and economist, asserts that these figures are most probably grossly exaggerated, as it would mean that every Chongryun Korean each year sent thousands of dollars to the North, which is not likely given the fact that most of them were, and still are, low income earners. Annual money flows were probably in the tens of millions rather than in the hundreds of millions, or billions—still considerable sums, though, given the size of the North Korean economy.[33] In the late 1990s, Japan's economic downturn also began to affect the *pachinko* industry. In 1996 alone, revenues shrank 7.5 percent for the first time in fifteen years, and, in 1997, seventy-six *pachinko* parlors filed for bankruptcy.[34] This meant that less money was going to North Korea.

While the colorful *pachinko* industry attracted the attention of the police and media the Chongryun was actively supporting North Korea in other, more subtle and clandestine ways. The Chongryun's eight-story Tokyo headquarters also has a basement, where the organization's bodyguards and special agents are given martial arts training. Many of them belong to an underground outfit called *haksupjo* in Korean— and *Gakushu-gumi* in Japanese—or literally "the study group." Candidates must submit recommendations from two members of "the study group" along with their applications, and, once accepted, new members "must arm themselves with the *juche* ideology, unconditionally practice the teachings of the Great Leader and the policies of the Korean Workers' Party, and safeguard the Great Leader with their own lives." Its five thousand carefully selected members also have to pledge to fulfill "the patriotic task of Chongryun," and "safeguard the organization from the subversive maneuverings of enemies."[35]

Some of those tasks and duties are to conduct intelligence operations in Japan, assist the infiltration of agents from North Korea, and divert advanced technology to Japan. *Gakushu-gumi* members are also considered cadre of the Korean Workers' Party, and as such stand above ordinary Chongryun Koreans, most of whom are probably blissfully unaware of the real nature of the organization's "study groups."[36] The suspicion is strong that without their assistance and preparatory ground work, the abduction of the Japanese youngsters in the late 1970s and early 1980s would probably have been impossible.

According to Japanese newspaper reports, North Korean spies in Japan—either *Gakushu-gumi* members or special agents sent by Pyongyang—hide out in towns next to bases in Japan belonging to the United States military or Japan's own Self-Defense Forces. Japanese intelligence suspects that some of them may even be working within those bases as laborers and contractors. Nuclear power plants are considered as important as the military bases, and kept under North Korean surveillance.[37] *Gakushu-gumi* activists are also expected to put into action directives issued by the leadership in Pyongyang. Known as *marsum*—or "words from the Supreme Power"—they usually come from Kim Jong Il himself. In September 1986 he issued the first such edict, code-named "*Marsum* of September," which ordered the Chongryun to "expand businesses . . . maximize profits, and remit them to the North Korean government as a gift."[38] North Korea's economy was beginning to deteriorate, and there was no better source of funds to tap than the loyal Koreans in Japan. The 1986 *marsum* marked the beginning of large-scale money-making operations by the Chongryun and Chongryun-affiliated organizations and enterprises in Japan.

In 1988, Pyongyang issued a new order, instructing its loyal followers in Japan to obtain chemicals and technology needed in North Korea's arms industries.[39] This was done through a host of front companies, run by Chongryun faithfuls or North Korean agents, and it was not such a difficult task. Anyone can walk into a computer store in Tokyo or Osaka and buy components and software. Chemicals, machine tools, and spare parts for military use can be obtained in the same way as North Korea's agents in Slovakia ordered and sent their goods: different companies order chemicals or technological equipment from a variety of suppliers, and taken one by one, there is nothing suspicious about those orders. Only when put together do they form a complete picture of what they are going to be used for.

Crackdowns on such activities have proved extremely difficult to implement. When the Japanese authorities made it harder to send money to North Korea though "normal" channels, stacks of Japanese 10,000-yen bills were hidden inside boxes of melons and other fruit, and loaded onto the *Mangyongbong-92*.[40] Or, with Ashikaga Bank out of the picture, remittances can be made to banks in China, Macau, or Hong Kong, and then forwarded to North Korea.[41] Electronic equipment could be shipped directly onboard the *Mangyongbong-92*, or indirectly through other North Korean front companies in China.

The Chongryun's clandestine business activities can sometimes be as convoluted at the operation Kim Kum Jin and Ri Sun Hui used to run from Bratislava. In November 2002, a Tokyo-based, Chongryun-affiliated company called Meishin, or Myongshin in Korean, attempted to export three power-control devices to North Korea. But when the company informed customs of the planned shipment, Japan's Ministry of Economy, Trade, and Industry responded that Meishin required special permission under Japanese regulations governing the export of dual purpose equipment that can be used in, or converted for use in, weapons of mass destruction. The power-control devices could, for instance, stabilize the flow of electric current to uranium-enrichment centrifuges. Meishin did not apply for such permission, but on April 4, 2003, it shipped those same devices to a Thai company, Loxley Pacific, which in turn was going to ship them to North Korea's Daesong General Trading Company. But customs in Hong Kong, where the ship stopped on its way to Bangkok, acted on a tip-off from the Japanese and seized the devices and returned them to Japan. Loxley Pacific, one of Thailand's leading telecommunications companies, has major interests in North Korea, and was therefore a perfect conduit for the stabilizers. But a spokesman for Loxley insisted that the devices were not destined for North Korea's nuclear program. "The electricity situation is poor in North Korea," he said. "They need stabilizers to avoid hurting their household appliances."[42]

The transfers of selected technological items may have become the main activity in recent years, as the flow of hard cash from Japan to North Korea began to drop considerably after 1989, and the large pool of formerly die-hard Chongryun loyalists has begun to shrink. In the late 1980s, the Japanese "bubble economy" burst, and the Chongryun Koreans—like all other people in Japan—suddenly had less money to spare.[43] Then, in 1994, Kim Il Sung died, and many Chongryun members began to look at the situation in the North as "gradually ambiguous."[44] It was obviously harder to relate to the younger, not particularly charismatic Kim Jong

Il than the old guerrilla fighter and father figure, Kim Il Sung.[45]

At the same time, South Korea could no longer be seen as a poor client of the United States. Until the mid-1970s, per capita GNP was said to be higher in the North than in the South. Even in 1976, the U.S. Central Intelligence Agency estimated that the North Korean economy was out-producing the South in almost every sector.[46] But that began to change in the late 1970s, as drastic reforms and bold initiatives by the authoritarian ruler Park Chung Hee started to show impressive results. He may have been a ruthless dictator, but the South Korean economy grew at a breathtaking pace.

South Korea's per capita GNP stood at a mere US$80 in 1960, or on the same level as poor African states. By the mid-1980s, it had increased to US$2,000, and in 1993 annual income per person was estimated at US$7,466 in the South—but only US$904 in the North, which was getting poorer as a result of the collapse of the Soviet Union and a sharp reduction in aid from China.[47] Then, in 1998, Kim Dae Jung was elected president of South Korea. Unlike many of his predecessors, he could not be accused of being a "U.S. puppet" or a "military dictator." In fact, Kim Dae Jung had been kidnapped, and almost murdered, in Japan in August 1973 by South Korean agents, assisted by local workers for the Chongryun's rival, the Mindan. In broad daylight, five Korean men had entered the hotel in Tokyo where Kim Dae Jung was staying, grabbed him in one of the corridors, and shoved him into an empty room, where he was beaten and drugged. Kim Dae Jong was driven to Osaka, and then taken in a high-speed boat in the middle of the night to a freighter at sea. Only a last minute intervention by the then U.S. ambassador in Seoul, Philip Habib, and Donald Ranard, a U.S. State Department official in Washington, forced the South Koreans to release the famous dissident. But contrary to what most Japanese—and Koreans—believe, they acted without approval from Washington.[48] Kim Dae Jung survived the ordeal to become the president of his country twenty-five years later.

***

The Chongryun received a further blow when Han Duk Su passed away in February 2001. He was ninety-four, and had been the Chongryun's undisputed leader since its inception in 1955—as well as a close friend of the late Great Leader, a frequent visitor to North Korea, and a member of its Supreme People's Assembly. His successor, So Man Sul, is also a Chongryun veteran, but he does not have nearly the same status in the Korean community as Han Duk Su had had for almost half a century.[49]

Nine months after the death of Han Duk Su, the Japanese police—for the first time ever—entered Chongryun's headquarters in downtown Tokyo. Though the raid had nothing to do with Han Duk Su, his being gone from the scene may have made the police more willing to take on the Chongryun. Its credit association had gone bankrupt and one of its senior officials, Kang Young Kwan, had been arrested on suspicion that he had diverted about US$6.5 million, perhaps to his own pocket, perhaps to North Korea.[50] More than forty other places were also searched, and almost one hundred people were taken in for questioning.

About four hundred Chongryun members gathered on the street outside the headquarters building to protest the raid, which the organization condemned as "nothing but a political suppression of Koreans in Japan and ethnic financial institutions of the Chongryun, a crackdown prompted by racial discrimination." The Chongryun went on to assert that "all (our) activities . . . are legitimate ones in line with the Japanese laws and there has been nothing illegal in the transactions with our credit institutions."[51]

The Chongryun seemed to overlook the fact that it was its own poor members who had been ripped off. Ostensibly set up to help the Koreans in Japan, the Chongryun's credit institutions were used to tap them for cash, which went to the North. Chongryun Koreans were asked to put money into a special account for "patriotic works," or to invest in North Korea's Rajin-Sonbong "economic and trade zone." They never saw the money again, or got any noteworthy returns on their investment. Others shipped computer chips and electronic goods to the North, and were never paid.[52] With the collapse of the bubble economy, and the slump in the *pachinko* industry, the importance of money still in accounts with the credit institutions grew—until the main one collapsed in November 2001.

In recent years, the Chongryun has tried hard to adjust to the changing times, and to recover from the shock caused by the revelations of the abduction issue. In a move in September 2002 which seemed to be aimed at depoliticizing the Chongryun in the eyes of the Japanese public, the organization's leadership decided to remove the portraits of the Great and Dear Leaders from its elementary and junior high schools. But it kept those on the walls of its higher education institutions, including the Korean University in Tokyo, and, of course, in all Chongryun offices across Japan.[53] The organization's various publications have also become glossier and now put a firmer emphasis on community work, Korean literature, sports, and music rather than being filled with stories extolling the virtues of Kim Il Sung, Kim Jong Il, and the invincibility of the *juche* idea.

It is hard to estimate the Chongryun's strength today, but the number of children attending its schools is down to 17,000 from a peak of 40,000 in the 1960s.[54] Membership— or rather affiliation, as Chongryun does not actually have card-carrying members—stands at perhaps a third of the Korean population in Japan, or a bit over 200,000. Some sources put the figure at between 100,000 and 150,000, still an impressive figure.[55] And although it is no longer as difficult as it used to be for foreign residents in Japan to acquire Japanese citizenship, many Chongryun Koreans have no interest in doing so, feeling that it would deprive them of their national identity.[56] The Chongryun, therefore, still provides them with a sense of belonging to what they see as their community.

But in order to survive in a changing world, the Chongryun has been compelled to move closer to its former rival, the Mindan, with the aim of creating an "all-Korean" movement in Japan.[57] On December 22 and 23, 2002, two hundred Koreans from both groups rallied together against the acquittal of two American soldiers by a U.S. military court on homicide charges over an accident in which two South Korean schoolgirls were killed. The Koreans who marched in the candlelight procession in Tokyo's Shinjuku ward also protested against the presence of U.S. troops in South Korea.[58] At the same time, cultural and sport exchanges between the Mindan and the Chongryun have become common.

The Chongryun may be weaker and tamer these days, but it still plays an important role in North Korea's strategic thinking. Two weeks before Japanese premier Koizumi made his historic visit to Pyongyang in September 2002, North Korea publicly ordered the Chongryun's "informal study groups" to disband—indirectly admitting that the activities of the *Gakushu-gumi* comprised a potential thorn in relations with Japan.[59]

But did they? Despite some setbacks and stricter controls, Japan remains an important source of money and technology for the North Korean regime. And why should Pyongyang give up its important espionage network in a country where many still look at North Korea as their spiritual homeland, even if the regime in Pyongyang today may not seem as much of an ideal as it was twenty or thirty years ago? As a young Chongryun member put it: "If your father comes home drunk, he's still your father and you have to respect him."[60] It is such loyalty that the North Korean regime is counting on for continued support.

CHAPTER 8

THE CAMPS AND THE REFUGEES

The writing on the archway across the dirt road says "Border Patrol of the Korean People, Unit 2915." But this is far from any of North Korea's frontiers. The nearest town, Yodok, is seven hours by truck from Pyongyang along a bumpy road that winds its way into the mountainous interior of South Hamgyong province in the center of the peninsula. And the sign does not fool anyone. Just to mention the name "Yodok" sends shivers down the spines of most North Koreans. Not without reason, Wolwangnyong, or King's Pass, in the mountains before the last stretch of road down to the narrow valley below is also called the Pass of Tears. Most people cross it in only one direction. This is not an ordinary border police outpost, but one of North Korea's most dreaded prison camps.[1]

Rows of uniformed soldiers, armed with Kalashnikovs, stand guard at the gates. Vicious Alsatians, held back by steel leashes, bark at anyone. Papers are checked, and trucks with prisoners in the back then drive across a ten-kilometer, uninhabited "buffer zone" before they enter the actual camp—an enormous, eighty-kilometer-long and eighty-kilomete-wide area surrounded by high mountains. The lowland parts are sealed off with electric fences, while, up in the mountains, barbed wire, traps, and mine fields make sure that no one can escape. And no one has managed to escape from Yodok. Many have tried, only to be caught and shot. This is the end of the road for tens of thousands of people, whom the regime in Pyongyang have branded "traitors of the fatherland."

Kang Chol Hwan was only nine when he, along with his sister, father, uncle, and grandmother, was sent to Yodok. His grandfather, Kang Tae Gyu, had been a local leader of the Chongryun in Kyoto, and he and some of his closest family members were among the many Koreans in Japan who decided to move to North Korea in the early 1960s. At first, they had been welcomed by the North Korean state and lived in relative comfort in Pyongyang. But one night in July 1977, grandfather did not come home from work. The family had no idea what had happened to him, and in North Korea no one dares to ask about sudden disappearances. A few weeks later, their home in Pyongyang was raided. An officer pulled out a document from which he read out loud, announcing that the grandfather had committed "a crime of high treason." As a consequence—and in line with the official philosophy of "collective responsibility"—his family had also to be arrested. Only the mother remained behind in Pyongyang.

Kang Chol Hwan spent ten years in Yodok—most of his childhood and his entire adolescence—and left it as a young man of nineteen. The family was never told what "acts of treason" Kang Tae Gyu had committed. But Kang Chol Hwan suspects that the reason was that the Chongryun's Kyoto cell, to which his grandfather belonged, had opposed the appointment of Han Duk Su as chairman of the organization in 1955. He was Kim Il Sung's choice, and the "dissidents" had, therefore, opposed not only Han Duk Su but the will of the Great Leader himself. That was a crime that could not be forgiven easily, even if it was committed almost two decades before the punishment was meted out.[2]

Following Kang Chol Hwan's release in 1987, he roamed around North Korea for a few years, then made it across the border to China. In August 1992 he managed to get on a ship to South Korea, where he now lives and works as a journalist for the daily *Chosun Ilbo*. Kang Chol Hwan is one of very few survivors from Yodok who have made it to the South, and his book, *Aquariums of Pyongyang: Ten Years in the North Korean Gulag*, is the most detailed account of life in a North Korean prison camp that has ever been published. "Aquariums" is an allusion to his love for fish as a child. He climbed aboard the truck that took him to Yodok, holding a small fish tank close to his chest. In the camp, the fish died one by one, as did many of his friends and fellow prisoners. Life means nothing in Yodok.

It is often argued that "refugee stories" are exaggerated and should not be believed, and Kang Chol Hwan and other North Koreans who have managed to escape from their country have been met with utmost skepticism from several quarters.[3] While it is evident that exaggerations have occured, we should not repeat the same mistake as the outside world did when refugees arrived from Nazi Germany in the 1930s, or from the Khmer Rouge's Cambodia in the 1970s, and told us about the horrors they had escaped from. By the time the truth came out, it was too late for the world to react.

At the same time, it is evident that those concocting stories about human rights abuses in North Korea are making it more difficult for witnesses to be taken seriously. One of the worst—and clumsiest—examples of this was provided in early 2004 by the otherwise well-respected British Broadcasting Corporation, the BBC, in a documentary called *Access to Evil*, which was shown in several countries. Over the years, several refugees have reported that political prisoners are used for vivisection experiments, to test new surgical techniques, and new medicines and other chemical agents.[4] The BBC film claimed that the smoking gun now had been found: a "Letter of Transfer" from the local State Security Agency of a labor camp called "Camp 22" saying that, "The above person is transferred to the security agency . . . for the purpose of human experimentation of liquid gas for chemical weapons."[5] The letter included the test subject's name, sex, date of birth, place of birth, and place of residence.

"Camp 22," which is also called Hoeryong after the North Hamgyong county where it is located, is indeed a well-known labor camp that even many outsiders have heard about. The document was marked "Top Secret," and was signed by an official. It also had a stamp affixed to it from the State Security Agency. But critical eyes—among them *Yonhap*, South Korea's official news agency, which is not noted for being sympathetic to the North—immediately pointed out the printed text on the document appeared faded while the text written in pen was much less damaged.

The paper was not of the type normally used in North Korea, and *Yonhap* as well as other South Korean sources, also noted that the direct translation of the agency in question that had stamped the document was "the National Protection Division," or, in Korean, the *Kukga-bowi-bu*. Between 1982 and 1993, that was the correct name of the agency in charge of, among other things, the country's labor camps. The problem was that this letter was dated "February 13, 91 Juche," or 2002, nine years after the name of the agency had been changed to "the National Security Protection Division," or the *Kukga-anjeon-bowi-bu*. South Korea's intelligence agencies reached the conclusion that the letter was most probably written, or dictated, by a North Korean refugee who had fled before 1993 and therefore was unaware of the name change.[6]

It was, of course, not entirely impossible that the person who signed the order had used an old stamp. But in strictly controlled North Korea where every civil servant is afraid of making mistakes, that was deemed extremely unlikely by South Korean sources. Combined with other discrepancies in the documentation it became quite clear that the question whether political prisoners have been used in experiments with biological and chemical weapons remains unanswered. But any attempt to find out the truth has been severely hampered by the BBC's highly dubious report.

Kang Chol Hwan does not mention such experiments in his book, nor did he in an interview with me in Seoul in May 2003. But other horrible things did happen. He recalls that he had his worst experience in Yodok in 1981, when he was only thirteen. The guards were bulldozing the top of a hill, and, as the machines tore up the soil, they unearthed hundreds of corpses. They had no bullet wounds, so the victims had most probably starved to death. The bones had scraps of human flesh on them and the stench was terrible. One of his friends vomited, and the young boys ran away, their noses tucked in their sleeves, trying to avoid the ghastly scent of flesh and putrefaction.[7]

Public executions were not uncommon in Yodok when Kang Chol Hwan was there, and he and other prisoners were always forced to watch the macabre spectacles. He especially remembers a wretched man, only skin and bones, being led to his execution without uttering a word or a sound: "It would have been easy to mistake him for an animal, with his wild hair, his bruises, his crust of dried blood, his bulging eyes. Then I suddenly noticed his mouth. So that's how they shut him up. They had stuffed it full of rocks. The guards were now tying him to a post with three pieces of rope: at eye level, around the chest, and at the waist. As they withdrew, the commanding officer took his place beside the firing squad. 'Aim at the traitor of the Fatherland . . . Fire!' The custom was to shoot three salvos from a distance of five yards. The first salvo cut the topmost cords, killing the condemned man and causing his head to fall forward. The second salvo cut the chords around his chest and bent him forward further. The third salvo released the tether, allowing the man's body to drop into the pit in front of him, his tomb. This simplified the burial."[8]

Lee Soon Ok, a woman who spent six years in Kaechon prison on charges of "government property embezzlement," recalls how prisoners were used to produce cheap items for export, a practice that is not uncommon even in neighboring China. In May 1988, the "export factory" in her prison began making women's brassieres for the Russian market. Over a period of six months, nine hundred thousand brassieres were produced for export. She also claims that the prisoners made doilies to export to Poland, sweaters for Japan, and paper roses for France.[9] They worked day and night, and were severely punished for the smallest offenses. A forty-year-old lady was put in solitary confinement for seven days because she stained some fabric—and solitary confinement in a North Korean prison means a small box, seventy centimeters wide and just over a meter high. Prisoners had to crawl into the box and could not stand or lie down.[10]

In 1998, the Seoul-based Center for the Advancement of North Korean Human Rights estimated that about two hundred thousand people are being held in more than ten different prison camps for such "crimes" as reading a foreign newspaper, listening to a foreign broadcast, complaining about the food situation, refusing an arbitrary request from an official, talking to foreigners, traveling to China or Russia without permission, or doing anything to "insult the authority" of Kim Jong Il.[11] A more recent report by the U.S. Committee for Human Rights in North Korea asserts there are between 150,000 and 200,000 inmates in North Korea's prison camps, and states that presumed offenders are "simply picked up and taken to an interrogation facility and frequently tortured to 'confess' before being sent to the political penal-labor colony."[12]

"Offenses" can often be minor transgressions of what is socially acceptable in North Korea. Kim Myung Jun, a young guide at the state-owned Koryo Hotel in Pyongyang, was arrested for an unauthorized conversation with a foreigner who was visiting North Korea. Two others, Han Sang Il and Chang Sung Ho, were arrested for disco dancing at the Ansang Bar in Pyongyang, an activity tolerated in foreigners but not in North Koreans.[13] A customer who went into the Cheil Department Store in Pyongyang—which is said to have been established by the Dear Leader, Kim Jong Il—and complained that there were no goods for sale was promptly reported by the salesperson to the authorities. The customer was sent to prison for "the crime of discontent."[14]

The number of main camps has in recent years been reduced to five, as the smaller ones have been closed down and the prisoners moved to bigger sites. Apart from Yodok, there are camps in Hoeryong in North Hamgyong province, Hwasong, Tongshin, and Kaechon north of Pyongyang. Yodok is believed to have nearly fifty thousand prisoners, and the same number is said to be held in the notorious Camp 22 in Hoeryong in the remote northeastern mountains.[15] The camp was expanded after two nearby facilities were closed down following a serious riot in 1987. The riot reportedly erupted in the smaller Onsong camp when a political prisoner working as a coal miner beat a State Security Agency operative to death in protest against brutal torture. Over two hundred other inmates who were at the scene then killed another security agent and in blind fury attacked the guard quarters across a hill. In a futile but brave sign of dissent, more than five thousand prisoners joined the uprising. Not surprisingly, guards equipped with machine guns encircled the camp. They fired for hours into the crowd. All the rioters were mowed down by the bullets, and their bodies were either burned or buried in mass graves in the nearby hills. Onsong was subsequently closed down, and the surviving prisoners disbursed to Camp 22 and some other larger camps.[16]

Conditions in Camp 22 have been described as even harsher than those in Yodok. About fifty thousand prisoners are reported to be living inside a three-meter-high electrified wire fence. Mine fields and deep traps with sharpened bamboo stakes in them have been dug along passages which escapees are expected to take. Control is enforced by supervisors and team heads selected from among the prisoners. Inmates are crammed into clusters of huts, each of which houses around thirty people. Everyone has to work from 5:00 a.m. to 7:00 p.m. in winter, and till 8:00 p.m. in summer. Hard labor is followed by the study of works by Kim Il Sung and Kim Jong Il, and nobody is allowed to move after 10:00 p.m. Each prisoner gets only three hundred grams of corn a day, and beatings occur frequently. And, as in Yodok, public executions, mostly of prisoners who have tried to escape, are routine events.[17] Female prisoners are often subjected to sexual abuse.[18]

Lee Soon Ok is not the only refugee who has testified that forced labor is part of the prison routine, and North Korea's huge population of prisoners is believed to be making a significant contribution to the country's economy. Inmates in Camp 22, for instance, are said to produce coal and livestock, and harvest apricots, a speciality of Hoeryong county. The nearby Chungbong District Coal Mine used to supply coal to the once important Kim Chaek Integrated Iron and Steel Works before production there ground to a halt in the late 1990s.[19] North Korea's most famous bicycle brand, *Kalmaegi*, or "Seagull," used to be made in Kaechon camp, partly for export to China, and in Yodok children are sent into the mountains to pick herbs, which are used in Chinese medicine and exported to Japan.[20]

***

The establishment of North Korea's own Gulag goes back to the purges in 1956, when many Yan'an veterans and Soviet Koreans were arrested for opposing Kim Il Sung. Initially, only real opponents to Kim Il Sung's regime were sent to the camps, but later they were filled with anyone who had committed an actual or imagined "crime against the fatherland."[21] Many have been arrested under a new criminal law that the Supreme People's Assembly passed in December 1974, and which went into effect on February 1, 1975. According to this law, "Counterrevolutionary crimes" are dealt with by this criminal law, but its 215 articles are often very vague, such as "concocting and disseminating reactionary ideologies (Article 56); acts of "not performing or shoddily performing assigned tasks" (Article 61); acts of "opposing the socialist state and antagonizing the revolutionary people" (Article 62); acts of "producing and distributing works of literature and art that reflect bourgeois cultures" (Article 111); acts of "hooliganism" (Article 146); and acts of "exaggerating, fabricating or passing unjust verdicts on criminal cases" (Article 147).[22]

Of these articles, number 56 is the most draconian. It stipulates the death penalty and forfeiture of all property on three accounts:

1.   Slander and vilification of policies of the party and the State by speech or gesture or the fabrication, dissemination and propagation of reactionary ideas and vicious rumors;

2.   The production, safe-keeping and dissemination of reactionary publications and written materials and,

3.   The writing of reactionary graffiti or the sending of a reactionary letter to the authorities.[23]

In effect, the article totally suppresses freedom of speech and expression as it makes even passing remarks about the party and the state punishable by death. In theory, a prisoner has the right to an attorney to defend himself, but Article 11 of the Legal Representation Law provides that an attorney's responsibility is to "Explain the nation's laws and regulations to the people, and to help the people obey these laws and regulations."[24] In other words, the duties of an attorney are to make sure the policies of the party and the state are understood and carried out by the people. North Korean lawyers usually serve to help persuade defendants to confess their crimes. Amnesty International has described North Korea as "a human rights disaster" ruled by a regime "that maintained rigid control of power while its economy collapsed and millions of its impoverished people faced starvation."[25] Even the last East German ambassador to Pyongyang, Hans Maretzki, concluded that the ordinary North Korean citizen is "powerless and without legal rights."[26]

But this has not prevented even Western lawyers from arguing the opposite. In October 2003, the U.S.-based National Lawyers Guild and the affiliated American Association of Jurists—both left-wing organizations—sent a delegation to North Korea at the invitation of the "Korean Democratic Lawyers Association." The visit resulted in an incredibly naive report that stated, "We were told there was no death penalty and that the maximum penalty for any crime is twelve years . . . A lack of death penalty was seen by the delegation as a sign of a civilized nation."[27] But even a book they refer to in their report, *The Criminal Procedures Act of the Democratic People's Republic of Korea*, mentions the death penalty, albeit with the reservation that it "may be executed only with the approval of the Central People's Committee of the Democratic People's Republic of Korea."[28] The same book, which is available in Pyongyang hotel bookstores, states that provincial courts may judge cases of "treason against the nation," which are "punishable with death or a maximum of fifteen years' reform through labor."[29] Friends of the North Korean regime abroad, it seems, have difficulty reading, and they have not done a particularly good job convincing the outside world that nothing is amiss in Workers' Paradise.

The huge number of political prisoners in North Korea has led many to believe that there must be an opposition against the regime. But that is hardly the case; most prisoners are sent to the camps because they have committed some very minor offense, which is used as an excuse for punishment. Mainly, the very existence of the dreaded camps serves as a tool to control the population, and to make sure they remain loyal to the regime. People subject to banishment are primarily those considered, in very general terms, harmful to the system. Most come from "the wavering class," and some from "the hostile class" of descendants of former landowners and private businesspeople, although they are decreasing in number.

Some attempts have been made to set up a provisional North Korean government in exile, notably by Hwang Jang Yop, the highest-ranking North Korean to defect to the South. A former president of the Kim Il Sung University in Pyongyang and, before his flight to the South in 1997, chairman of the Foreign Affairs Committee of the Supreme People's Assembly, Hwang Jang Yop has on several occasions tried to bring together prominent North Korean refugees in China, Russia, and South Korea and announce an alternative to Kim Jong Il's regime. Hwang Jang Yop has argued that there are internal forces in North Korea strong enough to oust Kim Jong Il—if given a proper external push.[30] But nothing has come of these efforts, and it seems unlikely that Hwang Jang Yop has any significant following inside North Korea.

The only challenge to the regime in Pyongyang may come from the country's Christian community. Christianity took hold in Korea at the beginning of the last century in a way it did not in Japan or China.[31] While small in number—only about 2 percent prior to World War II—the Christians tended to be better educated and more influential than any other religious group. Although Kim Il Sung himself came from a partly Christian family, the Christians became a target of his regime as early as the late 1940s. Most of them were imprisoned, or forced into exile. But somehow, a small Christian community has survived in North Korea. In 1988, the regime announced that it had started to guarantee freedom of religion, and two churches were built: the Bongsu Protestant Church and a Roman Catholic chapel in Chang-chung. Officially, North Korea has ten thousand Christians and five hundred home churches, but these are established for political purposes to show to visiting foreigners and to act as local partners of international aid organizations.[32] In reality, very few Christians dare to show their faith openly, although several refugees have testified that they have met practicing Christians in the labor camps.[33]

Many of the Korean returnees from Japan have also been considered "suspect" because of their past lives in a capitalist society. Even the famous opera singer Kim Yong Gil, who sang *O Sole Mio* when he spotted the North Korean coastline, ended up being condemned as a spy and sent to die in the now closed Senghori hard labor camp, reputedly one of North Korea's harshest when it was in operation.[34] Following the collapse of the Communist regimes in Eastern Europe, those who returned and told others what they had seen and heard abroad have also been targeted.[35] Any sign of possible dissent has been taken care of with utmost thoroughness.

***

The only alternative to blind obedience is to flee the country—also a crime under North Korea's law. The first North Korean refugees were workers who had been sent to the former Soviet Union to work in logging camps and mines in the wilderness north of Khabarovsk. Under a treaty signed in 1967 between then Soviet president Leonid Brezhnev and Kim Il Sung, North Korean labor was used to pay off Pyongyang's debt to Moscow, and to raise money for the North Korean regime. At one point the number of North Korean workers in the Siberian forest reached twenty thousand, but it is now down to a few thousand in accordance with an arrangement between North Korean officials, acting as brokers, and privately owned Russian logging companies.[36]

Following the collapse of the Soviet Union, hundreds of North Koreans began to escape from their work sites. Some managed to reach South Korea, but those who were apprehended were sent back to North Korea under a secret protocol signed by Moscow and Pyongyang. That protocol was declared illegal in 1993 by the chairman of the Human Rights Subcommittee of Russia's parliament, Sergei Kovalnov.[37] But as late as 2002, North Korean "illegals" in Russia were repatriated across the railway bridge that spans the Tuman River, the border between the two countries. A Russian border guard recalls how waiting North Korean security officials would drag the returnees away with meat hooks to their mouths and ears. Returnees from Russia are usually taken to the city jail in Chongjin, from which few have emerged alive.[38]

China turned out to be a better destination for North Korean refugees, mainly because they can hide among the ethnic Korean population in Yanbian across the border. But, if caught, they are also sent back to North Korea, risking imprisonment and torture, forced labor, and even execution. Even so, the flow of North Korean refugees to China has increased dramatically since the famine in the mid-1990s. No accurate numbers are available, but estimates range from 10,000 to 500,000. Most NGOs put the figure at around 300,000.[39] They are euphemistically called "defectors," as China has never recognized any political refugees from North Korea.

Helping the refugees is even deemed a criminal offense in China. In December 2001, an ethnic Korean in Yanbian was arrested in his home and fined 20,000 Renminbi (US$2,400) for harboring North Korean refugees in his house. In the same month, Chun Ki Won, a South Korean pastor, was arrested on the Sino-Mongolian border while he was assisting a group of twelve North Koreans trying to escape to Mongolia. He was jailed for seven months, and was expelled from China after a trial and a 50,000 Renminbi (US$6,000) fine.[40] In late October 2002, Hiroshi Kato, a Japanese humanitarian worker, was also arrested in China for helping North Korean refugees. The Chinese government even denied knowledge of his arrest for the first five days. He was released after a week in custody, and then only after strong representations had been made by the Japanese government.[41]

The plight of the North Korean refugees in China is one of the world's most hidden tragedies. The men are exploited and often not paid even the pitiful salaries they have been promised. Young North Korean women who went to China to seek a better life have ended up being raped and trafficked to other parts of China to be sold as "wives" or prostitutes.[42] In 2002, the Chinese authorities decided to strengthen border patrols and conduct house-to-house searches to find North Koreans hiding in villages across the border in China. A large detention center for the refugees was also built near the Tuman border river, where they are kept before being sent back to North Korea.[43] On the other side of the border, a string of new detention facilities have been set up to punish those forcibly repatriated to North Korea.[44]

The flow of North Korean refugees into China has strained relations between the two countries, as China has begun to show signs of impatience with Pyongyang's slow progress in dealing with the refugees and the exodus of hungry citizens. In an attempt to improve ties, a delegation led by Kim Yong Nam, chairman of the Standing Committee of the Supreme People's Assembly, visited China in June 1999, but this did not result in any change in the treatment of the refugees. According to the "Bilateral Agreement on the Maintenance of National Security and Public Order in the Border Area," which China and North Korea adopted in 1965, refugees are treated as criminals who should be repatriated. That agreement is still valid, and being enforced in the border areas.[45]

There is no doubt that most North Koreans in northeastern China are there because they have escaped economic misery in their home country, but the informal cross-border movement of people has also led to the emergence of a wide range of crime in the frontier areas. Alexandre Mansourov, a Russian-born associate professor at the Asia-Pacific Center for Security Studies in Honolulu and a specialist in Northeast Asian security issues, says that "cross-border human trafficking, polygamy, underage sex slavery, illegal opium production in the mountains, drug smuggling from Manchuria to the North, commercialization of asylum-seeking, contraband trade, black marketeering, local corruption, physical abuse, and violent crime all constitute part and parcel of the tragic North Korean refugee life in the Manchurian underground."[46] Long before they leave home, many North Koreans have already signed away to human smugglers the reward money they expect to get from the South Korean government once they eventually get there. Thousands end up being cheated, and, if they are female, being sold into the local sex industry.

Many North Koreans have therefore tried to escape deeper into China to escape detection by the Chinese authorities and exploitation by local gangsters—and to force their way into foreign missions in Beijing and elsewhere. On their own initiative, or assisted by other human traffickers, scores of North Koreans have made it into the South Korean embassy, and, in March 2002, twenty-five North Korean asylum seekers rushed into the Spanish embassy in Beijing. They were eventually allowed to continue to South Korea, but following the incident the Chinese authorities set barbed wire fences around several embassies in Beijing.

Appeals by the international community have had very little effect on the Chinese, and even international organizations such as the United Nations High Commissioner for Refugees, UNHCR, have been unable to provide the refugees with protection. One of the few organizations that has tried to work on behalf of the North Korean refugees is the France-based Médecins Sans Frontières, but even they have had to conclude that "neither China's repeated violation of international conventions nor desperate attempts by hundreds of North Koreans to seek asylum in foreign representations have resulted in measurable progress on the question of protection of North Korean refugees in search of asylum."[47]

Stricter surveillance around the embassies in Beijing has prompted many refugees to try to make it to third countries. In the late 1990s, a trickle of refugees, often helped by South Korean church groups, managed to escape to Mongolia, and from there continued by air to South Korea. In more recent years, North Korean refugees have traveled through China down to Southeast Asia, from where they are not likely to be deported back to North Korea. On July 31, 2003, ten North Koreans—including a four-year-old girl and a six-year-old boy—broke into the Japanese embassy in Bangkok and requested asylum. Ten days later, five North Korean women were given suspended three-month jail terms and fined 1,000 Baht (US$25) for entering Thailand illegally from Laos.[48] The refugees were later allowed to continue to South Korea.

The escape route down to Southeast Asia is the first example of a more organized North Korean refugee network, as it involves obtaining false identification documents, or being accompanied by escorts who know how to elude Chinese checkpoints. The journey from the North Korean border in northeastern China down through Laos to Thailand can take weeks, and it cannot be done without the involve-ment of some kind of clandestine organization. Norbert Vollertsen, a German doctor in South Korea, even admitted as much at a press conference in Seoul on August 2, 2003. He described the people he worked with as "a loose movement of several nationalities," mostly South Koreans but also Americans and Europeans, including retired diplomats, former journalists, and Christian missionaries.[49] Their aim, Vollertsen explained later, is to cause a flood of refugees which would bring down the North Korean regime in the same way as Communist East Germany collapsed in 1989–1990, at least in part because thousands had escaped through Hungary to the West. "China will become the Hungary of the Far East," Vollertsen said.[50]

But that is highly unlikely to happen. China does not even recognize the North Korean escapees as refugees, and has consistently refused to discuss the issue with international organizations. And, in September 2003, thousands of regular Chinese troops moved into new positions along the North Korean frontier, mainly because Beijing was getting concerned about the influx of refugees from across the border.[51]

It is also uncertain to what extent Vollertsen's "loose movement" has contacts inside North Korea, or if its contacts are confined to border areas in China. At his August press conference, he indicated that the latter is the case. He said that his group had plans to send "messages by balloon into North Korea, smuggling in radios, and a boat-people project to encourage people to flee by sea to South Korea."[52] If the network extended into North Korea, such measures would not have been necessary. The lack of any organized opposition inside North Korea puts the country apart from other totalitarian states, and shows clearly that the regime in Pyongyang is not about to fall or collapse. The Dear Leader may not be as charismatic and revered as his late father, but he remains firmly in power.

CHAPTER 9

THE FUTURE?

Disaster struck Ryongchon, a small North Korean railroad town just south of the Chinese border, on April 22, 2004. Two trains loaded with ammonium nitrate blew up during a shunting operation with fuel oil wagons, sending plumes of black, acrid smoke billowing into the sky. The blast obliterated the station and thousands of other buildings within a radius of four kilometers. More than 160 people died, at least 1,300 were injured, and thousands more made homeless in North Korea's worst accident in recent memory. Many of the dead and injured were children because several schools were located not far from the station. It was in the middle of the day, so the kids were having their lunch break and many were out on the streets around the station.

Foreign aid workers rushed to the disaster zone and were able to confirm what they had been told by the authorities in Pyongyang. One of the trains had got caught in an overhead electric cable, causing a spark that ignited the chemicals on the heavily-loaded train.[1] The area around the station had been reduced to ashes, and local hospitals were full of victims but acutely short of medicines, including painkillers and antibiotics.

The foreign media were quick to play up the fact that the accident was not immediately reported by the North Korean media. A North Korean defector based in Seoul told *Agence-France Presse* that "it is a rule for the North Korean propaganda mill not to talk about any accidents."[2] But on the same day as his comments appeared in the international press, the *Korean Central News Agency* released a dispatch saying that "an explosion occurred at Ryongchon . . . on April 22 due to the electrical contact caused by carelessness during the shunting of wagons loaded with ammonium nitrate and tank wagons." The report went on to say that the North Korean authorities appreciate "the willingness expressed by the governments of various countries and international bodies and organizations to render humanitarian assistance."

The foreign media were further discredited when it began to report wild speculations as to what could have caused the explosion. Several Western newspapers and media organizations highlighted the fact that Kim Jong Il's private train had passed through Ryongchon just before dawn on April 22. He was on his way back from Beijing, where he had attended talks with Chinese leaders about the nuclear standoff with the U.S. and other issues. So was it an assassination attempt?

The *New York Times*, reporting from Tokyo, even went as far as asking, "Where is the Dear Leader?" indirectly suggesting that he might have died in the explosion, but failing to take into account that Kim Jong Il makes very few public appearances in any circumstances.[3] To back up the claim that Kim Jong Il might have been closer to the accident than suggested, the *New York Times* mentioned that children accounted for many of the casualties because they ""were lined up to wave at the train of a passing dignitary."[4] All these speculations turned out to be completely groundless. South Korea's unification minister, Jeung Se Hyun, had a much more plausible explanation: "With Kim's special train going through, other trains were shunted to sidings—this is my speculation."[5]

Most foreign media missed the point that it was the first time the official North Korean news agency, and newspapers and the radio, were surprisingly open about a domestic disaster. One of the few who registered this was Norbert Vollertsen, the German doctor who had become one of the most outspoken critics of the Pyongyang regime. He saw parallels between the blast at Ryongchon and the 1986 nuclear disaster in Chernobyl that forced the Soviet Union to open up for Western aid and be more transparent, eventually—combined with other factors—leading to *glasnost*.[6]

Although that assumption may be overly optimistic, the KCNA's unusual frankness came at a time when North Korea's economic reforms were starting to bite. Pyongyang in April 2004 was a very different place from ten or even five years before. In August 2003, a new market opened in Tongil Street in a Pyongyang suburb, where hundreds of shoppers throng the narrow aisles between rows of tightly packed stalls stocked with snacks, foreign liquor, and a variety of fruit from locally grown apples and peaches to imported pineapples. There are also imported clothes from China, beer from Singapore and Japan, or dishwashing liquid from Thailand. Some stalls offer Chinese-made watches, shavers, TV sets, and washing machines.[7]

Other small signs of change were also evident. Apart from the cardboard and canvas kiosks, other enterprises were appearing along Pyongyang's streets at the beginning of 2004: an elderly woman selling farm goods from a bicycle or a man repairing shoes. These may be small, private enterprises and therefore insignificant, but put together with the stalls in the Tongil market, which are supposedly run by trading companies, workers' and farmers' organizations subordinate to the state, and the modest kiosks, they represent an entirely new trend in North Korea. Prices everywhere are regulated by the market, not the state; customers pay with cash, not coupons, and the salespeople are determined to make a profit.[8]

With consumerism has come the first hints of consumer culture. Mobile phones were still a rare sight in April 2004, but but those who have got them were proud to show off their new status symbols on street corners and in hotel lobbies, thanks to the Thai-owned telecommunications company Loxley Pacific, which is not only helping North Korea get controversial "stabilizers" into the country but also really developing a mobile phone network in a joint venture with the government in Pyongyang. At the end of May, however, the North Korean government ordered all its citizens—but not the country's foreign residents—to hand in their mobile phones. It is uncertain what prompted that move, but Pyongyang residents suggest that the phones had become just too popular, and the government, obsessed with wanting to control everything, felt that the new fad was getting out of hand.[9] Loxley remains in Pyongyang, and it is very likely that the mobile phone system will be restored once the government has found a way to monitor it in the same as it does the country's land lines.

And, in December 2003, the North Korean capital got its first commercial advertisement: billboards with pictures of a new car called *Huiparam*, or "the Whistle." Made with Italian Fiat components imported to South Korea and then to the North, it is assembled at a plant in the port city of Nampo as part of an inter-Korean joint venture with South Korea's Pyeongwha, or "Peace," Motor Company—and thus also an outcome of Kim Dae Jung's much-maligned Sunshine Policy. The car costs 8,000 Euros—the preferred foreign currency in North Korea—and is therefore well beyond the means of most North Koreans. But quite a few *Huiparams* can nevertheless be seen in the streets of Pyongyang, among second-hand cars imported from Japan and China.

So is the unthinkable really happening? Is North Korea, at long last, really moving towards a system like that of China, Vietnam, and Laos, in which the ruling Communist party retains political control while permitting the economy to operate relatively freely? There are three possible answers: The changes are insubstantial, they are substantial but not irreversible, or the reforms are for real and there is no turning back.[10] Those who hold the first view, which includes almost everyone in President Bush's administration, dismiss the new initiatives, arguing that North Korea is, and will remain, a rogue state, an obstacle to peace in the region that must be dealt with firmly. Most of them advocate sanctions to pressure the Pyongyang government to end its nuclear, chemical, and biological weapons programs, which it undoubtedly is pursuing. Siegfried Hecker's down-to-earth and factual report from Charles Pritchard's visit to North Korea in January 2004 said, "Officials of the DPRK ministry of foreign affairs claimed that the DPRK had weapons of mass destruction."[11]

Others recognize that economic changes have taken place, but argue that it is not the first time outside observers have predicted economic reform and then seen the government backtrack on its pledges. Open markets, or farmers' markets, have been tolerated off and on since the 1960s. And, after all the initial fanfare, nothing really came of the plans to set up free economic zones in Rajin-Sonbong and Sinuiju. In any case, real development could only take place in a climate of reduced nuclear tension with the U.S.[12]

The third way of looking at recent developments is shared by most foreign residents I met in Pyongyang a few days before the accident in Ryongchon. They believe the changes are real and that it would be extremely hard to turn the clock back to a decade ago. Tongil's market is not on the periphery, but in a Pyongyang suburb and accessible to anyone with money. A second market is being built, this time in the city center, and more are planned.[13] Further, the old farmers' markets have been renamed "consumers' markets," indicating that they will be allowed, even formally, to sell other daily necessities in addition to food. Foreigners are still not allowed to visit those markets, but from a distance some have observed that they are becoming more permanent. Roofed market stalls are being erected where people previously squatted with their wares on the ground in an open field.

In private conversations, North Korean officials toe the party line, saying they will "remain faithful to the socialist system," and not "copy the Chinese model," which they see as being far too liberal.[14] But change may be outrunning rhetoric. A directory published in 2003 by the government lists nearly two hundred new trading companies that appear to be small versions of South Korea's *chaebols*, conglomerates that export and import a variety of goods.[15] Although state-owned, they are autonomous and make their own deals with foreign business partners. According to the directory, one "corporation" exports marine products and embroidery and imports printing material and fishing tackle. Another exports seafood, instant noodles and sanitary ware and imports medicines, fertilizer, and construction material.

There is no doubt that these trading companies, and new light-industry enterprises, represent the future, if North Korea is ever going to develop economically. It has now been confirmed that the country's old heavy industry—steel and iron works—has more or less collapsed. Recent visitors to North Korea's "rust belt" in the northeastern provinces tell of huge, abandoned, crumbling factory buildings. What remains of the machinery is being dismantled and sold as scrap metal to China. Most of the workers have been sent to the countryside to grow badly needed food for themselves and for people in the cities.

But the new light-industry enterprises now rising will still have to face the same problem as those that caused the heavy industry to collapse: an acute shortage of electricity and rapidly collapsing infrastructure outside Pyongyang. The same goes for the vital mining industry, a huge potential foreign-currency earner. A study of the North Korean economy published by the Hong Kong and Shanghai Banking Corporation, HSBC, in February 2003 describes the situation as a vicious circle. One example cited in the study is coal, the main source of energy in the country: "Without an increase in the coal supply, sufficient energy cannot be generated to drive either the mines or the machine tool sector that are needed for coal production."[16] The circle cannot be broken without foreign assistance, the study concluded. That is not likely to be forthcoming as long as the nuclear stand-off with the U.S. continues, and even with a massive injection of foreign aid and with the soundest policies in place, it would be an almost insurmountable task to revitalize the North Korean economy.

Also in 2003, a team of foreign mining experts were invited to analyze minerals in the northeast to determine whether they were good enough to export. They were—but the nearby enrichment plant, bought from Sweden in the 1970s, had decayed to the point that it would cost millions of dollars to refurbish it. The railroad down to the nearest port, Chongjin, was in such a bad state that the locomotives could pull only one wagon at the time, otherwise the bridges would collapse. And Chongjin, one of North Korea's biggest port cities, goes without electricity most of the year.

So what is likely to happen in North Korea? The first scenario, which has been widely predicted by Western observers, is collapse. Lack of substantial economic development and political repression will lead to chaos and, eventually, the fall of Kim Jong Il's regime in Pyongyang in a way similar to that in which Romania's Nicolae Ceaucescu was ousted—and executed—in 1989.[17] Given the levels of control and mass mobilization in North Korea, this is not likely to happen. Most totalitarian states exercise power in three different ways. The first is through normative control: a state ideology around which the citizens are expected to rally. The second is through remunerations to high-ranking officials: financial and other privileges to ensure the continued loyalty of people who matter in the hierarchy. The third is by instilling fear in the population at large: massive punishment for dissent and even disobedience. North Korea has practiced—and still is practicing—all three measures of control, and has done so more successfully than other totalitarian states.

Sanctions, as proposed by some U.S. legislators, are also unlikely to create a situation where the government's control mechanisms break down. The continued survival of North Korea's highly militarized society shows that it can hold together against internal as well as external pressures, and the regime is more firmly in power than most outsiders believe. North Korea could also survive sanctions, even if they led to severe economic decline. Many Koreans—even South Koreans—point out that they are used to hardship, and that famine, suffering, and a strict social order are nothing new to them. For centuries they have suffered invasions and wars. In the 1930s, many landlords took 75 percent of the crop as "rent," and then sold it to the Japanese colonial authorities. According to a 1935 Japanese government publication, "these poor people are driven by hunger from place to place, making shelters in log cabins and keeping their bodies and souls together by planting grains and vegetables on the hillsides."[18] Today's prosperity in South Korea is an entirely new phenomenon.

A second possibility, if or rather when sanctions prove ineffective, is war and invasion, or at least "preemptive" military strikes by the U.S. against North Korea's nuclear installations, military bases, and defense industries. In a surprisingly candid interview with *Global Viewpoint* in August 2002, former Central Intelligence Agency director James Woolsey stated that "we had best get ready for war on the Korean peninsula. And only if we have a practical plan for war do we have the one chance of avoiding it—which is convincing the Chinese that if they don't take action to change the Kim Jong Il regime, we will."[19] It is unclear exactly what action the U.S. wants China to take, but it has been suggested that Beijing should offer asylum and a safe haven in exile for Kim Jong Il and his inner circle "to solve that problem."[20] But it would go against the very nature of Kim Jong Il and his men. They are extreme Korean nationalists, and that is far more than a veneer for public consumption.

Kim Jong Il is much more likely to dig in and stay in Pyongyang. And, according to Kim Myong Chol, a pro-Pyongyang Korean living in Japan and a former journalist of Chongryun's weekly *People's Korea*, he is also well prepared for war, which is the reason why most military installations are located underground and built to withstand even nuclear attacks.[21] There would be minimal damage, but such an attack would according to Kim Myong Chol most certainly provoke North Korea to fire, all at once, the 13,000 long-range guns and rocket launchers it has deployed along the DMZ.

Even if most of them were intercepted by America's and South Korea's advanced defense systems, many would still hit their targets and turn the area south of the DMZ, including

Seoul, "into a sea of fire, a hell on earth."[22] If North Korea was attacked, Kim Myong Chol argues, it would also give it an excuse to justify missile attacks on nuclear power stations in South Korea and "the neighbouring countries," presumably Japan, as well as "nuclear retaliation on the United States."[23] Kim Myong Chol may be overstating North Korea's military capabilities, but a nuclear holocaust could well be the final outcome of an attack on North Korea. Japan is well aware of this, and, in 2003, decided to buy a sophisticated anti-missile system from the U.S. to protect the country from potential attack from North Korea. The program, set to cost US$7 billion, makes Japan only the second of the major U.S. allies, after Israel, to invest in a missile defense system.[24]

Had the war in Iraq gone more smoothly for the U.S., it is not inconceivable that North Korea would have been next, as Woolsey more or less suggested in his interview with *Global Viewpoint*. And that would have been in line with President Bush's "war on terror," which he launched after the September 11, 2001 attacks in New York and Washington, and the subsequent inclusion of North Korea in "the Axis of Evil" along with Iraq and Iran. Acutely conscious of this, and to avoid the "nuclear holocaust scenario" that eventually would wipe out North Korea as well, Pyongyang has long been seeking a bilateral, nonaggression pact with the U.S. It dropped that demand in October 2003, settling for a letter from President Bush stating that he will never attack nor attempt to overthrow Kim Jong Il's regime. Such assurances must be forthcoming and relations between Pyongyang and Washington would have to be normalized before North Korea would abandon its nuclear ambitions, the North Koreans have argued.

Washington, on the other hand, has demanded that North Korea must dismantle its nuclear program before it would consider economic aid and diplomatic relations. In order to break the deadlock, representatives from North and South Korea, Japan, China, Russia, and the U.S. met in Beijing in August 2003. It was thought a regional approach would work, but the views of the U.S. and North Korea were so incompatible that a meaningful dialog proved impossible. A second round of talks in February 2004 ended equally inconclusively. Thus, some kind of military confrontation on the Korean peninsula is still a possibility. In the spring of 2004, hawks in the Bush administration were again raising the possibility of a military conflict on the Korean peninsula. "Once the threat posed by Iraq has been resolved, new threats in the form of Iran and North Korean and others need to be addressed," a U.S. official told the Hong Kong weekly *Far Eastern Economic Review*.[25] Continuous unrest and chaos in Iraq seems to be the Pyongyang regime's best assurance for survival.

Change could also come from within, and it could be violent. The South Korean president—and *de facto* dictator—Park Chung Hee was assassinated in 1979 by Kim Jae Kyu, the head of his own intelligence service. Kim Jae Kyu was prepared to sacrifice his own life—he was later executed—to save the country. Park Chung Hee had criticized him for failing to curb the political unrest that was sweeping the country at the time, an act that Kim Jae Kyu was convinced would only have exacerbated the situation, and strained relations with the U.S.

It is much less likely—but not inconceivable—that a similar event could occur in North Korea. And that would definitely lead to the collapse of the Kim Jong Il regime, because he *is* the regime. A mass uprising is not possible in North Korea, but a violent act by an individual, which would trigger a chain of events, cannot be ruled out. If that happened, however, the consequences for the country's neighbors would be disastrous. A flood of refugees to China and perhaps even across the DMZ, or by boat, to South Korea and Japan—followed by the astronomical cost for South Korea and others to rebuild the North. And who would neutralize North Korea's weapons of mass destruction, including the nukes and the missiles? The U.S., China, and most probably also Russia would be jockeying for influence over the strategically located peninsula, with Japan watching carefully from the sidelines. It is in nobody's interest to have a violent conflict in Korea, but it may be inevitable.

The weakness of this argument is that it assumes that Kim Jong Il is against reform, and that there are other forces pressing for change. Most foreign residents I met in Pyongyang in April 2004 believe that the opposite is true. The recent changes could not have been possible without his approval, they argue. They suggest there is a tug-of-war between conservative old-timers and more reform-minded younger officials, and that Kim Jong Il is on the side of the reformers at the same time as he is pursuing a delicate balancing act with older officials, mainly from the military. But, like everything else in North Korea, that remains unproven.

There is also, the foreign residents say, a genuine desire among many of the younger officials to steer North Korea's foreign trade away from counterfeit money, drugs, and fake cigarettes to more legitimate businesses. The emergence of all the new trading companies lends credence to this suggestion. But as long as North Korea continues to teeter on the brink of disaster, revenue from missile sales and smuggling will remain important sources of income—and continue to hamper North Korea's attempts to be accepted in the world community.

Politically, North Korea's long-term solution to the Korean crisis, and the question of reunification, is what it calls the "Koryo Federation System." The two Koreas would create a federation, or a confederation, while maintaining two economic and political systems and two governments.[26] This would be rather like the two athletic teams marching together and then competing separately at the 2000 Sydney Olympics. But due to the huge contrasts between life, society, and the economy in the North and the South, it is not clear how this could work in practice. "One country, two systems" may work with China and Hong Kong, but is not likely with two governments both claiming the entire country.

There is also the question of who really wants to see a unified Korea. With South Korea's industrial base and North

Korea's abundance of mineral resources, a united Korea could pose a potential economic threat to Japan once it has—if it can—overcome the cost of reunification. Tsuneo Akaha at the Center for East Asian Studies at the Monterey Institute of International Studies in the U.S. has also pointed out that "a nuclear-armed North Korea (or a nuclear-armed unified Korea) would be a direct threat to Japan's security."[27] And if the two Koreas became one country, and the U.S. troops remained, how would China react to having an immediate neighbor with an American military presence? China would moreover lose its influence, or what remains of it, in a strategically important neighboring country. A united Korea that would be closer to Washington than to Beijing would not be acceptable to the Chinese. And, conversely, Washington is most unlikely to give up its foothold on the peninsula and accept a neutral Korea.[28] The cold war may be over, but China, which is emerging as the main U.S. rival in the region, is just next door.

Despite all the emotional issues attached to the notion of a unified Korea, there is also a strong vein of opinion in South Korea that preserving the *status quo* is the most pragmatic way to proceed. A unification would simply be too costly, and could, as many economists have pointed out, wreck the South Korean economic miracle. Besides, North and South Korea have been separated for so long, and developed in such different directions, that it would be a social nightmare to try to live together again. Even the three thousand or so North Korean refugees in the South have difficulty adjusting to their new lives, and are often discriminated against. Their North Korean educational background makes it almost impossible for them to get qualified jobs in their new environment, and many South Koreans tend to regard them in general as country bumpkins.[29]

On the other hand, maintaining the *status quo* would only mean continued tension on the peninsula, more economic hardships in the North, and the need for more foreign aid. South Korea would also have to continue spending billions of dollars on defense, and keeping its nearly 700,000-strong army equipped and constantly battle-ready. Sooner or later, change—if not reunification—is bound to come, but how?

In the most optimistic scenario, Kim Jong Il may recast the interpretation of the *juche* idea and begin to emphasize *chajusong*, the concept of man's ability to take his own initiatives and be creative in, for instance, trade and commerce. That would be a face-saving way out of the immediate predicaments—and the dilemma of reform versus *juche*. Kim Myong Chol even believes the answer is, "Flap your wings again, *chollima!*"— that the fabled horse that was the symbol of the country's economic development in the 1950s and 1960s will fly again, now at an "unprecedentedly high speed."[30] That may be the dream of people in power in Pyongyang, but Kim Myong Chol's prediction is wildly optimistic and hard to take seriously. The *chollima* horse remains on its pedestal on a hill overlooking Pyongyang and its solid bronze wings show no sign of flapping. *Chollima* is history, and remembered only as the statue it is today. But it is very likely that further reforms will be introduced along the lines they were first introduced in 2002, and with a continued emphasis on the military-first policy. That means economic development will be strictly controlled and supervised in order not to get out of hand and undermine the authority of the state. A strong emphasis on nationalism will serve to justify the regime's existence, and make sure no political liberalization would follow in the wake of economic reform.

If North Korea opened up, even like China, where the free flow of information is increasing by the day, just imagine the trauma that many North Koreans would go through when they realized that their Dear Leader was not born in a log cabin on Mount Paekdu, as they had been told since they were children, but near a nondescript village in Siberia. Or that the Great Leader did not take part in the "liberation" of the Korean peninsula in 1945, but returned from five years in exile in Vyatskoye more than three weeks after the Soviet Red Army had captured Pyongyang. Or that Kim Jong Suk was actually a very shy housewife, not a general and a master shot.

In China, people began to reevaluate Mao Zedong's role in Chinese history and society only a few years after his death. Books with titles like *Mao Zedong: Man, Not God* are now being sold openly even in government bookstores.[31] Ten years after his death, Kim Il Sung is still worshiped as a god, and that is not likely to change as long as Kim Jong Il is alive. After all, he reigns because of his father's legacy—and he is also part of the official mythology with all its legends and fanciful tales. It is too early to say, but maybe the third generation of the Kim clan would dare to take a fresh look at the country's history. For the time being, it is only realistic to expect more frankness when it comes to disasters such as the blast in Ryongchon. It may not turn out to be North Korea's Chernobyl, but it was nevertheless a small step forward and should be recognized as such. For once, the KCNA was more accurate in its reporting than the foreign media.

So the economy may change, but, for the foreseeable future, not the politics. At the same time, it is almost impossible to gauge to what extent North Korea is really developing economically as there are no official statistics. The World Bank and the International Monetary Fund are not present in Pyongyang and have not conducted any recent studies of the North Korean economy, but trade statistics from North Korea's trading partners show an interesting pattern. The U.S. may be contemplating sanctions, but trade with China, South Korea, and Thailand is definitely increasing. Thailand especially has emerged as an important trading partner, now ranking fifth after China, South Korea, Japan, and the European Union. The two-way trade with Thailand increased to US$16.5 million in 2002, up from US$129 million the previous year, and is still rising. The Thai Customs Department reports trade at US$214 million in the first ten months of 2003.[32] Thailand exported rice, fish products, fuel oil, textiles, and machinery to North Korea while it imported fertilizer, optical equipment, and some iron and steel. In may appear odd that Thailand would import fertilizer from North Korea and export fuel oil. But this seems to indicate barter deals, which are favored by the North

Koreans: in exchange for oil, they give fertilizers to their Thai partner, who, in turn, sells them—these locally produced chemicals of questionable quality, or chemicals received as aid from the South—at a favorable price to countries such as Laos, Cambodia or Burma.

Trade with Japan, though, is decreasing, mainly because of stricter controls imposed on Chongryun-affiliated companies. But anecdotal evidence suggests that another group of "overseas" Koreans are beginning to play a role in North Korea's economic development: the Koreans across the border in China.[33] The two million Chinese Koreans may be near perfect and more equal trading partners for the North Koreans, who may find it difficult to relate to the much richer South Koreans and their superior familiarity with the outside world. The Chinese Koreans, too, have lived through austere socialism, but many of them have now become successful businessmen and businesswomen. Much of the cross-border trade between northeastern China and Russia, for instance, is in the hands of Chinese Koreans. The Chinese authorities may be wary of similar contacts over the North Korean border, where the Chinese Koreans are dealing with people of their own kin. South Korean sources believe that the Chinese want "their" Koreans to be Chinese first and foremost, then members of an ethnic minority. Increased cooperation between the two million Koreans in China and North Korea could create, at least in an economic sense, a "Greater Korea," which China's central authorities would most probably look upon with disapproval. But it is happening and it may be a development that it is impossible for anyone to stop.

In the final analysis, the foreign residents in Pyongyang may be right in saying that North Korea's economic reform program is also unstoppable, but its success or failure hinges on the outcome of the nuclear confrontation with the U.S. The present situation on the Korean peninsula, and even more so its future, therefore remains one of the most complex issues facing the world today. And it is an issue to which there is no obvious solution. Whatever has been suggested seems to fail on its own improbability. The first step, however, is to demystify North Korea, to try to understand where the regime came from, and how it has managed to remain in power for so long. And that necessitates a more critical approach than the stifling political correctness that has followed in the wake of the Sunshine Policy. The rest should be up to the Koreans themselves. It is, after all—despite centuries of foreign meddling—their country.

CHRONOLOGY

1910

August 29: The Korea-Japan Annexation Treaty marks an end to the rule of the Yi (Chosun) Dynasty and finalizes Japan's takeover of Korea, which began in 1905. The Yi (Chosun) Dynasty had ruled Korea since 1392 replacing the old Koryo Dynasty, which was founded in 935 (and from which comes the name Korea in foreign languages; today, North Korea calls the country "Chosun" while South Korea calls itself "Hanguk," a term dating back to the 1890s.) While it was an independent kingdom for centuries, Chinese influence was always strong, and many foreigners who visited the country in the late nineteenth century found it "more Confucian than China." Japan's occupation ushered in a completely new era of foreign rule, industrialization—and severe political repression.

1912

April 15: Kim Il Sung is born in Mangyongdae near Pyongyang. His name at birth is Kim Song Ju. The family moves to Manchuria in 1917, returns to Pyongyang in 1923–1925, then moves back to Manchuria.

1925

April 17: The first Korean Communist Party is formed in Seoul.

1930

July: Kim Song Ju takes the name Kim Il Sung after his release from prison for anti-Japanese activities.

1932

April 25: Kim Il Sung organizes the first anti-Japanese guerrilla unit in Manchuria. Officially, this is seen as the founding date of the Korean People's Army.

1933–1939: Small-scale guerrilla activities occur in Manchuria and along the Manchurian-Korean border. On June 4, 1937, Kim Il Sung and a force of 150 guerrillas (the Japanese claimed 80) cross the border into Korea and attack the small town of Pochonbo (Pojon). Several Japanese policemen are killed, town offices are raided, and Kim Il Sung delivers a speech in the town before retreating to Manchuria.

1940

December: Kim Il Sung and a group of Korean guerrillas from Manchuria retreat across the border into the Soviet Union.

1941: Secret Korean and Chinese resistance bases are set up at Vyatskoye northeast of Khabarovsk, and near Nikolsk (Ussuriysk) north of Vladivostok. Kim Il Sung commands the Korean contingent with the rank of captain. He marries Kim Jong Suk.

1942

February 16: Kim Jong Suk gives birth to a son in Vyatskoye. He is given the Korean name Kim Jong Il and is also called Yura (a colloquial form of Yuri) in Russian.

1945

July 26: The Potsdam Declaration demands an unconditional surrender of Japan and states that Korea should be independent.

August 15: Japan announces its unconditional surrender.

August 26: The Soviet Red Army marches into Pyongyang.

September 2: The Allied Powers announce that Korea will be divided into a Northern and a Southern half occupied by the Soviet Union and the United States respectively.

September 4: Kim Il Sung leaves Vyatskoye by plane for Vladivostok.

September 19: Kim Il Sung arrives in Wonsan by boat from Vladivostok.

1946

February: The last remaining Koreans in Vyatskoye return to North Korea.

August 28: The First Congress of the North Korean Communist Party is held in Pyongyang. The party becomes the North Korean Workers' Party with Kim Bu Tong as chairman and Kim Il Sung as vice chairman.

1948

February 8: The Korean People's Army is formally established.

August 15: The Republic of Korea is founded in the U.S.-occupied South.

September 9: The Soviet-occupied North becomes the Democratic People's Republic of Korea with Kim Il Sung as its first premier.

1949

June 30: The North Korean Workers' Party and the South Korean Workers' Party merge to become the Korean Workers' Party (KWP) with Kim Il Sung as chairman.

September: Kim Jong Suk, Kim Il Sung's wife, dies while delivering a stillborn baby.

1950

June 25: The Korean War breaks out.

1953

July 27: A cease-fire agreement is signed at Panmunjom, ending the Korean War. A demilitarized zone (DMZ) is set up to separate North from South Korea.

1955

May 25: The General Association of Korean Residents in Japan, or Chongryun, is formed in Japan.

December 15: Kim Il Sung's main political rival, Pak Hon Yong, is sentenced to death and executed for "espionage" and "treason."

December 28: Kim Il Sung delivers a speech launching his *juche* idea.

1956

April 23–29: The KWP holds its Third Congress. Kim Il Sung is reelected chairman.

June 1–July 19: Kim Il Sung visits the Soviet Union, East Germany, Hungary, Czechoslovakia, Bulgaria, Albania and Mongolia to strengthen relations with the Communist bloc. He comes back almost empty handed.

August 30–31: The KWP Central Committee meets in Pyongyang. Kim Il Sung is almost ousted, but reasserts power and purges the party.

1957

November 3–21: Kim Il Sung visits the Soviet Union to attend the fourtieth anniversary of the October Revolution. Kim Jong Il travels with him. It is Kim Jong Il's first foreign trip since he arrived in North Korea in 1946.

1959

January 21–February 9: Kim Jong Il undertakes his second trip abroad, accompanying his father to Moscow where they meet Soviet leader Nikita Khrushchev.

February 13: The Japanese government decides to repatriate ethnic Koreans in Japan to North Korea.

December 16: The repatriation of Koreans from Japan begins. Eighty-two thousand Koreans and six thousand Japanese citizens (most of them wives of Koreans) are repatriated before the program ends in 1967.

1963

Kim Il Sung officially marries his second wife, Kim Song Ae.

1965

April 10–20: Kim Il Sung visits Indonesia together with Kim Jong Il to attend the Non-aligned Conference.

1968

January 21: North Korean commandos infiltrate Seoul in an attempt to assassinate South Korean president Park Chung Hee. The mission fails.

January 23: North Korean patrol boats seize the U.S. intelligence ship *Pueblo*, killing one crew member and capturing eighty-two. The crew was released eleven months later.

November 4: A group of thirty North Korean commandos infiltrate the east coast of South Korea.

1969
December 11: A South Korean airliner carrying fifteen passengers and crew is hijacked to North Korea.

1970
April 3: North Korea provides sanctuary to nine members of the Japanese Red Army who hijacked a Japanese airliner on March 31. The plane makes an emergency landing at Seoul's Kimpo airport, and heads for Pyongyang after releasing all ninety-nine passengers aboard.
June: North Korean patrol boats seize a South Korean broadcast vessel with twenty crew members onboard off the west coast of the peninsula.
November 2–13: The Fifth Congress of the KWP is held in Pyongyang. Kim Il Sung is relected general secretary.

1972
January: Kim Il Sung proposes an inter-Korean peace treaty.
July 4: North and South Korea announce an agreement to end hostilities and work together toward peaceful reunification of the nation.
August 30: Inter-Korean Red Cross talks are held in Pyongyang.
September 13: A second round of inter-Korean Red Cross talks are held in Seoul.
December 25–28: The Supreme People's Assembly elects Kim Il Sung president of the DPRK.

1973
November 15: A North Korean delegate delivers a speech at the United Nations General Assembly for the first time in history.

1974
February: The Central Committee of the Korean Workers' Party establishes Kim Jong Il's position as successor to his father.
August 15: South Korean president Park Chung Hee narrowly escapes an assassination attempt by a Korean from Japan. The president survives, but his wife is killed.
November 15: A North Korean infiltration tunnel dug across the DMZ is discovered.

1975
March 19: A second infiltration tunnel dug under the DMZ is discovered.

1976
August 18: Two U.S. army officers are beaten to death in an attack by thirty axe-wielding North Korean soldiers in the Joint Security Area of Panmunjom in the DMZ.

October: North Korean embassy personnel are expelled from Denmark, Norway, and Finland for smuggling alcohol and cigarettes. In Denmark drugs were also involved. The North Korean ambassador in Sweden is recalled for being engaged in similar activities.

1978
October 17: A third North Korean infiltration tunnel dug under the DMZ is discovered.

1980
May 7: Kim Il Sung visits Yugoslavia to attend the funeral of Marshal Tito, then travels to Romania.

October 10: During its Sixth Congress, KWP formalizes Kim Jong Il's position as his father's successor.

1981
June: A North Korean spy boat is sunk off the coast of Sosan. Nine North Koreans are killed and one captured alive.

1982
March 31: Kim Jong Il presents a paper about the *juche* idea to mark his father's seventieth birthday.

September 15–26: Kim Il Sung visits China where he holds talks with Chinese leader Deng Xiaoping.

November 1: Libyan leader Muammar Al-Qadafi visits Pyongyang and meets Kim Il Sung.

1983
June 2–12: Kim Jong Il visits China at the invitation of Hu Yaobang, general secretary of the Communist Party of China.

October 9: North Korean agents attempt to assassinate South Korean president Chun Doo Hwan on a visit to Burma's capital Rangoon. They fail but eighteen high-ranking South Korean officials are killed in a bomb explosion.

November 15: The first ever inter-Korean economic conference is held at Panmunjom.

1986

September 5: The North Korean authorities announce that 150,000 soldiers from the army will be mobilized at "economic construction sites."

October 27: Kim Il Sung holds talks with Soviet leader Mikhail Gorbachev in Moscow.

1987

November 29: A South Korean airliner with 115 people on board explodes in the air over the Andaman Sea near Burma. The North Korean agent who planted the bomb is arrested in Bahrain and extradited to South Korea on December 15.

1988

January 12: North Korea announces that it will not participate in the 1988 Olympics to be held in Seoul.

January 20: The U.S. places North Korea on the list of countries supporting international terrorism.

1989

July 1–8: In a late attempt to counter the Seoul Olympics, the thirteenth World Festival of Youth and Students is held in Pyongyang. It is attended by twenty thousand participants from 170 countries.

1990

March 3: A fourth North Korean infiltration tunnel under the DMZ is discovered.

September 4–7: The first round of inter-Korean talks is held in Seoul. Several other rounds of talks are held later in the year.

November 2: North Korea and the Soviet Union sign an accord under which imports and exports have to be paid in hard currency, ending barter trade between the two countries.

December 15–17: North Korea and Japan hold talks in Beijing for the normalization of diplomatic relations between the two countries.

1991

March 11–12: North Korea and Japan hold a second round of talks for the normalization of diplomatic relations between the two countries.

September 18: North and South Korea become full members of the United Nations.

December 10–13: North Korean prime minister Yon Hyong Muk arrives in Seoul via Panmunjom to attend talks with his South Korean counterpart. They sign an agreement on reconciliation, nonaggression, and exchanges and cooperation.

December 24: Kim Jong Il becomes supreme commander of the Korean People's Army.

December 28: North Korea declares a 621-square-kilometer area in Rajin-Sonbong in the northeast a "free economic and trade zone." Foreign investors are invited to set up businesses in the zone.

1992

January 26: North Korea and China sign an accord stating that hard currency is to be used in trade between the two countries.

May 11: Hans Blix, director general of the International Atomic Energy Agency (IAEA), visits a laboratory in Yongbyon north of Pyongyang and later reveals that it is in fact a nuclear plant that could be converted into a nuclear reprocessing facility.

October 5: North Korea adopts the Law on Foreign Investment, the Law on Foreign Enterprises, and a Law on Contractual Joint Ventures.

1993

March 15: South Korean president Kim Young Sam tells his government to halt economic assistance to the North until the nuclear question is resolved.

April 7: The Fifth Session of the Ninth Supreme People's Assembly convenes in Pyongyang and elects Kim Jong Il as chairman of the National Defense Commission.

June 2: Talks are held in New York between North Korea and the United States to deal with North Korea's nuclear program.

1994

March 1: An IAEA inspection team arrives in Pyongyang to check on North Korea's nuclear facilities.

June 13: North Korea withdraws from the IAEA.

June 16: Former U.S. president Jimmy Carter travels to Pyongyang, where he meets Kim Il Sung. They agree to arrange an inter-Korean summit in the North Korean capital. South Korean president Kim Young Sam prepares to visit the North.

July 8: Kim Il Sung dies of a heart attack. The summit is canceled.

August–September: Severe food shortages are reported from many parts of North Korea.

October 21: North Korea and the Unites States sign an agreement in Geneva under which Washington and its allies will build two light-water reactors and supply 500,000 tons of heavy oil annually in return for Pyongyang's freezing its nuclear program. The Korean Peninsula Energy Development Organization (KEDO) is formed to implement the program. North Korea also accepts inspection of its nuclear facilities.

1995

April 28–30: An International Sports and Culture Festival is held in Pyongyang.

June 4–10: North Korea sends a trade delegation to the United States to promote economic cooperation between the two countries. In North Korea, the food distribution system collapses.

December 12: KEDO and North Korea agree on the supply of light-water reactors.

1996

March 23: Interpol and the Cambodian police apprehend a man carrying a North Korean diplomatic passport under the name Kim Il Suu. He turns out be Yoshimi Tanaka, a wanted member of the Japanese Red Army who hijacked an airplane to North Korea in 1970. The arrest followed a raid on an office in Cambodia's capital Phnom Penh in search of counterfeit U.S. dollar bills.

June 14: North Korea and KEDO sign an agreement for the implementation of the light-water reactor program.

September 18: A North Korean submarine is discovered on the east coast of South Korea. Eleven of the twelve-man crew are found to have committed suicide while one is captured alive.

December 11: North Korea's foreign minister, Kim Yong Nam, is interviewed by a German television network and concedes that his country's economy is on the verge of collapse. Widespread famine is reported from the North.

1997

February 12: Hwang Jang Yop, secretary of the KWP's Central Committee, defects to the South.

July 8: On the third anniversary of Kim Il Sung's death, North Korea introduces its own *juche* calendar with 1912, the birth year of Kim Il Sung, as its initial year. His birthday, April 15, is declared the "Day of the Sun."

August 19: A ground-breaking ceremony is held for the two 1,000 MW light-water reactors provided by KEDO.

October 8: The Central Committee and the Central Military Commission of the KWP announces the appointment of Kim Jong Il as general secretary of the Korean Workers' Party.

1998

February 25: Kim Dae Jung, a former dissident, is sworn in as president of South Korea. He decides on conducting a "Sunshine Policy" towards the North.

April 11: Inter-Korean talks are held in Beijing for the first time since the death of Kim Il Sung.

June 22: A North Korean midget submarine is seized after it was spotted entangled in fishing nets off the South Korean coast, south of the DMZ. When brought ashore three days later, nine crew members were found dead inside from an apparent group suicice.

August 31: North Korea fires a new three-stage Taepodong-1 missile over Japan.

September 5: The Supreme People's Assembly elects Kim Jong Il chairman of the National Defense Commission.

October 30: Kim Jong Il holds talks in Pyongyang with Chung Ju Yung, the founder of South Korea's Hyundai Business Group.

November 18: The first cruise ship from South Korea sails to the North with South Korean tourists bound for Mount Kumgang. This is the first time South Korean tourists have been allowed to visit the North since the end of the Korean War. The tours are organized by Hyundai.

1999

January 7: The defense ministers of Japan and South Korea agree in Seoul to jointly counter missile and other threats from North Korea.

January 28: The South Korean government announces a five-year plan to turn the DMZ into a world peace park.

February 13: President Kim Dae Jung says his government will seek inter-Korean dialog in "the nearest possible time."

April 18: Former South Korean president Roh Tae Woo reveals that he was invited to Pyongyang by Kim Il Sung, and that he pursued an inter-Korean summit through secret exchanges of envoys during his time in power from 1988–1993.

June 3: South Korea's intelligence chief, Lim Dong Won, announces that South and North Korea have signed an agreement to hold vice-ministerial-level talks in Beijing from June 21.

June 14–15: South and North Korean naval vessels clash in the West Sea (which the Japanese call the Sea of Japan, a term much resented in Korea) after a nine-day naval confrontation off South Korea's western coast. One North Korean torpedo boat caught fire and sank with its entire crew onboard, while five others were heavily damaged. Two or more South Korean vessels sustained minor damage.

June 22: The inter-Korean talks in Beijing collapse, partly because of the naval clash in the West Sea.

July 18: South Korean intelligence officers say North Korea is strengthening its naval bases along the west coast of the peninsula with armored artillery and multiple rocket launchers.

August 12: Inter-Korean friendship soccer matches open in Pyongyang.

September 2: North and South Korean business leaders agree to conduct joint research involving financial reform.

September 18: A South Korean White Paper for 1999 estimates North Korea's chemical weapons stockpile at 2,500 to 5,000 tons.

October 2: Hyundai Group founder Chung Ju Yung returns from Pyongyang, where he met Kim Jong Il and agreed to pursue the Mt. Kumgang tourism project and the construction of an industrial complex.

December 1: Former Japanese prime minister Tomichi Murayama visits Pyongyang and the two sides agree to resume talks to normalize relations.

2000

January 4: North Korea and Italy establish diplomatic relations.

March 9: North Korea rejects a request from the United States to stop providing shelter for members of the now-defunct Japanese Red Army, a terrorist group that hijacked a Japanese airliner to Pyongyang in 1970.

March 10: Kim Dae Jung issues a declaration in Berlin offering aid to rebuild North Korea's infrastructure.

April 8: Kim Dae Jung announces that an inter-Korean summit has been set for June 12–14.

May 8: Diplomatic relations between North Korea and Australia are restored.

May 29–June 1: Kim Jong Il travels to China by train. He stays there for three days and meets President Jiang Zemin and Premier Zhu Rongji.

June 13–15: South Korean president Kim Dae Jung visits Pyongyang to hold talks with Kim Jong Il.

July 19–20: Russian leader Vladimir Putin visits Pyongyang.

July 29: The first post-summit North-South ministerial talks are held in Seoul.

September 2: Japan announces that it will provide 400,000 tons of rice to North Korea under the auspices of the World Food Program.

September 11: The leader of North Korea's Asia-Pacific Committee, Kim Yong Sun, heads a delegation to Seoul to discuss a return visit to Seoul by Kim Jong Il.

September 15: Athletes from North and South Korea march under a single flag at the opening of the Sydney Olympics, but then compete separately.

September 26: South Korea decides to provide North Korea with 300,000 tons of rice and 200,000 tons of corn.

October 23–25: U.S. secretary of state Madeleine Albright visits Pyongyang and holds talks with Kim Jong Il.

December 10: At a ceremony in Oslo, Norway, Kim Dae Jung is awarded the Nobel Peace Prize for his "lifelong work for democracy and human rights in South Korea and East Asia in general, and for peace and reconciliation with North Korea in particular."

2001

January 1: The official North Korean media calls for "new thinking" in the country's economic management.

January 15: North Korea and the Netherlands establish diplomatic relations.

January 15–20: Kim Jong Il visits China. He tours factories, the Pudong industrial complex in Shanghai as well as the city's stock exchange.

February 2: Pyongyang and Seoul agree on a plan to reconnect the railways between the two Koreas.

February 6: Canada and North Korea establish diplomatic relations.

February 7: Germany and North Korea establish diplomatic relations.

February 8: South and North Korea agree on guidelines on how to connect the railways between the two countries.

March 1: Spain and North Korea establish diplomatic relations.

May 1: Kim Jong Il's first son, Kim Jong Nam, is caught at Tokyo's Narita airport traveling on a false passport. He is deported to China.

May 2: A delegation from the European Union led by Swedish prime minister Göran Persson visits Pyongyang.

June 18: North Korea demands a meeting with the United States to demand compensation for the delayed construction of light-water reactors promised by KEDO.

June 27: Turkey and North Korea establish diplomatic relations.

July 26–August 18: Kim Jong Il travels by train through Russia to Moscow and St. Petersburg.

September 3: Chinese president Jiang Zemin visits North Korea.

September 19: North and South Korea agree to resume family reunions.

November 27: North Korean troops fire gunshots at a South Korean guard post inside the DMZ.

December 15: North Korean defense minister Kim Dong Shin meets Chinese Chief of General Staff, Gen. Fu Quanyou, to exchange views on the Korean situation.

December 22: A North Korean ship is sunk by Japanese Coast Guards in Japanese waters. The Japanese determined it to be a spy vessel that was also carrying amphetamines.

2002

January 29: In his State of the Union speech, U.S. president George W. Bush says that Iraq, Iran and North Korea form an "Axis of Evil" that is a threat to America's security.

February 8: North Korea hits back by calling the United States the "empire of [the] devil."

February 20: George W. Bush visits South Korea and the DMZ and says that he supports a dialog with North Korea.

February 21: President George W. Bush meets Chinese president Jiang Zemin in Beijing and both agree to work on the reunification of Korea.

March 15: China allows twenty-five North Korean asylum seekers to leave the Spanish embassy in Beijing for South Korea via the Philippines.

May 31–June 30: The FIFA World Cup is cohosted by Japan and South Korea. The soccer games, in which South Korea did very well, also attracted a lot of attention in North Korea.

July 1: North Korea announces that it will restructure its state enterprises. It is interpreted as a first step toward economic reform.

July 2: Taiwanese law enforcement agents seize 79 kg of Southeast Asian heroin during a raid in the port city of Keelung. The heroin was smuggled from North Korea.

August 20–24: Kim Jong Il visits the Russian Far East by train.

September 17: Japanese prime minister Junichiro Koizumi visits Pyongyang and meets Kim Jong Il, who admits that his country kidnapped and abducted thirteen Japanese citizens from 1977 to 1983 to help train North Korean spies. Five are still alive. The admission causes an outrage in Japan, and a backlash against the Chongryun.

September 23: Yang Bin, a Dutch-Chinese entrepreneur, is appointed governor of "the Sinuiju Special Administrative Region" near the Chinese border. Private enterprise will be allowed inside the special economic zone.

September 25: South Korean opposition lawmaker Eom Ho Sung alleges that Seoul sent US$400 million to the North to secure the inter-Korean summit in June 2000. He claims that the secret fund was channeled through Hyundai Merchant Marine. A political storm erupts in South Korea following the allegation.

October 4: Chinese authorities arrest Yang Bin and charge him with contract fraud and bribery.

October 15: The five surviving Japanese, who were abducted to North Korea in the late 1970s and early 1980s, are allowed to return to Japan, but their children and the American husband of one of the abductees remain behind in Pyongyang.

October 16: According to the United States, North Korea has revealed to US assistant secretary of state James Kelly in Pyongyang that it has pursued its nuclear program despite a 1994 pledge to shelve it.

October 26: Kim Dae Jung, U.S. president George W. Bush, and Japanese prime minister Junichiro Koizumi urge North Korea to dismantle its secret nuclear program and to come into full compliance with all its international nuclear commitments.

November 14: The U.S. announces that the five hundred thousand tons of heavy oil that it has promised to supply North Korea annually in return for Pyongyang's pledge to freeze its nuclear program will no longer be delivered.

December 9: Spanish marines patrolling the sea south of the Arabian peninsula intercept a North Korean ship carrying fifteen Scud missiles and other equipment to Yemen. The ship, with its cargo, is later allowed to continue to its destination.

December 12: North Korea says it will restart the Yangbyon nuclear reactor.

December 19: Roh Moo Hyun, close associate of Kim Dae Jung, wins the presidential election in South Korea and vows to continue the Sunshine Policy.

December 22: North Korea removes the IAEA's monitoring devices at Yangbyon.

December 27: North Korea announces that it will expel the IAEA's inspectors.

December 28: The United States threatens North Korea with an economic blockade.

2003

January 7: North Korea warns the United States that it will consider economic sanctions "a declaration of war."

January 8: South Korea's Unification Ministry announces that North Korea will be short of more than 2 million tons of grain to feed its population.

January 10: North Korea withdraws from the nuclear nonproliferation treaty.

February 14: Kim Dae Jung admits that his government helped arrange a US$200 million payment to North Korea before the 2000 summit.

February 25: Roh Moo Hyun is sworn in as South Korea's president. North Korea fires a short-range missile into the East Sea (called the Yellow Sea in China and on most international maps.)

February 26: Predicting a U.S.-led invasion of Iraq is "just a matter of time," North Korea says it could be the U.S. military's next target and urges its armed forces to be ready for war.

April 19: Australian commandos board a Tuvalu-registered North Korean ship off the coast of Victoria. A total of 50 kg of heroin from Southeast Asia's Golden Triangle is seized from the ship and another 75 kg, which had been dropped ashore, is found later.

April 27: South and North Korean officials meet in Pyongyang. The South Koreans demand that the North abandon its suspected nuclear weapons program.

June 9: North Korea admits publicly for the first time that it is seeking nuclear weapons, but puts the blame on the United States for the need to develop a strong deterrent.

July 14: A Chinese court sentences Yang Bin, the deposed "governor" of the "Sinuiji Special Administrative Region," to eighteen years in jail. He is also fined 2.3 million yuan (US$277,100).

July 18: The *Asian Wall Street Journal* reports that China believes North Korea now has enough plutonium to build a nuclear bomb.

July 31: North Korea abandons its long-standing demand for one-on-one talks with the United States.

August 4: The head of Hyundai, Chung Mong Hun, commits suicide over the North Korean payoff scandal.

August 27–29: Representatives from North and South Korea, Japan, China, Russia and the United States meet in Beijing to defuse the nuclear crisis. North Korea then dismisses the six-nation talks as "not only useless but harmful in every respect."

September 9: North Korea celebrates its fifty-fifth anniversary with big parades and a mass rally in Pyongyang, but no new missiles or other military hardware are displayed. Only civilians and lightly armed soldiers march through the streets of the capital.

October 8: More than a thousand South Koreans are taken by twenty-eight buses into Pyongyang over a newly constructed road from the South to the North.

October 9: North Korea demands Japan be excluded from the six-nation nuclear talks.

October 22: North Korea denounces South Korea for agreeing to send troops to Iraq.

October 29: Pyongyang says it will settle for a written pledge from President Bush not to attack North Korea rather than a bilateral nonaggression pact.

October 29: China's second-highest-ranking politician, Wu Bangguo, begins a three-day visit to Pyongyang to ease the tension on the Korean peninsula.

November 1: A group of U.S. lawmakers, whose trip to North Korea was canceled by President Bush, send a scathing letter to the White House, complaining of "arrogant and disrespectful" treatment of his security advisers. North Korea accuses the U.S. military of conducting at least two hundred spy flights against it in October.

December 19: Japan announces that it is buying a sophisticated anti-missile system from the U.S. Although North Korea is not mentioned, the decision is seen as a move to protect Japan from potential attack from North Korea.

2004

January: A U.S. delegation led by Charles "Jack" Pritchard visits North Korea in the first week of January and spends several days visiting Yongbyon. They are shown an empty holding pond from which eight thousand fuel rods have been removed. On January 15, Pritchard addresses a gathering in Washington and says that he was told all the rods had been reprocessed, allowing North Korean scientists to make plutonium bombs.

February 2: The founder of Pakistan's nuclear weapons program, Dr. Abdul Qadeer Khan, confesses to leaking nuclear secrets to North Korea, Iran, and Libya.

February 5: The Pakistani president, Gen. Pervez Musharraf, pardons Dr. Kahn for leaking nuclear secrets. Musharraf reiterates "there was no official involvement in the proliferation."

February 28: Another round of six-nation talks between North and South Korea, Japan, China, Russia, and the United States ends in Beijing with no firm agreement being made. However, North Korea hints that it may agree to give up its nuclear program in exchange for aid.

April 14: U.S. vice president Dick Cheney visits Beijing and hands Chinese officials new evidence of North Korea's weapons capabilities.

April 15: Dick Cheney arrives in South Korea warning of the risk of a nuclear arms race in the region if pressure is not brought to bear on North Korea to dismantle its nuclear programs. He also says that the North Korean government thrives on terror and points to the fate of toppled Iraqi leader Saddam Hussein for threatening the U.S.

April 18: The North Korean media describes Dick Cheney as "mentally deranged."

April 19: Kim Jong Il arrives in Beijing by train on a four-day visit for talks with Chinese president Hu Jintao and military chief Jiang Zemin. China urges North Korea to soften its stance towards the U.S. and Kim Jong Il offers to scrap nuclear plans if the U.S. alters its "hostile" policies towards North Korea.

April 22: At least 160 people are killed and a 1,300 are injured when a train carrying ammonium nitrate explodes at Ryongchon railroad station near the Chinese border in North Pyongan province. North Korea appeals for help from the international community.

May 22: Japanese prime minister Junichiro Koizumi pays a second visit to Pyongyang. Five children of Japanese who were abducted to North Korea in the late 1970s and early 1980s are allowed to join their parents, who returned to Japan in October 2002.

May 31–June 3: Yet another round of talks on North Korea's nuclear program closes with agreement to meet again in September and only marginal progress. North Korea threatens to test a nuclear bomb if it does not get substantial aid from the international community. For its part, the U.S. tables its first offer to North Korea since Bush became president: a step-by-step dismantling of North Korea's plutonium and uranium weapons programs in return for aid and security guarantees and easing of its political and economic isolation. The proposal may turn out to be a non-starter as North Korea does not admit to having a uranium enrichment program.

July 9: Charles Robert Jenkins, a U.S. soldier who disappeared into North Korea in 1965 and later married one of the Japanese women who were abducted in the 1970s, is allowed to leave the country. He travels to Indonesia, where he is reunited with his wife who was among those who left for Japan in

May. They travel on to Japan on July 18 and Jenkins surrenders to the U.S. army in Tokyo on September 11.

July 27–28: About 450 North Korean refugees, who have made it through China to Vietnam, are flown from Vietnam to South Korea. It was the biggest mass defection to South Korea since the end of the 1950–53 Korean War.

August 27: Koh Young Hee, the favorite consort of Kim Jong Il, is rumored to have died in Pyongyang. The rumor is yet to be confirmed.

September 9: As North Korea celebrates its national day, satellites pick up images of a huge mushroom-shaped cloud over Kimhyungjik county near North Korea's border with China.

September 16: Foreign diplomats are taken to the site of the explosion and are told a hydroelectric dam was being built and the cloud was a result of explosions to clear the area. They conclude that the explosion was not, as first suspected, a nuclear test. The South Koreans, however, say the site the diplomats were taken to was some distance from the site of the mysterious cloud.

WHO'S WHO

ABBREVIATIONS

CC   Central Committee
KU   Kim Il Sung University
KWP Korean Workers' Party
PB   Politburo
SPA Supreme People's Assembly

CHANG SONG TAEK

Born in 1946. Educated at KU, Pyongyang. Delegate to the 8th (1986), 9th (1990), and 10th (1998) SPAs. Deputy Director of the CC of the KWP, 1996–. Married to Kim Jong Il's sister, Kim Kyong Hui. Visited South Korea as a delegate of the North after the June 2000 Kim-Kim summit.

CHANG SONG U

Born in 1933. Educated at Kim Il Sung Military University. Member of the CC of the KWP, 1980–. Delegate to the 8th (1986), 9th (1990), and 10th (1998) SPAs. Army general in 1992. Director of the Political Department of the Ministry of Public Security, 1992. Commander of the 3rd Army Corps 1995. Chang Song Taek's brother.

CHO MYONG ROK

Born in 1930 in Manchuria. Educated at Mangyongdae Revolutionary School. Trained as a pilot in the Soviet Union. Member of the CC of the KWP in 1974. Commander of the air force in 1978. Member of the Central Military Commission in

1980. General of 1982, and vice marshal and director general of the General Political Bureau of the Korean People's Army in 1995. Delegate to the 8th (1986), 9th (1990), and 10th (1998–) SPAs. Vice marshal in 1995 and first vice chairman of the National Defense Commission in 1998, of which Kim Jong Il is chairman. Visited the United States in October 2000 and met Madeleine Albright. Signed a joint statement with the United States on October 12, 2000, at the White House.

CHUNG JU YUNG

Born in 1915 in the small farming village of Asan in the Tongchon area of Kangwon province, in what later became North Korea. Moved to Seoul where he in 1945 set up the Hyundai ("modern") Auto Repair Company, which later grew to become one of South Korea's largest conglomerates. Entered politics in the 1992 election, but failed to be elected president. Instrumental in forging business links between the two Koreas, and in 1998 became the first South Korean civilian to enter North Korea without a military escort when he and his sons crossed the DMZ with five hundred head of cattle that were donated to feed the villagers of Asan. Passed away in 2001. A year later, Hyundai was accused of acting as a conduit for South Korean government funds going to Pyongyang to pay for the June 2000 North-South summit. His son and successor as head of Hyundai, Chung Mong Hun, committed suicide in August 2003 over the payoff scandal.

HAN DUK SU

Born in 1907 in North Kyongsang province. Left for Japan in 1927. Became a leader of the Korean community in Japan and played a decisive role in forming the pro-Pyongyang General Association of Korean Residents in Japan, or Chongryun, in 1955. Chairman of Chongryun until his death in Tokyo in 2001. Represented Chongryun in the SPA from 1967 till his death.

HO KA I

Born in 1908 in Khabarovsk as Aleksei Ivanovich Hegai. Active in Komsomol, the Communist youth movement, and left for central and European Soviet Union in 1933. Studied in Moscow. Returned to the Far East in 1936, but was deported to Central Asia in 1937. Sent to Soviet-occupied northern Korea in 1945 and played a significant role in the creation of the Democratic

People's Republic of Korea. First secretary of the CC of the KWP in 1949. Perceived by Kim Il Sung as a rival, he was ousted from power in 1951 and, according to the official version, "committed suicide" in 1953.

HONG IL CHUN

Kim Jong Il's first wife. Mother of Kim Hye Suk (daughter). Vice minister of general education, 1982. Delegate to the 8th SPA (1986). President of Kim Hyongjik University of Education, 1991–. Member of the South-North Social Cultural Cooperative and Exchange Joint Committee, 1992–.

HONG SUNG NAM

Born in 1924 in Kangwon province. Educated at KU and the Prague Engineering College, Czechoslovakia. Director of the Heavy Industry Department of the KWP in 1971. Vice prime minister in 1973, member of the CC of the KWP in 1982. Alternate member of the PB of the KWP in 1982, dismissed from the PB in 1984 but reinstated in 1986. Chairman of the State Planning Commission in 1982. Delegate to the 9th (1990) and 10th (1998) SPAs. Prime minister since 1998.

HWANG JANG YOP

Born in 1923 in Pyongyang. Educated in Moscow. Head professor at KU, 1954; president of KU in 1965. Chairman of the SPA in 1972 and 1982. Secretary of the CC of the KWP in 1985. Chairman of the Foreign Affairs Committee of the SPA until he defected to South Korea in 1997. The highest-ranking North Korean official to defect to the South.

HYON CHOL HAE

Born in 1934. Alternate member of the CC of the KWP in 1991, full member in 1993. Chairman of the South Hamgyong Province People's Committee in 1990. Delegate to the 10th SPA. General and deputy director of the General Political Bureau of the Korean People's Army. A close confidant of Kim Jong Il.

KANG SOK JU

Born in 1939 in Pyongyang. Vice foreign minister in 1983 and first vice foreign minister from 1986. Alternate member of the CC of the KWP in 1988, full member 1991–. Delegate to the 7th

(1986) and 10th SPAs (1998). Represented North Korea in nuclear talks with the United States, signed the Agreed Framework on the nuclear issue on October 21, 1994 in Geneva on behalf of North Korea. The other signatory was Robert Gallucci, ambassador at large of the United States.

KIM CHAEK

Born in 1904 in South Hamgyong province. Studied in Moscow, joined the Chinese communists in Shanghai in the 1920s and Kim Il Sung in Manchuria in the 1930s. Vice premier and minister of industry in independent North Korea's first government. Field commander of the Korean People's Army during the Korean War. Killed in action in 1950. The largest iron and steel mill in North Korea, the Kim Chaek Integrated Iron and Steel Works, is named after him.

KIM DU NAM

Born in 1928. Educated at Mangyongdae Revolutionary School. Member of the CC of the KWP, 1980. General and military secretary to Kim Il Sung. Delegate to the 7th (1982), 8th (1986), and 9th (1990) SPAs. Member of the Central Military Commission of the KWP, 1994–. Brother of Kim Yong Nam.

KIM IL CHOL

Born in 1933 in Pyongyang. Educated at Mangyongdae Revolutionary School. Vice commander of the navy, 1974; commander of the navy, 1978. Member of the CC of the KWP 1980–. Delegate to the 7th (1982) and 10th (1998) SPAs. Appointed general in 1992 and vice marshal in 1997. Minister of the People's Armed Forces 1998–.

KIM IL SUNG

Born on April 15, 1912 in the village of Mangyongdae near Pyongyang. His original name was Kim Song Ju, but he changed it to Kim Il Sung in 1930. Organized the first anti-Japanese guerrilla unit in Manchuria in 1932. Fought the Japanese in Manchuria and along the Korean border for almost a decade. Retreated into the Soviet Union in the winter of 1940. Stayed in the village of Vyatskoye near Khabarovsk until the end of the war. Returned to Korea in September 1945. Vice chairman of the North Korean Workers' Party from 1946–1949; Chairman of the KWP from 1949 until his death in 1994. First premier of North Korea, 1948, chairman of the Military Committee, 1950. President from 1972 to 1994.

KIM JONG CHUL

Born in 1981. Son of Kim Jong Il and Koh Young Hee. Educated in Switzerland. Possible successor to Kim Jong Il.

KIM JONG IL

Born on February 15, 1942 in the village of Vyatskoye north of Khabarovsk in the Soviet Union. First son of Kim Il Sung and Kim Jong Suk. Also given the Russian name Yura (a colloquial form of Yuri). Educated at Mangyongdae Revolutionary School and KU, from where he graduated in 1964. KWP secretary in charge of organization, propaganda, and agitation in 1973. Named successor to his father in 1974, a decision that was finalized in 1980. Member of the PB of the KWP in 1980. Member of the SPA since 1982. First deputy chairman of the National Defense Commission in 1990. Supreme commander of the Korean People's Armed Forces in 1991. Appointed marshal in 1992 and chairman of the National Defence Commission in 1993. Became general secretary of the KWP in 1997.

KIM JONG JU

Born in 1922. Educated in Moscow. Chief of the Organization-Guidance Department of the KWP, 1954. Member of the CC of the KWP, 1961–. Member of the PB of the KWP, 1969–. Vice premier, 1974. Delegate to the 10th (1998) SPA. Honorary vice chairman of the Standing Committee of the SPA, 1998–. Kim Il Sung's younger brother.

KIM JONG NAM

Born in 1971. Son of Kim Jong Il and Song Hye Rim. Possible successor to Kim Jong Il.

KIM JONG OON

Born in 1983. Son of Kim Jong Il and Koh Young Hee. Possible successor to Kim Jong Il.

KIM JONG SUK

Born in 1917 in Hoeryong, Hamgyong province. Joined Kim Il

Sung's guerrilla force in 1935 as a kitchen helper. Married Kim Il Sung in the Soviet Union, most probably in 1941. Died while delivering a stillborn baby in 1949 in Pyongyang. Posthumously elevated to "Mother of the Revolution" in 1974, and a museum was built for her in Hoeryong.

KIM KYONG HUI

Born in 1946 in Pyongyang. Daughter of Kim Il Sung and Kim Jong Suk. Educated at KU, Pyongyang. Member of the CC of the KWP, 1988–. Delegate to the 9th (1990) and 10th (1998) SPAs. Director of the Light Industry Department of the KWP, 1994–. Director of the CC of the KWP, 1995–. Married to Chang Song Taek.

KIM PYONG IL (1)

Born in 1944 in the village of Vyatskoye north of Khabarovsk in the Soviet Union. The second son of Kim Il Sung and Kim Jong Suk, he was also given the Russian name Sura (a short form of Alexander). Drowned in Pyongyang in 1947.

KIM PYONG IL (2)

Born in 1954 in Pyongyang. Son of Kim Il Sung and Kim Song Ae. Educated at KU in Pyongyang. Director of the Ministry of the People's Armed Forces, 1984. Ambassador to Bulgaria, 1988. Ambassador to Finland, 1993. Ambassador to Poland, 1997–.

KIM SONG AE

Born in 1924. Kim Il Sung's second wife. Chairwoman of the CC of the Korean Democratic Women's Union, 1965. Member of the Standing Committee of the SPA, 1972 and 1990. Member of the CC of the KWP, 1980. Delegate to the 7th (1982), 8th (1986), and 9th (1990) SPAs.

KIM TU BONG

Born in 1889 in Kijang, Kyongsang province. A linguist and a philologist, he joined the Korean Communist movement in the 1920s. Chairman of the North Korean Workers' Party from 1946–1949. Held many other important posts, including that of president of KU, until he was purged in 1958.

KIM YONG CHUN

Born in 1932. Alternate member of the CC of the KWP in 1980. General in 1990 and vice marshal in 1995. Chief of staff of the

Korean People's Army in 1995 and member of the National Defense Commission in 1998. Delegate to the 10th SPA (1998).

KIM YONG NAM

Born in 1928 in North Hamgyong province. Educated at KU, Pyongyang, and in Moscow. Director of the International Department of KWP, 1961 and 1972. Member of the CC of the KWP, 1970–. Member of the PB of the KWP, 1980–. Vice premier, 1983. Foreign minister, 1983. Delegate to the 7th (1982), 8th (1986), 9th (1990), and 10th (1998). SPAs. Chairman of the Standing Committee of the SPA, 1998–.

KIM YONG SUK

Born in 1947. Kim Jong Il's second wife. Mother of two daughters.

KIM YONG SUN

Born in 1934 in South Pyongan province. Educated at KU and in Moscow. Ambassador to Egypt 1970. Member of the CC of the KWP, 1980. Director of the International Department of the KWP, 1988. Chairman of the Anti-Nuclear Peace Committee, 1989–. Chairman of the Korean Committee for Solidarity with World Peoples, 1990–. Delegate to the 9th (1990) and 10th (1998) SPAs. Alternate member of the PB of the KWP, 1992–1993. Led the North Korean side during South-North talks in 1994. Secretary of the KWP, 1994. Chairman of the Asia-Pacific Peace Committee, 1994. Chairman of the Council for the Peaceful Reunification of the Fatherland, 1998.

KOH YONG HEE

Born in 1953. A dancer of the Mansudae Dance Troupe and Kim Jong Il's second mistress. Mother of Kim Jong Chul (son), Kim Jong Oon (son), and a daughter. Rumored to have died in August 2004.

PAK CHAE GYONG

Born in 1933 in North Hamgyong province. Alternate member of the CC of the KWP since 1993. Chief of the propaganda department of the Ministry of the People's Armed Forces in 1994; full general in 1997. Delegate to the 10th (1998) SPA. One of the fastest rising officers in the Korean People's Army, he often accompanies Kim Jong Il on inspection tours of military facilities.

PAK GI SO

Member of the CC of the KWP in 1986. Delegate to the 9th (1990) and 10th (1998) SPAs. Full general in 1990; vice marshal in 1997. Member of the Central Military Commission of the KWP, 1998–. Often accompanies Kim Jong Il on inspection tours of military facilities.

PAK HON YONG

A founding member of the first Korean Communist Party in 1925 and the best-known Communist leader in Korea during the Japanese occupation, operating underground in the South. Fled to the North in 1946. Vice chairman of the party, vice premier and foreign minister of the first North Korean cabinet. Arrested along with twelve other party members in 1953 and charged with "treason" and "espionage activities for the United States." Sentenced to death and executed in 1955 or 1956.

PANG HAK SE

A former Soviet police officer who arrived in North Korea in 1946 to become head of the Section of Political Defense of the State, or, in effect, chief of North Korea's secret police. Among the masterminds behind the purges of the 1950s and 1960s. One of few former Soviet Koreans who never lost Kim Il Sung's trust. Member of the CC of the KWP in 1980 and chairman of the Supreme Court until the late 1980s. Died in 1992.

SONG HYE RIM

Born in 1937. An actress of the Korean Art Film Studio and Kim Jong Il's first mistress. Mother of Kim Jong Nam. Died in Moscow in 2002.

Note: Ilpyong Kim in his *Historical Dictionary of North Korea* gives different years of birth for some of the individuals above: Cho Myong Rok (1924), Kim Il Chol (1928), Kim Yong Chun (1922), and Kim Yong Nam (1925). The years in this "Who's Who" corresponds to those in *Korea Manual*, the annual yearbooks of the *Yonhap* news agency, South Korea.

NOTES

INTRODUCTION

1. Marcus Noland, "Reasonable reunification Costs Are Estimated at $1.5 Trillion for 10 Years," *Korea Economic Weekly*, Nov. 4, 1996.

2. Charles Wolf, "How Much for One Korea?" *Asian Wall Street Journal*, Oct. 2, 2000. Wolf is generally more optimistic than other observers, and believes some of these figures are exaggerated. See also Manfred Wagner, "Six Years After German Reunification: What Are the Lessons for Korea?" Paper presented at the International Conference on International Economic Implications of Korean Unification, Seoul, June 28–29, 1996.

3.This is an exact quote from a South Korean diplomat I interviewed in October 2001. See Bertil Lintner, "Coming in From the Cold?" *Far Eastern Economic Review*, Oct. 25, 2001.

4. *World News Connection* (U.S. Dept. of Commerce), "North Korean Military Engages in Foreign Currency Earning," June 3, 2001.

5. *Korea Times*, July 25, 2001.

6. Ed Cropley, "'Dear Leader' for Dinner," *Bangkok Post*, Dec. 27, 2003.

7. Bertil Lintner, "Coming In From the Cold?" *Far Eastern Economic Review*, Oct. 25, 2001, and "Corrections," *Far Eastern Economic Review*, Nov. 8, 2001. For a while, the Tongjiang Foreign Trade Corporation advertised the medicine on its now defunct website.

8. *Far Eastern Economic Review*, Oct. 25, 2001. The article is based on numerous interviews with foreign diplomats and North Korea watchers.

9. Heather Smith and Yiping Huang, "What Caused North Korea's Agricultural Crisis?" Paper presented to a conference on Sept. 6–7, 2000, at The Australian National University, Canberra.

10. *Far Eastern Economic Review*, Oct. 25, 2001.

11. Ibid.

12. Anthony Spaeth, "Kim's Rackets," *Time* (Asia), June 9, 2003.

13. "Police Seize 198 Bricks of Heroin," *Taipei Times*, July 3, 2002.

14. Jay Solomon and Jason Dean, "Heroin Bust Point to Source of Funds for North Koreans," *Wall Street Journal*, April 23, 2003, and "SAS Nabs North Korean Drug Ship," *The Australian*, April 21, 2003.

15. Elissa Hunt, "Macau Link to Drug Ship," *Herald Sun* (Australia), Nov. 20, 2003.

16. The Tuman or Duman (Duman-gang) is the Korean name of the river. It is called the Tumen in China and Russia.

17. "North Korea Opening (Sh-h-h!) a Casino," New York Times, July 31, 1999. See also Bertil Lintner, *Blood Brothers: The Criminal Underworld of Asia*, New York: Palgrave, Macmillan, 2003, pp. 84–85. I also visited the Russian side of the border, opposite Rajin-Sonbong, in May 2003, and interviewed Russian border guards who had visited the casino.

18. For a detailed account of Yeung's business and underworld connections, see Fredric Dannen, "Partners in Crime," *New Republic*, July 14 and 21, 1997.

19. I stayed at the Yanggakdo Hotel in April 2004 and also visited the casino.

20. "Lessons from Lippo," *Wall Street Journal*, Feb. 27, 1998.

21. "North Korea Calls Ship Seizure 'Piracy.'" *CBSNews.com*, Dec. 12, 2002.

22. "Brigandish Piracy of the U.S. Imperialists," *Democratic People's Republic of Korea*, no. 4/2003.

23. Tito Drago, "U.S. Should Explain Libya Missile Shipment," *Inter Press Service*, Dec. 9, 2003.

24. For a complete list of North Korean missile systems and missile sales, see Bertil Lintner, "North Korea's Missile Trade Helps Fund Its Nuclear Program," *YaleGlobal Online*, May 5, 2003.

25. Ibid. and Larry Niksch, "North Korea's Nuclear Program," Washington: Congressional Research Service, Jan. 22, 2003.

26. Pierre Rigoulot, "Crimes, Terror, and Secrecy in North Korea." In Stéphane Courtois et al., *The Black Book of Communism*, Cambridge, Massachusetts and London, England: Harvard University Press, 1999, pp. 559.

27. These arguments came up in numerous discussions I had with academics and policy makers in South Korea in 2002 and 2003. But since these were private discussions, I have opted to summarize their arguments rather than identify individuals.

28. Based on my own observations in Pyongyang in April 2004, and discussions with diplomats, aid workers, and other foreign residents in the city.

CHAPTER 1   THE SUMMIT THAT SHOOK THE WORLD

1. A video recording of Kim Dae Jung's arrival in Pyongyang in June 2000 and some other meetings, which are described below, is in my possession.

2. The "Reunification Dogs" were featured on the website of the *People's Korea* (published by pro-Pyongyang North Koreans in Japan) in June 2000.

3. *Economist*, June 15, 2000.

4. Suh-Kyung Yoon, "Dollars and Sentiments,"*Far Eastern Economic Review*, June 22, 2000.

5. Moon Chung In, "Understanding the DJ Doctire: The Sunshine Policy and the Korean Peninsula," in Moon Chung In and David Steinberg, *Kim Dae-jung Government and Sunshine Policy: Promises and Challenges*, Seoul: Yonsei University Press, and Asian Studies Program, Georgetown University, 1999, p. 37.

6. Ibid., p. 37.

7. Ibid., p. 39.

8. Ibid., p. 39.

9. James Folley, "Prospect for rapprochement on the Korean Peninsula," *Jane's Intelligence Review*, March 2001.

10. Ibid.

11. Shim Jae Hoon, "No Turning Back," *Far Eastern Economic Review*, June 22, 2000.

12. *Associated Press*, Sydney, Sept. 15, 2000, and *People's Korea*, Sept. 27, 2000.

13. Selig Harrison, "The Kim Dae Jung Government, the Sunshine Policy, and the North-South Summit," in Moon Chung In and David Steinberg, *Korea in Transition: Three Years under the Kim Dae-jung Government*, Seoul: Yonsei University Press, and Asian Studies Program, Georgetown University, 2002, p. 77.

14. This and other quotes from Madeleine Albright are from an interview she gave to *Global Viewpoint* on Jan. 9, 2003. See http://www.digitalnpq.org/global_services/global%20viewpoint/01-09-03.html

15. Address by Gunnar Berge, Oslo City Hall, Dec. 10, 2000.

16. "The Nobel Lecture given by The Nobel Peace Laureate 2000, Kim Dae Jung, Oslo, Dec. 10, 2000." http://www.nobel.no/eng_lect_2000k.html

17. "Political Storm Erupts Over Alleged Secret Fund for inter-Korean Summit," Agence France-Presse, Seoul, Sept. 26, 2002.

18. *Korea Herald*, Sept. 27, 2002.

19. Larry Niksch, Korea: "U.S.-South Korean Relations—Issues for Congress," Congressional Research Service, Library of Congress, Washington, March 5, 2002, p. 9. Also interview with Larry Niksch and Raphael Perl, Washington, Dec. 2 and 3, 2003.

20. *Seoul Chungang Ilbo*, Feb. 2, 2003. Internet version in English on Feb. 3, 2003.

21. Bertil Lintner, "The Macau Connection," *Far Eastern Economic Review*, Oct. 25, 2001.

22. Richard Saccone, *Koreans to Remember: 50 Famous People Who Helped Shape Korea*, Elizabeth, New Jersey, and Seoul: 1998, p. 132.

23. "Korea: U.S.-South Korean Relations—Issues for Congress," March 5, 2002, p. 9.

24. *Chung Ju Yung, 1915–2001*, http://obits.com/chungjuyung.html

25. *Straits Times* (Singapore), Sept. 27, 2002.

26. *Korea Times*, Oct. 4, 2002.

27. *Korea Herald*, Sept. 27, 2002.

28. *Korea Times*, Oct. 4, 2002.

29. *Post Courier: Charleston Net.*, Feb. 15, 2003, http://charleston.net/stories/021503/wor_15summit.shtml

30. *Korea Times*, Aug. 6, 2003.

31. For a full text of the Agreed Framework, see Michael O'Hanlon and Mike Mochizuki, *Crisis on the North Korean Peninsula: How to Deal With a Nuclear North Korea*, New York: McGraw-Hill, 2003, pp. 177–181.

32. Ilpyong J. Kim, *Historical Dictionary of North Korea*, Lanham, Maryland, and Oxford: The Scarecrow Press Inc., 2003, p. 102.

33. Larry Niksch, "North Korea's Nuclear Weapons Program," Congressional Research Service, Library of Congress, Washington, Jan. 22, 2003, p. 1.

34. Bruce Cumings, "North Korea: The Sequel." Paper presented at a North Korea symposium in Berlin, Germany, June 25, 2003, pp. 17–18.

35. Quoted by *Agence-France Presse*, Seoul, June 9, 2003.

36. "North Korea's Nuclear Weapons Program." Jan. 22, 2003, p. 1.

37. Cumings, op. cit., p. 19.

38. Ibid., p. 3.

39. Unmesh Kher, "Accounted for, at Last," *Time* (Asia), Sept. 30, 2002.

40. For the full text of the "DPRK-Japan Pyongyang Declaration," see *Korea Today* (Pyongyang), Nov. 2002.

41. Haruki Wada, "Re-examining the Alleged Abductions of Japanese," *Sekai*, Jan. and Feb. 2001.

42. "Japanese Returnees Receive Family Letters," *Associated Press*, Tokyo, August 2, 2003.

43. I visted Osaka, Kyoto and Tokyo in February 2003, and interviewed several current and former members of the Chongryun, including Kum Ki Do of its International Affairs Department in Kyoto, and Ri Sang Yong, a reporter for its English-language newspaper, *People's Korea*.

44. Noland, Marcus Noland, "Famine and Reform in North Korea." Paper produced by the Institute for International Economics, July 2003, p. 14.

45. Bradley Babson, "The North Korean Economy and Possibilities for Reform." Paper prepared for the seventeenth Annual Conference on Korea-U.S. Studies, Seoul, Oct. 14–15, 2002.

46. See also "Through a Glass, Darkly," *The Economist*, March 13, 2004.

47. The Amnok is called the Yalu River in Chinese.

48. "China Detains Yang Bin, Head of NK's Special Economic Zone," *Agence-France Presse*, Beijing, Oct. 4, 2002.

49. "Sinuiju Designated as H.K.-Type Special Zone: First Market Economy Experience in DPRK," *People's Korea*, Sept. 28, 2002.

50. Ibid. See also Michael Schuman, "Bizarre SAR," *Time* (Asia), Oct. 7, 2002.

51. David Murphy, "Own Goal," *Far Eastern Economic Review*, Oct. 10, 2002.

52. "Yang Bin to be Dismissed," *Chosun Ilbo*, Oct. 9, 2002.

53. *Far Eastern Economic Review*, Oct. 10, 2002.

54. *Agence-France Presse*, Beijing, Oct. 4, 2002.

55. "Yang Bin Convicted of Fraud, Sentenced to 18 Years," *People's Daily* (online), July 14, 2003.

56. Babson, op. cit.

CHAPTER 2 THE FAMINE AND THE *JUCHE* IDEA

1. Interview with Kim Mi Ran, Seoul, July 27, 2003. Kim Mi Ran is not her real name; she asked me to use this name to protect her relatives who are still in North Korea. Also, interview with Park Yong, another North Korean refugee, Seoul, July 26, 2003.

2. Andrew S. Natsios, *The Great North Korean Famine: Famine, Politics, and Foreign Policy*, Washington D.C.: United States Institute of Peace Press, 2001, p. 93. Also interview with Park Yong, a North Korean refugee, Seoul, July 26, 2003. See also Marcus Noland, "Famine and Reform in North Korea," paper published by the Institute for International Economics, July 2003, pp. 12–13.

3. This and other descriptions from the Chongjin area of North Hamgyong, interview with Park Yong, Seoul July 26, 2003.

4. Philo Kim, "The Social Impact of the Food Crisis in North Korea," in Gill-Chin Lim and Namsoo Chang (eds.), *Food Problems in North Korea: Current Situation and Possible Solutions*, Seoul: Oruem Publishing House, 2003, p. 152.

5. Varroll Bogert, "Days of Hunger," *Newsweek* (Asia), May 5, 1997.

6. Käthi Zellweger, "Caritas in Nordkorea—für menschliche Würde und Gerechtigkeit," paper presented at a North Korea symposium in Berlin, Germany, June 25, 2003, p. 6.

7. Interview with Park Yong, Seoul, July 26, 2003.

8. Philo Kim, op. cit., p 155.

9. Ibid., p. 155.

10. Noland, op. cit. 13.

11. Natsios, op. cit., p. 212 and 215.

12. Ilpyong J. Kim, *Historical Dictionary of North Korea*, Lanham, Maryland, and Oxford: The Scarecrow Press Inc., 2003, p. 40.

13. Hazel Smith, "Improving Intelligence on North Korea," *Jane's Intelligence Review*, March 2004.

14. Noland, op. cit., p. 12.

15. "It's Tough Living as North Koreans," *Keys* (Network for North Korean Democracy and Human Rights), vol. 11, Autumn 2002.

16. Zellweger, op. cit., p. 6.

17. "North Korea: Notes from Pyongyang," *Asian Economic Insight* (from the Hong Kong and Shanghai Banking Corporation), vol. 117, Nov. 2002.

18. Gregory Elich, "Targeting North Korea," http://www.globalresearch. ca/articles/ELI212A.html, Dec. 31, 2002, p. 5.

19. Noland, op. cit., p. 6.

20. "People are Hungry," *Focus: Asia Pacific* (the International Federation of Red Cross and Red Crescent Societies), issue 23, Dec. 2000. The article gives metric tonnes: 8 million, 3.5 million, 4.3 million, and 3 million.

21. Ilpyong J. Kim, op. cit., p. 40.

22. *Focus: Asia Pacific,* Dec. 2000.

23. Interview with Eigil Sørensen of the World Health Organization, Pyongyang, April 19, 2004.

24. Quoted in Natsios, op. cit., p. 83.

25. Ibid. p. 83.

26. Quoted in Song Du Yul, "Eine verlorene Dekade? Nordkoreas Wirtschaftslage und die sozio-politische Folgen," paper presented at a North Korea symposium in Berlin, Germany, June 25, 2003, p. 2. "Rodong" can also be spelt "Nodong" and means labor in Korean. It is also the name of a missile produced in North Korea.

27. *Kim Il Sung: Short Biography*, vol. 2, Pyongyang: Foreign Languages Publishing House, 1973, pp. 118–119.

21. Ilpyong J. Kim, op. cit., p. 63. There is a misprint in Kim's book, it says that Kim Il Sung first used the term *Juche* in a speech on December 28, 1995. It should be December 28, 1955.

21. *Kim Il Sung: Short Biography*, pp. 118–119.

30. Ibid., p. 119.

31. Natsios, op. cit., pp. 41–42.

32. Interview with Shim Jae Hoon, Seoul, Nov. 11, 1996.

33. Elich, op. cit., p. 6.

34. Natsios, op. cit., p. 85.

35. *Focus: Asia Pacific,* Dec. 2000

36. Erik Cornell, *North Korea Under Communism: Report of an Envoy to Paradise*, London and New York: Routledge Curzon, 2002, p. 45.

37. Grace Lee, "The Political Philosophy of Juche," *Stanford Journal of East Asian Affairs*, vol. 3, no. 1, Spring 2003, p. 108.

38. Bruce Cumings, *Korea's Place in the Sun: A Modern History*, New York and London: W.W. Norton and Company, 1997, p. 110.

39. Ibid., p. 404.

40. *Korean Central News Agency*, Nov. 23, 1978. Quoted in ibid, p. 411.

41. *The Juche Idea and Man's Destiny*, Pyongyang: Foreign Languages Publishing House, 1989, pp. 66–67.

42. Ibid., p. 61. See also Kim Chang Ha, *The Immortal Juche Idea*, Foreign languages Publishing House, 1984.

43. Ilpyong J. Kim, op. cit., p. 124.

44. Ibid., pp. 63–64.

45. Kim Jong Il, *On the Juche Philosophy*, Pyongyang: Foreign Languages Publishing House, 2002, p. 80.

46. See, for instance, Brian Hook (ed.), *The Cambridge Encyclopedia of China*, Cambridge, London, New York, New Rochelle, Melbourne, Sydney: Cambridge University Press, 1982, p. 113.

47. Cornell, op. cit., p. 119.

48. *White Paper on Human Rights in North Korea*, Seoul: Korea Institute for National Unification, 2001, p. 35.

49. Natsios, op. cit., p. 208. South Korean sources give other percentages for the three classes: The "core class," about 30 percent; the "wavering class," 45 percent; and the "hostile class," about 27 (or 25) percent, *White Paper on Human Rights in North Korea*, pp. 34–35.

50. Helen-Louise Hunter, *Kim Il-song's North Korea*, Westport, Connecticut, and London: Praeger, 1999, pp. 111 and 214.

51. Hunter, op. cit., p. 19.

52. Lee, op. cit., p. 111.

53. Quoted in Hunter, op. cit., pp. 17 and 19.

54. Hans Maretzki, *Kim-ismus in Nordkorea: Analyse des letzten DDR-Botschafters in Pjöngjang, Böblingen* (Germany): Anita Tykve Verlag, 1991, p. 110.

55. Hunter, op. cit., p. 18.

56. Dae-sook Suh (Suh Dae Sook), *Kim Il Sung: The North Korean Leader*, New York: Columbia University Press, 1988, p. 317.

57. I visited the Tower of the Juche Idea on April 18, 2004, and also took the elevator to the top.

58. Natsios, op. cit., p. 166.

59. Ibid., pp. 167–168.

60. Interview with Richard Ragan, country director of the World Food Program, Pyongyang, April 19, 2004.

61. Ibid., p. 192.

62. Ibid., p. 86.

63. Ibid., pp. 175–176.

64. Ilpyong J. Kim, op. cit., p. 40.

65. Natsios, op. cit., p. 172.

66. Fiona Terry, "Feeding the Dictator," *Guardian*, Aug. 6, 2001.

67. Noland, op. cit., p. 11.

68. Ibid., p. 13.

69. Press Release from the International Federation for Human Rights, FIDH: "Misery and Terror: Systematic Violations of Economic, Social and Cultural Rights in North Korea," Dec. 19, 2003.

70. Ibid., p. 13.

71. Interview with Ragan and other WFP officials, Pyongyang, April 19, 2004.

72. Interviews with WFP officials and foreign diplomats, Pyongyang, April 19, 2004.

73. Quoted in ibid., p. 98.

74. Interviews with Park Yong and Kim Chul Yong, North Korean refugees, Seoul, July 26, 2003.

75. Ilpyong J. Kim, op. cit., p. 42.

76. According to several foreigners I met in Pyongyang in April 2004.

77. Quoted in Natsios, op. cit., p. 99.

78. Ibid., p. 99.

79. Philo Kim, op. cit., pp. 158–159.

80. Ibid., p. 160.

81. *Kim Il Sung: Condensed Biography*, Pyongyang: Foreign Languages Publishing House, 2001, p. 284.

82. Interview with Song Du Yul, Berlin, Aug. 28, 2003.

83. Noland, op. cit., p. 26.

CHAPTER 3 THE GREAT AND DEAR LEADERS

1. Andrei Lankov, *From Stalin to Kim Il Sung: The Formation of North Korea, 1945–1960*, New Brunswick, New Jersey: Rutgers University Press, 2002, p. 54. Lankov, a Russian who was an exchange student in North Korea in 1984–85, says that some sources give other dates for Kim Il Sung's crossing into the Soviet Union. His date, December 1940, is based on an interview with N.G. Lebedev, a Soviet political officer who stayed with the Koreans in Siberia during the war. Local historians in the Russian Far East mentioned the same date when I visited Khabarovsk and Vyatskoye in May 2003. However, Suh Dae Sook, the author of an outstanding biography of Kim Il Sung, gives a different date for Kim Il Sung's retreat into the Soviet Union. He says that he arrived there soon after the death of his Chinese comrade Wei Zhengmin on March 8, 1941. But by that date, Kim Il Sung was most certainly already in the Soviet Union. Lankov, however, suggests that Kim Il Sung crossed the Amur River into the Soviet Union. But the Amur forms the border more than 700 kilometers north of Vladivostok. It is unlikely that the guerrillas had trekked that far from their bases along the Manchurian-Korean frontier.

2. Lankov, op. cit., p. 55.

3. Before World War II broke out in Europe, Japanese and the Soviet forces had fought fierce battles near a river called Khalkhin Gol or Nomonhan on the Mongolia-Manchukuo (Manchuria) border. Japanese troops marched into Siberia in May 1939, but were stopped by the Soviets in July. The Hitler-Stalin pact of August 1939 brought the fighting to an end and led to a Soviet-Japanese dÈtente as well. On April 13, 1941, a formal Soviet-Japanese Neutrality Pact was signed, which even survived the collapse of the Hitler-Stalin

pact. See John J. Stephen, *The Russian Far East: A History*, Stanford, California: Stanford University Press, 1994, pp. 235–236.

4. Interview with Tatiana Kirpichenko (chief of the Department of Local Research and Studies at the Far Eastern State Scientific Library in Khabarovsk), Vyatskoye, May 15, 2003,

5. A Russian army officer showed me the ruins of Kim Il Sung's command post, and what remained of the trenches and the air strip in Vyatskoye in May 2003.

6. Interview with Kirpichenko, Vyatskoye, May 14, 2003.

7. See Lankov, op. cit., p. 56, and Suh Dae Sook (Dae-sook Suh), *Kim Il Sung: The North Korean Leader*, New York: Columbia University Press, 1988, p. 50.

8. Alexej Klimentyevitch Cherny, *Ostayus Dalnevostochnikom* (in Russian; "I will always be a Far Easterner"), Khabarovsk: Etnos DV, 1998, p. 223.

9. Lankov, op. cit., p. 57, and interviews with Kirpichenko as well as local villagers in Vyatskoye, May 14, 2003.

10. Interview with Augustina Vardugina, Vyatskoye, May 14, 2003.

11. Interview with Kirpichenko, Vyatskoye, May 14, 2003.

12. Suh, op. cit., p. 334.

13. *Kim Il Sung: Condensed Biography*, Pyongyang: Foreign Languages Publishing House, 2001, p. 94.

14. Ibid, p. 95, and *Kim Il Sung: Short Biography, Vol. 1*, Pyongyang: Foreign Languages Publishing House, 1973, p. 267.

15. Peter Carlson, "Sins of the Son: Kim Jong Il's North Korea Is in Ruins, But Why Should that Spoil His Fun?" *Washington Post*, May 11, 2003.

16. Kim Gang Il, *The Leader Kim Jong Il*, Pyongyang: Foreign Languages Publishing House, 1990, p. 3.

17. See, for instance, *Kim Il Sung: Short Biography, Vol. 1*, p. 293.

18. For a picture of the log cabin and "information" about the slogans on the trees, see http://www.vnc.nl/korea/pkt-ss.htm. See also http://www.simonbone.com/pyongyang.html

19. *Korean Central News Agency* (Pyongyang), "Slogan-bearding trees praising Kim Jong Suk," Dec. 24, 1999.

20. Quoted in Stanislav Glukmov, "The Biggest Secret of the Democratic People's Republic of Korea: Kim Jong Il is Our Fellow Countryman;" *Khabarovski Express* (weekly in Russian), Feb. 21–28, 2001.

21. Lankov, op. cit., p. 55.

22. Selig Harrison, *Korean Endgame: A Strategy for Reunification and U.S. Disengagement*, Princeton and Oxford: Princeton University Press, 2002, p. 13.

23. Robert Scalapino and Chong-sik Lee, *Communism in Korea: The Movement*, Seoul: Ilchokak under the auspices of the Center for Japanese and Korean Studies, University of California, Berkeley, 1992, p. 222. The village was then called Pojon, but was renamed Pochonbo after 1945.

24. Suh, op. cit., p. 52.

25. Scalapino and Lee, op. cit., p. 227. See also Suh, op. cit., p. 52, and Hans Maretzki, *Kim-ismus in Nordkorea: Analyse des letzten DDR-Botschafter in Pjöngjang*, Böblingen: Anita Thyke Verlag, 1991, p. 14.

26 "North Korea Today, for American Eyes Only (G-2, American Army Forces in Korea, August, 1947)," in *An Anthology of Selected Pieces from the Declassified File of Secret U.S. Materials in Korea Before and During the Korean War*, Seoul: National Reunification Board, 1981. Referred to in Lankov, op. cit., p. 55.

27. Scalapino and Lee, op. cit., p. 228.

28. Lankov, op. cit., p. 55. See also Scalapino and Lee, op. cit., p. 227: "There is no hard evidence that any such person (an "older" Kim Il Sung) ever existed."

29. Scalapino and Lee, op. cit., p. 324.

30. Ibid., p. 228.

31. Ibid., p. 228 and 206.

32. Lankov, op. cit., pp. 50–51.

33. Scalapino and Lee, op. cit., p. 204.

34. Suh, op. cit., p. 5.

35. Ibid., p. 6.

36. Lankov, op. cit., p. 52.

37. Scalapino and Lee, p. 205.

38. Ibid., p. 162.

39. *Kim Il Sung: Short Biography, Vol. 1*, p. 88.

40. Ibid. p. 139. See also Suh, op. cit., p. 12, and Scalapino and Lee, op. cit., p. 212.

41. Suh, op. cit., p. 15.

42. Scalapino and Lee, op. cit., p. 223.

43. I visited the old Korean area of Posiet southwest of Vladivostok in May 2003, and met several Koreans who had returned to the Far East from Central Asia. A good source was Yelisaveta Chun, a pediatrician at the local hospital in Kraskino, whom I interviewed there on May 22, 2003. Her parents were born in Posiet, but deported to Central Asia in 1937. Chun was born in Uzbekistan, and returned with her family to the Far East in 1993. See also Lee Kwang Yu, *Overseas Koreans*, Seoul: Jimoondang Publishing Company, 2000, pp. 140–142.

44. For a succinct account of this period in Korea's history, see Bruce Cumings, *Divided Korea: United Future*, Ithaca, New York: Foreign Policy Association, 1995, pp. 31–36, and Bruce Cumings, *Korea's Place in the Sun: A Modern History*, New York and London: W.W. Norton and Company, 1997, pp. 195–236.

45. For more detailed accounts of those four groups of Korean communists, see Lankov, op. cit., pp. 78–81, and Adrian Bozo, *The Guerrilla Dynasty: Politics and Leadership in North Korea*, Sydney: Allen and Unwin, 1999, pp. 13–15.

46. Lankov, op. cit., p. 144.

47. Suh, op. cit., p. 69.

48. Ibid., p. 89, and Lankov, op. cit., p. 87.

49. Lankov, op. cit., pp. 2–3, and Suh, op. cit., p. 62.

50. Lankov, op. cit., p. 127.

51. Suh, op. cit., p. 101.

52. Ibid., p. 102.

53. Lankov, p. cit.. p. 38.

54. Cumings, *Divided Korea: United Future?*, p. 35.

55. Cumings, *Korea's Place in the Sun*, p. 290.

56. Lankov, op. cit., p. 91.

57. Ibid., p. 150.

58. Ibid., p. 95.

59. Ibid., p. 97.

60. Ibid., pp. 100–101, and Suh, op. cit., pp. 134–136

61. Lankov, op. cit., p. 101.

62. Ibid., p. 38.

63. Suh, op. cit., p. 149, and Ilpyong Kim, op. cit., pp. 10–11.

64. For a detailed account of the 1956 crisis, see Lankov, pp. 154–193. See also Suh, op. cit., pp. 149–157, and Ilpyong Kim, op. cit., pp. 10–11.

65. *Kim Il Sung: Short Biography II*, Pyongyang: Foreign Languages Publishing House, 1973, p. 131.

66. Scalapino and Lee, p. 463, and Lankov, op. cit., p. 103.

67. Lankov, p. 102.

68. Ilpyong Kim, op. cit., p. 23.

69. Cumings, *Korea's Place in the Sun*, p. 413.

70. For a background to North Korea's *vinalon* industry, see *Korea in the 20ᵗʰ Century: 100 Significant Events*, Pyongyang: Foreign Languages Publishing House, 2002, p. 130.

71. "Juche (Self-reliance) Fiber Vinalon," *Chosun Ilbo*, April 29, 2001.

72. Cumings, *Korea's Place in the Sun*, pp. 423–425,

73. *Kim Il Sung: Short Biography I*, pp. 1–6.

74. Suh, op. cit., p. 279.

75. Kim Ok Sun, *Kim Jong Suk: The Anti–Japanese Heroine*, Pyongyang: Foreign Languages Publishing House, 1997, pp. 75–77.

76. Suh, op. cit., p. 5

77. I visited Mangyongdae on April 15, 2004. See also Erik Cornell, *North Korea Under Communism: Report of an Envoy to Paradise*, London and New York: Routledge Cutzon, 2002, p. 123.

78. Ibid., p. 26.

79. See Martezki, op. cit., in which there are several references to "der grosse Führer."

80. Cornell, op. cit., p. 88.

81. *Tangun: Founder-King of Korea*, Pyongyang: Foreign Languages Publishing House, 1994, p. 65.

82. Ibid., p. 65, and *Pyongyang Review*, Pyongyang: Foreign Languages Publishing House, 1995, p. 27.

83. *Tangun: Founder-King of Korea*, p. 134.

84. Ibid., p. 30.

85. Ilpyong Kim, op. cit., pp. 130–131.

86. Suh, op. cit., p. 280.

87. Aidan Foster-Carter, "Freedom Fighter or Traitor?" *Asia Times* (online), Oct. 9, 2003, and "Indictment of Song Du Yul," *Korea Times*, Nov. 20, 2003.

88. Interview with Song Du Yul, Berlin, August 28, 2003. During this interview, Song Du Yul told me that the 1991 visit to Pyongyang was his first visit to North Korea, and that he had only traveled to the country on one more occasion, Kim Il Sung's funeral in 1994. This was obviously not true, and it was only later clear that I had actually interviewed an alternate member of the KWP's politburo.

89. Interview with Song Du Yul, August 28, 2003.

90. Ilpyong Kim, op. cit., p. 115.

91. Suh, op. cit., p. 191.

92. Ibid., pp. 197–202.

93. Don Oberdorfer, *The Two Koreas: A Contemporary History*, New York: Basic Books, 1997, p. 150

94. Ilpyong Kim, op. cit., p. 132.

95. I visited the Kumsusan Memorial Palace on April 15, 2004. See also *Korea in the 20th Century: 100 Significant Events*, Pyongyang: Foreign Languages Publishing House, 2002: "the Kumsusan area [has been] rebuilt into the most sacred temple of Juche." (p. 161.)

96. Cumings, *Korea's Place in the Sun*, p. 416.

97. Ibid., p. 75.

98. Cumings, *Korea's Place in the Sun*, p. 416.

99. Cumings, *Divided Korea: United Future*, p. 55.

100. Suh, op. cit., p. 284. Martezki, the last East German ambassador to Pyongyang, denies that Kim Jong Il underwent any schooling or other training in East Germany. Maretzki, op. cit., p 56.

101. Suh, op. cit., p. 284.

102. Op. cit., p. 284, and Ilpyong Kim, op. cit., pp. 102–103.

103. Suh, op. cit., p. 386.

104. *Korea Annual 2002*, Seoul: Yonhap News Agency, 2002, p. 834.

105. Suh, op. cit., p. 242.

106. Suh, op. cit., p. 193.

107. Roald Savelyev, "Leadership in North Korea and the Nuclear Program," in James Clay Moltz and Alexandre Mansourov (eds.), *The North Korean Nuclear Program: Security, Strategy, and New Perspectives from Russia*, New York and London: Routledge, 2000, p. 116.

108. Ilpyong Kim, op. cit., p. 132.

109. According to BBC video tapes of the summit, which are in my possession.

110. *Agence-France Presse*, Tokyo July 24, 2003, "Kim's Sushi Chef Goes Underground." In 2003, the chef, who uses the pseudonym Kenji Fujimoto, published a book (in Japanese) about his experiences in North Korea entitled

"Kim Jong Il's Chef." See also "I Was Kim Jong Il's Cook," *Atlantic Monthly*, Feb. 2004 (excerpts from Fujimoto's book translated from the Japanese by Makiko Kitamura.)

111. James Brooke, "Kim Jong Il, the *bon vivant*," *New York Times*, Dec. 4, 2002.

112. Although Konstantin Pulikovsky is named as the author of the book, it was actually written by two Vladivostok-based Russian journalists. I met both of them in Vladivostok in May 2003. On condition of anonymity, they told me about the book and their own meetings with Kim Jong Il.

113. Suh, op. cit., p. 284.

114. Martezki, op. cit., p. 109.

115. Mike Thomson, "Kidnapped by North Korea," *BBC News*, March 5, 2003.

116. "North Korean movies' Propaganda Role," *BBC News*, Aug. 18, 2003.

117. *BBC News*, March 5, 2003.

CHAPTER 4 THE ARMY AND THE PARTY

1. Teruaki Ueno, "North Korea Hails Army and 'Impregnable Fortress.'" *Reuters* (Pyongyang), April 25, 2002.

2. "U.S. Slammed as 'Empire of devil.'" *Reuters* (Seoul), Feb. 8, 2003.

3. Wayne Kirkbride, *North Korea's Undeclared War; 1953–*, Seoul, New Jersey: Hollym, 1994, p. 30.

4. Ibid., p. 30.

5. Alex Vatanka, "North Korea Special Report," *Jane's Sentinel*, Feb. 20, 2003, p. 39.

6. Suh Dae Sook, "Military First Politics of Kim Jong Il," *Asian Perspective* (Kyungnam University, South Korea), vol. 26, no. 3, 2002.

7. *Korea Central News Agency*, Pyongyang, Feb. 15, 2001.

8. Suh, op. cit.

9. Ibid.

10. Ibid.

11. Don Oberdorfer, *The Two Koreas: A Contemporary History*, New York: Basic Books, 1997, p. 237

12. Vatanka, op. cit., p. 23.

13. "North Korea Conjures up Magic Circle," *Reuters* (Seoul) Oct. 25, 2001.

14. Ilpyong Kim, *Historical Dictionary of North Korea*, Lanham, Maryland and Oxford: Scarecrow Press, 2003, p. 81.

15. Helen-Louise Hunter, *Kim Il-song's North Korea*, Westport, Connecticut: Praeger, 1999, pp. 48–49.

16. I visited the Mangyongdae Schoolchildren's Palace on April 17, 2004.

17. Sung Chul Yang, *The North and South Korean Political Systems: A Comparative Analysis*, Elizabeth, New Jersey, and Seoul: Hollym, 1999, p. 223.

18. Vatanka, op. cit., p. 23.

19. Robert Scalapino and Chong-sik Lee, *Communism in Korea: The Society*, Berkeley, Los Angeles and London: University of California Press, 1972, pp. 793–794.

20. John Feffer, *North Korea, South Korea: U.S. Policy at a Time of Crisis*, New York: Seven Stories Press, p. 59.

21. *Korea Central News Agency*, Pyongyang, July 8, 2001.

22. *Korea Central News Agency*, Pyongyang, April 17, 2002.

23. *Reuters*, Seoul, April 17, 2002.

24. Vatanka, op. cit., p. 39.

25. Kongdan Oh and Ralph Hassig, *North Korea Through the Looking Glass*, Washington D.C.: Brookings Institution Press, 2000, p. 105.

26. Joseph Bermudez, *Shield of the Great Leader: The Armed Forces of North Korea*, Sydney: Allen and Unwin, 2001, p. 83.

27. Hunter, op. cit., p. 131.

28. Vatanka, op. cit., p. 79.

29. Bermudez, op. cit., p. 84.

30. Ibid., p. 83.

31. Kirkbride, op. cit., p. 58.

32. Interviews with WFP officials, Pyongyang, April 19, 2004.

33. "North Korean Agencies," http://exastriscientia.fateback.com/northkorea.htm

34. Vatanka, op. cit., p. 77.

35. Ibid., p. 79.

36. Vatanka, op. cit., p. 77.

37. Suh Jae Jean, "Class Conflict and Regime Crisis in North Korea," in Moon Chung In, ed., *Understanding Regime Dynamics in North Korea*, Seoul: Yonsei University Press, p. 207.

38. According to Pyongyang residents I met there in April 2004.

39. Bermudez, op. cit., p. 182.

40. Roald Savelyev, "Leadership Politics in North Korea and the Nuclear Program," in James Clay Moltz and Alexandre Mansourov, *The North Korean Nuclear Program: Security, Strategy, and New Perspectives from Russia*, New York and London: Routledge, 2000, p. 116. See also Selig Harrison, *Korean Endgame: A Strategy for Reunification and U.S. Disengagement*, Princeton and Oxford: Princeton University Press, 2002, p. 61. Harrison says that Chang Song Taek has three influential brothers: Chang Song Woo, Chang Song Kil, and Chang Song U. However, Chang Song Woo is just another spelling of Chang Song U.

41. Gordon Fairclough, "Kim Clan," *Wall Street Journal*, Oct. 9, 2003.

42. This is a summary of discussions I held with several foreign residents in Pyongyang, April 2004.

43. All accounts of Kim Jong Il's wives, mistresses, and children are very sketchy and often unreliable. The details here come from a variety of sources, for instance a long article about Kim Jong Il and his family in the Oct. 9, 2002 issue of the *Sapio* magazine (Japan), and a book in Korean written by

Lee Young Gook, a former bodyguard of Kim Jong Il, and published by Sidaejungsin in Seoul in 2002.

44. An English translation of the article is available at http://www.kimsoft. com/1997/namok.htm

45. Aidan Foster-Carter, "Whither the Web?" *Asia Times* (online), March 1, 2001, John Larkin, *AsiaInt* press release Sept. 7, 2001, and John Larkin, "Preparing for Cyberwar," *Far Eastern Economic Review*, Oct. 25, 2001.

46. Adriana Lee, "Secret Lives," *Time* (Asia), June 30, 2003.

47. "Second Son Being Groomed as Heir Apparent," *Chosun Ilbo*, Feb. 18, 2003.

48. Ibid.

49. "Kim's Sushi Chef Goes Underground," *Agence France-Presse* (Tokyo), July 24, 2003.

50.*Wall Street Journal*, Oct. 9, 2003.

51. *Far Eastern Economic Review*, Oct. 25, 2001.

52. Sarah Buckley, "North Korea's Secretive 'First Family.'" *BBC News* (online), Oct. 29, 2003.

53. Suh, op. cit.

54. Ibid.

55. Ibid.

CHAPTER 5 THE MISSILES AND THE NUKES

1. The story was first reported in the Slovak daily *Sme*, Sept. 6, 2002. See also Bertil Lintner and Steve Stecklow, "Murky Trail Shows How Arms Trade Helps North Korea," *Wall Street Journal*, Feb. 6, 2003, and Bertil Lintner and Steve Stecklow, "Paper Trail Exposes Missile Merchants," *Far Eastern Economic Review*, Feb. 13, 2003. That story was the result of a four-month investigation which I did in October 2002–January 2004.

2. Ibid.

3. "Staats Schutzbericht: Nachrichtendienste Nordkoreas," Vienna, Austria, 1997 report, 7.1. A second, more recent Austrian police report ("Verfassungsschutzbericht 2001: Staats-, Personen- und Objektschutz," Bundesministerium für Inneres, Vienna, Sept. 2002) also expressed concern about the presence of the bank in Vienna, but no one has been able to close it down.

4. *Sme*, Sept. 6, 2002

5. *Far Eastern Economic Review*, Feb. 13, 2003.

6. *Wall Street Journal*, Feb. 6, 2003, *Far Eastern Economic Review*, Feb. 13, 2003., and interview with Western diplomat who insisted on anonymity, Bangkok, Jan. 10, 2003.

7. Communication with Joseph Bermudez, Jan. 17, 2003.

8. Interview with Western diplomat, Bangkok, Jan. 10, 2003.

9. Ibid.

10. Quoted in Joseph Bermudez, *Shield of the Great Leader: The Armed Forces of North Korea*, Sydney: Allen and Unwin, 2001, p. 238.

11. Ibid., p. 249, and *Wall Street Journal*, Feb. 6, 2003.

12. Bermudez, *Shield of the Great Leader*, p. 252.

13. Ibid., p. 253.

14. Ibid., p. 262. The Rodong missile is more commonly known in the West by its South Korean spelling, Nodong. The word means "labor" and is always spelled with an "r" in the North, for instance in *Rodong Shinmun*, the party newspaper.

15. Douglas Jehl, "Iran Is Reported Acquiring Missiles," *New York Times*, April 8, 1993.

16. Bermudez, *Shield of the Great Leader*, pp. 252–253.

17. For an excellent overview of relations between North Korea and Pakistan, see Joseph Bermudez, "Ghauri Missile Cooperation," paper dated May 21, 1998.

18. Bermudez, *Shield of the Great Leader*, p. 271.

19. "Pakistan Denies Report of Nuclear Deal with North Korea," *Agence-France Presse*, Islamabad, Nov 25, 2002.

20. David Sanger and James Dao, "U.S. Says Pakistan Gave Technology to North Korea," *New York Times*, Oct. 18, 2002.

21. "My Enemy's Enemy," *Economist*, Oct. 4, 2003.

22. Julian West, "Pakistan Murder Exposes Nuclear Link," *Sunday Telegraph* (London), Nov. 1, 1998.

23. *Times of India*, Sept. 30, 1999,and Ranjit Devraj, "North Korea: China Also to Blame, Reminds India," *Asia Times* (online), Oct. 23, 2003.

24. Communication with an Asian diplomat who was based in Islamabad at the time of the murder, April 20, 2003. See also *Sunday Telegraph*, Nov. 1, 1998.

25. *New York Times*, Jan. 24, 2004.

26. The *Economist* wrote in its Feb. 14, 2004 issue: "Many Pakistanis are convinced that Mr. Khan has been used as a scapegoat to shield the army and intelligence hierarchy from the proliferation scandal."

27. "Khan Gave Secrets to Iran, North Korea," *Agence France-Presse*, Islamabad, Feb. 2, 2004.

28. David Sanger and William Broad, "High Praise for Gen. Musharraf," *New York Times News Service*, Feb. 7, 2004.

29. Alex Vatanka, "North Korea: Special Report," *Jane's Sentinel Security Assessment*, Feb. 20, 2003, p. 46.

30. Bruce Cumings, *Korea's Place in the Sun: A Modern History*, New York and London: W.W. Norton and Company, 1997, p. 290.

31. Natalya Bazhanova, "North Korea's Decision to Develop an Independent Nuclear Program," in James Clay Moltz and Alexandre Mansourov, eds., *The North Korean Nuclear Program: Security, Strategy, and New Perspectives from Russia*, London and New York: Routledge, 2000, p. 16

32. Quoted in ibid., p. 45, and in Bermudez, *Shield of the Great Leader*, p. 213.

33. Georgiy Kaurov, "A Technical History of Soviet-North Korean Nuclear Relations," in Moltz and Mansourov, op. cit., p. 16.

34. Ibid., p. 16.

35. Larry Niksch, "North Korea's Nuclear Weapons Program," Library of Congress, Congressional Research Service, updated Nov. 5, 2003, p. 6.

36. Georgiy Kaurov in Moltz and Mansourov, op. cit., p. 16.

37. Larry Niksch, "North Korea's Nuclear Weapons Program," Library of Congress, Congressional Research Service, Washington, Jan. 22, 2003, p. 5.

38. Alexander Zhebin, "A Political History of Soviet-North Korean Nuclear Cooperation," in Moltz and Mansourov, op. cit., p. 36.

39. Kaurov in Moltz and Mansourov, op. cit., p. 19.

40. Ibid., p. 16.

41. Larry Niksch, "North Korea's Nuclear Weapons Program," p. 8.

42. Ibid., p. 7.

43. Zhebin in Moltz and Mansourov, op. cit., p. 35.

44. Valery Denisov,"Nuclear Institutions and Organizations in North Korea," in Moltz and Mansourov, op. cit., p. 25.

45. Bermudez, *Shield of the Great Leader*, p. 216.

46. Kaurov in Moltz and Mansourov, op. cit., p. 16.

47. Zhebin in Moltz and Mansourov, op. cit., p. 36.

48. Bermudez, *Shield of the Great Leader*, p. 215.

49. Ibid., p. 220.

50. Vatanka, op. cit., p. 50.

51. *Proletären,* no 42/2003 (Oct. 17, 2003). *Proletären* is published by a small Swedish party called the Communist Party Marxist-Leninists (the Revolutionaries), which maintains close links with North Korea.

52. Siegfried Hecker, "Senate Committee on Foreign Relations Hearings on 'Visit to the Yongbyon Nuclear Research Center in North Korea,'" Jan. 21, 2004.

53. Peter Landers, Susan Lawrence and Julian Baum, "Hard Target," *Far Eastern Economic Review*, Sept. 24, 1998

54. Bermudez, *Shield of the Great Leader*, p. 280. Other sources say the missile flew 1,380 km from the North Korean coast (Shim Jae Hoon, "Fire, Backfire," *Far Eastern Economic Review*, Sept. 10, 1998.)

55. Ibid., p. 282.

56. Ibid., pp. 225–228. See also Vatanka, op. cit., p. 52.

57. Ibid., p. 231.

58. Ibid., p. 231.

59. Ibid., p. 233.

60. Ibid., p. 234.

61. Vatanka, op. cit., p. 54.

62. Aidan Foster-Carter, "Analysis: North Korea's Move," *BBC News* (online), April 16, 2003.

63. Donald MacIntyre, "Kim's War Machine," *Time* (Asia), Feb. 24, 2003.

64. Analysis by Bazhanova in Moltz and Mansourov, op. cit., p. 137.

65. "North Korea Using Missile Threat to Pry Economic Gains From Japan," *Korea Herald*, Aug. 27, 1999.

66. *British Broadcasting Corporation*, "Profile: Abdul Qadeer Khan," Dec. 23, 2003. Dr. Khan was born in Bhopal, India, in 1935 and emigrated to Pakistan in 1952, following the partition of the Subcontinent five years earlier. He graduated from the University of Karachi before moving to Europe for further studies in West Germany and Belgium. In the 1970s, Dr. Khan worked at a uranium enrichment plant run by the British-Dutch-German consortium Urenco. He returned to Pakistan in 1976 and Zulfikar Ali Bhutto almost immediately put in charge of the nation's nuclear program. In 2003, the U.S. imposed sanctions on his Khan Research Laboratories for the alleged transfer of missile technology from North Korea.

CHAPTER 6   THE MISSIONS

1. John Brown, "North Korean Envoys in Stand-off After Harboring Wanted Man," *Phnom Penh Post*, April 5–18, 1996.

2. Ibid.

3. Helen-Louise Hunter, *Kim Il-song's North Korea*, Westport, Connecticut, and London: Preager, 1999, p. 88, and interview with Julio Jeldres, Sihanouk's official biographer, Bangkok, March 27, 2003. Jeldres stayed with Sihanouk in his North Korean residence on several occasions in the 1980s and 1990s.

4. Interview with Julio Jeldres, March 27, 2003.

5. Hunter, op. cit., p. 27.

6. "Note For the Record," *Cabinet de Samdech Norodom Sihanouk*, Pyongyang, April 12, 1986.

7. Patrick Falby and Lon Nara, "Fish Hijack Ship Not Really Ours—Government," *Phnom Penh Post*, Nov. 22–Dec. 5, 2002.

8. Kim Gooi, "Lost Passports Lands Malaysian in Center of International Counterfeit Probe," *Nation* (Bangkok), May 2, 1997, and communication with Kim Gooi (now in Penang, Malaysia), Oct. 26, 2003.

9. Bill Bainbridge, "Ship Registry Award Sparks Controversy," *Phnom Penh Post*, Jan. 17–30, 2003.

10. Joseph Bermudez, *Terrorism: The North Korean Connection*, New York: Crane and Russack, 1990, p. 55.

11. Ibid., p. 88 and 123, and Bruce Hoffman, "Creatures of the Cold War: the JRA," *Jane's Intelligence Review*, Feb. 1997.

12. Bermudez, op. cit., p. 89.

13. Ibid., p. 94.

14. Ibid., p. 112.

15. Ibid, pp. 68–69.

16. Ibid., p. 71.

17. Ibid., p. 74.

18. Tore Forsberg, *Spioner och Spioner som Spionerar på Spioner*, Stockholm: Hjalmarson and Högberg, 2003, pp. 440–441, and 449. Forsberg is a retired special branch officer, who confirmed in the letter to the author in October 2003 that Carillo had indeed been trained in North Korea, but it was not clear exactly when.

19. Bermudez, op. cit., p. 80.

20. Matthew Vella, "Sex, English and Pianoforte—Kim's Maltese Holiday," *Malta Today*, July 27, 2003.

21. Bermudez, op. cit., pp. 129–130.

22. Bermudez, op. cit., p. 130. A Western Red Cross official met Kang Min Chul in Insein in 2000 and confirmed that he is in good health.

23. The whole story of the bombing is described by Kim Hyun Hee in her book, *The Tears of My Soul*, New York: William Morrow and Company, 1993.

24. Ibid., cover page.

25. Ibid., p. 110.

26. Bermudez, op. cit., p. 54.

27. Alexander Platkovskiy, "Nuclear Blackmail and North Korea's Search for a Place in the Sun," in James Clay Moltz and Alexandre Mansourov, *The North Korean Nuclear Program: Security, Strategy, and New Perspectives from Russia*, New York and London: Routledge, 2000, p. 95. Platkovskiy, however, says that forty thousand visitors attended the festival—and that it was held in August 1989, which is erroneous.

28. Kim Hyun Hee, op. cit., p. 69.

29. Interview with Pak Ku Po of Zokwang Trading, and another official who did not give his name, Macau, Sept. 12, 2001.

30. John Pomfret, "North Korea's Conduit for Crime," *New York Times*, April 25, 1999.

31. David Kaplan, "The Wiseguy Regime," *U.S. News and World Report*, Feb. 15, 1999.

32. "North Korea Perfects Fake Bills," *Far Eastern Economic Review*, March 6, 2003.

33. David Kaplan, "The Far East Sopranos," *U.S. News and World Report*, Jan. 27, 2003.

34. Bermudez, op. cit., p. 126.

35. Hunter, op. cit., p. 135.

36. For a detailed account of the 1976 smuggling crisis, see Erik Cornell, *North Korea Under Communism: Report of An Envoy to Paradise*, London and New York: Routledge Curzon, 2002, pp. 61–68.

37. Ibid., pp. 62–63.

38. Ibid., p. 67.

39. Raphael Perl, "North Korean Drug Trafficking: Allegations and Issues for Congress," Congressional Research Service, Library of Congress, Washington D.C., Sept. 14, 1999. Perl mentions "34 verifiable incidents involving drug seizures in at least 14 countries" but that was in 1999. The number of incidents is now about 50, see Anthony Speath, "Kim's Rackets,"

Time (Asia), June 9, 2003. The number of countries is 16, according to U.S. *News and World Report*, Feb. 16, 1999.

40. "Washington File: Congressional Report on North Korean Threat (House North Korea Advisory Group report), Nov. 3, 1999, and *Time* (Asia), June 9, 2003.

41. See introduction.

42. "Observers Disagree on How Official the North Korean Drug Trade Is," *Sydney Morning Herald*, May 5, 2003.

43. Burma's opium production is a matter of dispute. The United Nations Office on Drugs and Crime puts the 2002 figure at 820 tonnes, Sanong Chinnanon, "The Road to Opium Elimination in the Wa Special Region," *Eastern Horizons* (UNODC bulletin), March 2003. Other, independent estimates are higher as the UNODC does not have access to all opium-growing areas in Burma.

44. The United Nations has several "drug eradication programs" inside the UWSA-controlled territory along the Sino-Burmese border. See *Eastern Horizons*, March 2003.

45. Frank Downs, "Myanmar and North Korea: Birds of a feather?" *Asia-Pacific Defence Reporter*, vol. 29, no. 7 (Oct. 2003).

46. Hugh Williamson, "Land of Hunger Linked to Crime in Quest For Cash," *Gemini News Service*, Aug. 5, 1997.

47. "North Korean Drug Trafficking," Joint Interagency Task Force West Assessment, U.S. Department of Defense, May, 2000, p. 8.

48. Marcus Noland, "North Korea's External Economic Relations: Globalization in 'Our Own Style,'" in Samuel Kim and Tai Hwan Lee, *North Korea and Northeast Asia*, Lanham, Boulder, New York, Oxford: Rowman and Littlefield Publishers, p. 173.

49. Joseph Bermudez, "Criminalization of the Democratic People's Republic of Korea," *Jane's Intelligence Review*, March 2001.

50. Douglas Farah and Thomas Lippman, "The North Korean Con-nection," *Washington Post*, March 26, 1999.

51. Ilpyong Kim, *Historical Dictionary of North Korea*, Lanham, Maryland, and Oxford: The Scarecrow Press, 2003, p. 45.

52. I have a list of more then twenty such companies, but for legal reasons the names of those companies cannot be disclosed.

53. Jay Solomon and Hae Won Chi, "Mysterious Source of Kim's Power," *Wall Street Journal*, July 18, 2003.

54. "Kim Jong Il has Slush Fund of 2 Billion Dollars," *Korea Times*, Feb. 20, 2000.

55. The family-owned Macau bank cannot be named for legal reasons.

56. "North Korea's Financial Institutions," U.S. Embassy, Seoul, Flash Fax Document Number: 5711, April 1995.

57. Ibid. and *Time* (Asia), June 9, 2003.

58. Interview with Ri Do Sop, Hong Kong, Sept. 11, 2001.

59. Bertil Lintner, "The Macau Connection," *Far Eastern Economic Review*, Oct. 25, 2001.

60. Aidan Foster-Carter, "Beware of Defective Tales of Defectors," *Asia Times* (online), May 21, 2003, and "KCNA Refutes Sheer Lies Spread by South Korea," *Korean Central News Agency* (Pyongyang), May 19, 2003.

61. *Asia Times* (online), May 21, 2003, and "KCNA Refutes Sheer Lies Spread by South Korea," *Korean Central News Agency* (Pyongyang), May 19, 2003.

62. *Asia Times* (online) May 21, 2003, and "Watch Out, Kim Jong Il, the Heat is On!" *Association for Asian Research*, June 12, 2003.

63. Doug Struck, "Korean Scientists Defect in China," *Washington Post*, April 21, 2003.

64. State Department Daily Briefing, April 21, 2003, http://www.state.gov/r/pa/prs/dpb/2003/19778.htm

65. All these figures are from John Jennings, *The Opium Empire: Japanese Imperialism and Drug Trafficking in Asia, 1895–1945*, Westport, Connecticut and London: Praeger, 1997, pp. 34–37.

66. Raphael Perl, op. cit., p. 4. See also *Time* (Asia), June 9, 2003: "North Korea has anywhere from 4,200 to 7,000 hectares under poppy cultivation."

67. Bermudez, *Jane's Intelligence Review*, March 2001, and "North Korean Opium Seizure in Australia," *Asia Security Monitor*, April 21, 2003: "The U.S. State Department's annual report on the worldwide drugs trade claims that the North Korean regime cultivates opium illicitly, refines it into heroin, and also makes methamphetamines as a state-organized and state-directed activity aimed at earning revenue."

68. Raphael Perl, "Drug Trafficking and North Korea: Issues for U.S. Policy," Congressional Research Service, Library of Congress, Washington D.C., Dec. 5, 2003.

69. *Kyodo News Agency*, March 28, 2002.

70. *Korean Central News Agency* (Pyongyang), Oct. 30, 2003.

71. Stephen Lunn, "The Korean Connection," *Australian*, April 22, 2003.

72. Jay Solomon and Jason Dean, "North Korea: Heroin Busts Point To Source Of Funds For North," *Wall Street Journal*, April 23, 2003.

CHAPTER 7 THE CHONGRYUN

1. "Sweeping Anti-Chongryun Campaign in Japan," *People's Korea*, Dec. 13, 2001.

2. Masakazu Honda, "Cold War Relic?: Under Fire," *Asahi Shimbun*, Sept. 27, 2002.

3. "Koreans Suffer Attacks, Blackmail Due to Abductions Issue," *People's Korea*, Oct. 12, 2002.

4. Unmesh Kher, "Accounted for, at Last," *Time* (Asia), Sept. 30, 2002.

5. "North Korea High-Tech Espionage," *Mednews*, March 22, 1993. See also Bertil Lintner, "It's Hard to Help Kim Jong Il," *Far Eastern Economic Review*, March 27, 2003, and "General Association of Korean Residents in Japan

(Chosen Soren)," *FAS Intelligence Resource Program*, http://www.fas.org/irp/world/dprk/chosen_soren/

6. "Facts About Chongryun," *People's Korea*, 1997. http://pk/003rd_issue/chongryun/contents.htm

7. Ibid.

8. Interview with Kum Ki Do of the Chongryun's international affairs department in Kyoto, Kyoto, Feb. 24, 2003. I visited Osaka, Kyoto, and Tokyo in February 2003 and interviewed several current and former members of the Chongryun. See also "Japanese Bank to Suspend Remittances to Pyongyang," *NK.Chosun.com*, April 3, 2002, and *Far Eastern Economic Review*, March 27, 2003.

9. Mary Jordan and Kevin Sullivan, "Pinball Wizards Fuel North Korea," *Washington Post*, June 7, 1996.

10. Nicholas Walker, "The Year Pachinko Blinked," *Asahi Shimbun*, Jan. 1, 1997.

11. For a background to the Koreans in Japan, see Michael Weiner, "Narratives of Exclusion: Korean *hibakusha*," in Michael Weiner, ed., *Japan's Minorities: The Illusion of Homogeneity*, London and New York: Routledge, 1997, pp. 79–107; "Japan's Minorities: Burakumin, Koreans, Ainu," Report 3, 1974, Minority Rights Group, London; and Sonia Ryang, *North Koreans in Japan: Language, Ideology, and Identity*, Boulder, Colorado: Westview Press, 1997, pp. 6 and 80.

12. Ryang, op. cit., pp. 2 and 89.

13. Ibid., p. 90.

14. Ibid., p. 90.

15. Ibid., p. 88.

16. Aidan Foster-Carter, "'North Koreans in Japan: A Dying Breed?" *Asia Times* (online), March 17, 2001.

17. For short biography of Han Duk Su, see "Chairman Han Duk Su of Chongryun Passes Away," Special issue, *People's Korea*, 2001.

18. See picture in Ryang, op. cit., after p. 67.

19. Ibid., pp. 102–103.

20. Ibid., p. 107.

21. Ibid., p. 94.

22. "Laments from North Korea," *Life and Human Rights* (the Society to Help Returnees to North Korea/Citizens' Alliance to Help Political Prisoners in North Korea, Seoul), New Year, 1997.

23. Kang Chol Hwan, *Aquariums of Pyongyang: Ten Years in the North Korean Gulag*, New York: Basic Books, 2001, p. 23.

24. Ryang, op. cit., p. 113. Ryang says a total of about 82,000 Koreans and 6,000 Japanese citizens (most of them Japanese wives of Koreans) were repatriated. According to *Life and Human Rights*, 93,000 Koreans and 1,831 Japanese wives went to North Korea from 1959 to 1967.

25. Ibid., p. 98, and interview with Sonia Ryang, Baltimore, Feb. 14, 2003.

26. Donald MacIntyre and Sachiko Sakamaki, "Squeezing the Little Guy," *Time* (Asia), Dec. 6, 1999.

27. Ryang, op. cit., pp. 89–91.

28. For a detailed account of the assassination attempt and its immediate aftermath, see Don Oberdorfer, *The Two Koreas: A Contemporary History*, New York: Basic Books, 1997, pp. 47–55.

29. Ryang, op. cit., p. 100.

30. *Time* (Asia), Dec. 6, 1999.

31. Nicholas Eberstadt, "Financial Transfers from Japan to the DPRK: Estimating the Unreported Flows." Paper, undated, but written in the late 1990s.

32. *Time* (Asia), Dec. 6, 1999.

33. Eberstadt, op. cit.

34. Emily Tornton, "Lady Luck Is Frowning on Pachinko: The Vast Pinball Gambling Industry Looks Set For a Long Decline," *Business Week*, Sept. 8, 1997.

35. Ryang, op. cit., pp. 104–105.

36. Interview with former *Gakushu-gumi* member who insisted on anonymity, Tokyo, Feb. 22, 2003.

37. "The Weekly Post Special: Passenger Liner Smuggled (U.S.)$2.5 Billion from Japan to North Korea," *Weekly Post* (Japan), Dec. 2–8, 2002.

38. Ibid.

39. Ibid.

40. Ibid.

41. Interviews with former Chongryun members, Tokyo, Feb. 22, 2003.

42. Sebastian Moffett and Shawn Crispin, "Japan Suspects Firm Has Ties With Pyongyang," *Asian Wall Street Journal*, May 13, 2003.

43. Eberstadt, op. cit.

44. Interview with Kim Hyeon Il of the Chongryun's student organization, Kyoto, Feb. 24, 2003.

45. Sonia Ryang also emphasized this aspect of the changing attitudes of the Chongryun Koreans, interview, Baltimore, Feb. 14, 2003.

46. Ryang, op. cit., p. 127.

47. Ibid., p. 127.

48. See Donald Ranard (the son of the State Department official with the same name), "Kim Dae Jung's Close Call: a Tale of Three Dissidents." *Washington Post*, Feb. 26, 2003.

49. Interview with Kim Hyon, ex-Chongryun member, Tokyo, Feb. 22, 2003.

50. "Tokyo Police Raid N Korea HQ," *BBC News*, Nov. 29, 2001.

51. "Sweeping Anti-Chongryun Campaign in Japan; Ethnic Banks' Bankruptcy Develops into Political Repression," *People's Korea*, Dec. 13, 2001.

52. *Time* (Asia), Dec. 6, 1999.

53. "Chongryun Schools to Ax Kim Portraits," *Asahi Shimbun*, Sept. 10, 2002.

54. Booyeon Lee, "For Parents, Sudents, Heritage Trumps a Fading Ideology," *Asahi Shimbun*, Nov., 8, 2002. See also Ryang, op. cit., p. 24.

55. *Asahi Shimbun*, Sept. 27, 2002.

56. Interview with Kum Ki Do, Kyoto, Feb. 24, 2003.

57. Ibid.

58. Boonyeon Lee, "Korean Students Rally Against U.S.," *Asahi Shimbun*, Dec. 23, 2002.

59. *Far Eastern Economic Review*, March 27, 2003. See also http://www. vuw.ac.nz/~caplabtb/dprk/NK_japan.htm#september02.

60. Interview with Kim Hyeon Il, Kyoto, Feb. 24, 2003.

CHAPTER 8 THE CAMPS AND THE REFUGEES

1. This description of Yodok and other details below are based on an interview with Kang Chol Hwan, Seoul, May 11, 2003. Kang is also the author of *Aquariums of Pyongyang: Ten Years in the North Korean Gulag*, New York: Basic Books, 2000.

2. Interview with Kang Chol Hwan. Seoul, May 11, 2003.

3. See, for instance, Philip Gourevitch, "Alone in the Dark," *New Yorker*, Sept. 8, 2003: "Refugees' stories are often treated with suspicion as a source of reliable information on the places they've fled. Desperate people, who have proved willing to risk just about everything to get out, may have reason to exaggerate, or to tell you what they think you want to hear, or to be pushing the agenda of one or another political faction to which they belong. But in the late nineties, as the number of malnourished North Koreans in northeast China swelled from the thousands to the tens of thousands and into the hundreds of thousands, their accounts of the conditions that had driven them to risk their lives and escape had a cumulative authority that defied disbelief."

4. See for example, "I Survived a 10-Year Prison Term in North Korea," undated testimony by a North Korean refugee, and interview with Kim Sang Hun, a South Korean human rights activist who is helping North Koreans escape to the South, Seoul, May 24, 2003.

5. Interview with Kang Chol Hwan. Seoul, May 11, 2003.

6. See http://marmot.blogs.com/korea/2004/02/camp_22_documen.html, and www.freenorthkorea.net/archives/ freenorthkorea/000978.html

South Korean journalists and officials I contacted after the documentary was shown were convinced that the document was a forgery.

7. Interview with Kang Chol Hwan, Seoul, May 11, 2003. See also Kang, op. cit., p. 102.

8. Kang, op. cit., p. 139.

9. Lee Soon Ok, *Eyes of the Tailless Animals: Prison Memoirs of a North Korean Woman*, Bartlesville, OK: Living Sacrifice Book Company, 1999, pp. 70–72, and Murray Hiebert, "Putrid Penal System." *Far Eastern Economic Review*, Oct. 30, 2003.

10. Lee, op. cit, pp. 70–72.

11. "Voices from the North Korean Gulag," in *Journal of Democracy*, July 1998.

12. David Hawk, "The Hidden Gulag: Exposing North Korea's Prison

Camps," report by U.S. Committee for Human Rights in North Korea, Oct. 22, 2003.

13. *Life and Human Rights*, no. 2, 1997 (Citizens' Alliance to Help Political Prisoners in North Korea, Seoul).

14. "Defector's Testimony," mimeograph by Ahn Hyuk, a former political prisoner who escaped to South Korea in 1992.

15. Interview with Kang Chol Hwan. Seoul, May 11, 2003.

16. "5,000 Prisoners Massacred at Onsong Concentration Camp in 1987," *Chosun Ilbo*, Dec. 20, 2002.

17. "Hoeryong Concentration Camp Holds 50,000 Inmates," *Chosun Ilbo*, Dec. 5, 2002. See also John Larkin, "Exposed—Kim's Slave Camps," *Far Eastern Economic Review*, Dec. 12, 2002.

18. "I Survived a 10-Year Prison Term in North Korea," undated testimony by a North Korean refugee, and interview with Kim Sang Hun, a South Korean human rights activist who is helping North Koreans escape to the South, Seoul, May 24, 2003.

19. *Chosun Ilbo*, Dec. 20, 2002, and *Far Eastern Economic Review*, Dec. 12, 2002.

20. Interview with Kang Chol Hwan, Seoul, May 11, 2003.

21. *White Paper on Human Rights in North Korea*, Seoul: Korean Institute for National Unification, 2001, p. 104.

22. *North Korea's Criminal Law*, Seoul: Institute of North Korea Studies, 1991, p. 11.

23. Ibid., p. 24.

24. *White Paper on Human Rights*, p. 29.

25. *Amnesty International*, Issue Brief No. 20, Feb. 2003, "North Korea: A Human Rights Disaster," and "Amnesty Slams North Korea," *Bangkok Post*, May 29, 2003.

26. Hans Meretzki, *Kim-ismus in Nordkorea: Analyse des letzten DDR-Botschafters in Pjöngjang*, Böblingen: Anita Tyke Verlag, 1991, p. 97.

27. http://www.nlg.org/korea/Reports_Statements.html

28. *The Criminal Procedures Act of the Democratic People's Republic of Korea*, Pyongyang: Foreign Languages Publishing House, p. 53. It also states, "The death penalty is executed after the receipt of a death warrant, and the confiscation of property must be carried out within one month of the day of the receipt of the confiscation warrant and be notified to the court concerned." (p. 54.)

29. Ibid., p. 33.

30. "The Real Hwang Jang Yop." Paper by Hahn Ho Suk, president, Center for Korean Affairs, 1998. http://www.kimsoft.com/korea/whang-r.htm

31. Bruce Cumings, *Korea's Place in the Sun: A Modern History*, New York and London: W.W. Norton and Company, 1997, pp. 230–231.

32. *White Paper on Human Rights*, p. 59.

33. See "I Survived a 10-Year Prison Term in North Korea," and Lee Soon Ok, op. cit., p. 103.

34. Kang, op. cit., p. 23.

35. *White Paper on Human Rights*, p. 112.

36. Interview with Arman Dumikyan, local field coordinator for the World Wildlife Fund, Khabarovsk, May 16, 2003.

37. *White Paper on Human Rights*, p. 131.

38. I visited the bridge on the Tuman River on May 22, 2003, guided by a Russian border guard who asked not to be named.

39. *China Rights Forum*, no. 3, 2002.

40. "From Bad to Worse: Chronology of Events Surrounding North Korean Refugees' Situation in China," report by Médecins Sans Frontières, Jan. 2003.

41. Interview with Kim Sang Hun, Seoul, May 24, 2003.

42. *China Rights Forum*, no. 3, 2002, and *White Paper on Human Rights*, p. 126. Also interviews with Kim Mi Ran and Lee Jong Suk, female refugees from North Korea, Seoul, July 27, 2003.

43. *China Rights Forum*, no. 3, 2002.

44. Murray Hiebert, "Putrid Penal System," *Far Eastern Economic Review*, Oct. 30, 2003.

45. Ibid.

46. Alexandre Mansourov, "Giving Lip Service With an Attitude: North Korea's China Debate," in *Asia's China Debate*, Honolulu, Asia Pacific Center for Security Studies, Dec. 2003, p. 9–5.

47. "Urgent Appeal For The Protection of North Korean Refugees in China," Médecins Sans Frontières, Jan. 2003.

48. "Asylum-seekers Want to Go to South Korea, Motives Unclear," *Bangkok Post*, Aug. 2, 2003, and "Five North Koreans Get Suspended Jail After Illegal Entry," *Bangkok Post*, Aug. 10, 2003.

49. "Activist Network Says it Aided Koreans," *Nation* (Bangkok), Aug. 3, 2003.

50. Martin Nesirky, "North Korean Refugees Pose Diplomatic Dilemma," *Reuters* (Seoul), Oct. 14, 2003.

51. *Reuters* (Beijing), Sept. 15, 2003.

52. "More Asylum Seekers 'On Way,'" *Bangkok Post*, Aug. 3, 2003.

CHAPTER 9 THE FUTURE?

1. E-mail communication with Pyongyang-based foreign aid workers after the accident.

2. "Pyongyang silent over details of accident," *Agence-France Presse*, Seoul, April 23, 2004.

3. James Brooke, "Where is Kim Jong Il and What Caused the Blast?" *New York Times* and the *International Herald Tribune*, April 29, 2004.

4. Ibid. The paper went on to quote Robyn Lim, "a conservative military analyst in Japan" as saying, "So let's ask why half the casualties were kids and why so many of them had facial/eye injuries . . . this might indeed be

consistent with the theory that they were lined up." Pictures of injured and very scruffy-looking North Korean children in hospitals in Ryongchon hardly lended credence to the assumption that they had been out to greet a passing dignitary.

5. *Reuters*, Dandong, China/Seoul, April 23, 2004.

6. "Rail Disaster Could Force North Korean Turnaround," *Reuters*, Seoul, April 26, 2004.

7. I visited the Tongil Street market on April 14, 2004.

8. Based on my impressions of Pyongyang in April 2004.

9. E-mail communication with Pyongyang residents, June 2004.

10. I addressed these and other related issues in my cover story about North Korea for the *Far Eastern Economic Review*, May 13, 2004.

11. Siegfried Hecker, "Senate Committee on Foreign Relations Hearing on 'Visit to the Yongbyon Nuclear Scientific Research Center in North Korea.'" Jan. 21, 2004.

12. Jasper Becker, author of *Rogue State: The Continuing Threat of North Korea*, was very dismissive of North Korea's reform program when I met him in Beijing on April 21, 2004. Don Oberdorfer, journalist-in-residence at Johns Hopkins University's Nitze School of Advanced International Studies in Washington D.C. and author of *The Two Koreas: A Contemporary History*, expressed a more balanced view in an e-mail message on April 20, 2004, saying that although there is no guarantee that the changes are not irreversible, "the domestic economic changes in North Korea are among the only moving parts in a diplomatic situation which has seemed unyielding and unchanging for many months."

13. I saw the site which was being cleared for the new market when I visited Pyongyang in April 2004.

14. Conversations with government officials, Pyongyang, April 13–20, 2004.

15. *PRK Korea Trade Directory*, Pyongyang: Committee for the Promotion of International Trade of the Democratic People's Republic of Korea, 2003.

16. *HSBC: Asian Economic Insight*, vol. 117, Feb. 14, 2003.

17. For a discussion about this and other scenarios, see Robert Scalapino, "Korea: The Options and Perimeters," in Tsuneu Akaha, *The Future of North Korea*, London and New York: Routledge, 2002, pp. 9–25.

18. Quoted in Andrew Natsios, *The Great North Korean Famine: Famine, Politics, and Foreign Policy*, Washington D.C.: United States Institute of Peace Press, 2001, p. 117.

19. "What Intelligence Crisis?" *Global Viewpoint*, reproduced in *Bangkok Post*, Aug. 31, 2003.

20. Marcus Noland, *Avoiding the Apocalypse: The Future of the Two Koreas*, Washington D.C.: Institute for International Economics, 2000, p. 231.

21. Kim Myong Chol, *Kim Jong Il: Day of Having Korea United. North Korean Scenario for War and Peace*, Pyongyang: Foreign Languages Publishing House, 2001.

22. Ibid., p. 117.

23. Ibid., p. 121.

24. "Analysis: Japan's Missile Defence," *British Broadcasting Corporation*, Dec. 19, 2003.

25. "U.S. Hawks Look to Korea Post-Iraq," *Far Eastern Economic Review*, May 27, 2004.

26. *HSBC: Asian Economic Insight*, vol. 93, July 4, 2002. See also Ilpyong Kim, *Historical Dictionary of North Korea*, Lanham, Maryland, and Oxford: The Scarecrow Press, 2003, p. 82.

27. Akaha Tsuneo, "Japan's Policy Toward North Korea," in Akaha, ed., op. cit., p. 81.

28. See for instance James Clay Moltz, "U.S. Policy Interests and the Concept of Korean Neutrality," in ibid., pp. 64–76.

29. Interview with Kim Chul Yong and Park Yong, North Korean refugees, Seoul July 26, 2003.

30. Kim Myong Chol, op. cit., pp. 131–132.

31. Quan Yanchi *Mao Zedong: Man, Not God*, Beijing: Foreign Languages Press, first printing 1992, then reprinted twice. The book is based on recollections by Li Yinqiao, Mao's bodyguard.

32. *Far Eastern Economic Review*, May 13, 2004. The figures come from KOTRA (Korea Trade Investment Promotion Agency), a South Korean government agency, and from the Thai Customs Department's website.

33. I met a group of Chinese Koreans in Pyongyang in April 2004. They were private businessmen setting up a joint venture with a small North Korean state corporation to manufacture tiles and sanitary ware. They told me such small-scale joint ventures are quite common these days.

ANNOTATED BIBLIOGRAPHY

Books and Independent Studies

Akaha Tsuneo (ed.). *The Future of North Korea*. London and New York, Routledge, 2002. 178p. A collection of essays by ten South Korean, American, German, Japanese, and Russian authors about possible future scenarios for North Korea.

Becker, Jesper. *Rogue State: The Continuing Threat of North Korea*. New York: Oxford University Press, 2004. 288p. An account of the North Korean famine and its aftermath as well as a critical look at the North Korean regime by a British correspondent based in Beijing.

Bermudez, Joseph S. *North Korean Special Forces*. London: Jane's Information Group, 1988. 160p. A unique account of an important unit in the North Korean army.

——. *Terrorism: The North Korean Connection*. New York: Crane and Russack, 1990. 220p. An excellent overview of North Korea's links to various international terrorist organizations.

——. *Shield of the Great Leader: The Armed Forces of North Korea*. Sydney: Allen and Unwin, 2001. 375p. A detailed account of North Korea's armed forces, intelligence services, and defense industries by an author and lecturer on North Korean defense and intelligence affairs.

Breen, Michael. *Kim Jong Il: North Korea's Dear Leader*. Singapore: John Wiley and Sons (Asia), 2004. 200p. A critical portrait of North Korea's leader written by a Seoul-based correspondent.

Buzo, Adrian. *The Guerrilla Dynasty: Politics and Leadership in North Korea*. Sydney: Allen and Unwin, 1999. 323p. An analysis of factional conflicts within the North Korean leadership, and how Kim Il Sung and his family have remained in power. By a former Australian diplomat in North Korea who now teaches Korean Studies at Monash University, Australia.

Cha, Victor D., and David C. Kang. *Nuclear North Korea: A Debate on Engagement Strategies*. New York: Columbia University Press, 2003.

265p. Arguments for a new U.S. policy of engagement with North Korea by two Asian-American academics.

Cornell, Erik. *North Korea Under Communism: Report of an Envoy to Paradise.* London and New York: Routledge Curzon, 2002. 196p. An insightful account of North Korean politics as well as day-to-day life in North Korea by a Swedish former chargé d'affaires to North Korea.

Cumings, Bruce. *Divided Korea: United Future?* Ithaca, New York: Foreign Policy Association, 1995. 88p. A comprehensive account of South and North Korean politics, and the colonial legacy that has shaped the political landscape on the Korean peninsula.

———. *Korea's Place in the Sun: A Modern History.* New York and London: W. W. Norton, 1997. 527p. An excellent history of Korea from the mid-nineteenth century to the 1990s.

———. *North Korea: Another Country,* New York and London: The New Press, 2003. 241p. An in-depth look at North Korea today and Washington's North Korea policy.

Eberstadt, Nicholas. *Korea Approaches Reunification.* Armonk, New York, and London: M. E. Sharpe, 1995. 180p. The author, a prominent American Korea specialist at the American Enterprise Institute in Washington D.C., examines the possibility of a reunification of Korea.

———, and Richard J. Ellings (eds.). *Korea's Future and the Great Powers.* Seattle and London: University of Washington Press, 2001. 361p. Thirteen scholars analyze South and North Korea's relations with the four great powers of the Pacific: Russia, China, Japan, and the United States.

Feffer, John. *North Korea South Korea: U.S. Policy at a Time of Crisis.* New York: Seven Stories Press, 2003, 199pp. An overview of the current situation on the Korean peninsula. From 1998 to 2001, the author worked with the American Friends Service Committee, Tokyo, to establish a conflict resolution program for Korea, and to facilitate exchanges between the U.S. and North Korea.

Harrison, Selig S. *Korean Endgame: A Strategy for Reunification and U.S. Disengagement.* 409p. Princeton and Oxford: Princeton University Press, 2002. An informative and sometimes very personal account of North Korea's political system and relations with the United States by a former *Washington Post* bureau chief in Northeast Asia.

Henriksen, Thomas H., and Jongryn Mo (eds.). *North Korea After Kim Il Sung: Continuity or Change?* Stanford, California: Hoover Institution Press, 1997. 179p. Papers from a conference on North Korea convened at the Hoover Institution in 1996. By thirteen different authors.

Hunter, Helen-Louise. *Kim Il-song's North Korea.* Westport, Connecticut and London: Preager, 1999. 262p. An in-depth study of North Korean society by a former analyst with the Central Intelligence Agency.

Institute of North Korean Studies. *North Korea's Criminal Law.* Seoul: INKS, 1991. 74p.

Kang Chol Hwan. *Aquariums of Pyongyang: Ten Years in the North Korean Gulag*. New York: Basic Books, 2001. 238p. The author, now a staff writer for the *Chosun Ilbo* in Seoul, was in the Yodok concentration camp from the age of nine to nineteen.

Kil Soong Hoom, and Moon Chung In (eds.). *Understanding Korean Politics: An Introduction*. Albany, New York: 2001. 366p. An overview of Korean politics by a group of Korean and Korean-American scholars.

Kim Hyun Hee. *The Tears of My Soul*. New York: William Morrow and Company, 1993. 183p. The autobiography of a North Korean agent who was responsible for the blowing up of a South Korean airliner in 1987.

Kim Ilpyong J. *Historical Dictionary of North Korea*. Lanham, Maryland, and Oxford: The Scarecrow Press, 2003. 212p. A very useful dictionary of personalities, institutions, and events by a professor of political science at the University of Connecticut and president of the International Council of Korean Studies.

Kim, Solomon, and Tai Hwan Lee (eds.). *North Korea and Northeast Asia*. Lanham, Boulder, New York, Oxford: Rowman and Littlefield Publishers, 2002, 278pp. A reappraisal of the changing relationship between North Korea and its neighbors in the post–cold war era. Contributions by eight South Korean and American scholars.

Kirkbride, Wayne A. *North Korea's Undeclared War: 1953–*. New Jersey and Seoul: Hollym, 1994. 96p. An account of North Korea's covert war against the South by a retired U.S. Army Lieutenant Colonel.

Koo, Hagen (ed.). *State and Society in Contemporary Korea*. Ithaca and London: Cornell University Press, 1993. 258p. Seven of the most highly regarded Korea specialists examine the evolution of state-society relations in both North and South Korea since the end of World War II.

Korea Institute for National Unification. *White Paper on Human Rights in North Korea*. Seoul: KINU, 2001. 142p.

Lankov, Andrei. *From Stalin to Kim Il Sung: The Formation of North Korea 1945–1960*. New Brunswick, New Jersey: Rutgers University Press, 2002. 202p. An account of Kim Il Sung's rise to power by a Russian-born former exchange student in North Korea.

Lee Soon Ok. *Eyes of the Tailless Animals: Prison Memoirs of a North Korean Woman*. Bartlesville, Oklahoma: Living Sacrifice Book Company, 1999. 160p. The author survived six years of brutal treatment in prison before she managed to escape to South Korea in 1995.

Lim Gill Chin, and Namsoo Chang (eds.). *Food Problems in North Korea: Current Situation and Possible Solutions*. Seoul: Oruem Publishing House, 2003. 264p. A group of South Korean, Chinese, and American scholars examine the food crisis in North Korea.

McCormack, Gavan. *Cold War, Hot War: An Australian Perspective on the Korean War*. Sydney: Hale and Iremonger, 1983. 191p. An account of the Korean War by a Australian-born British academic who is more sympathetic to Pyongyang's position than other Western scholars.

————.*Target North Korea: Pushing North Korea to the Brink of Nuclear Catastrophe.* New York: Nation Books, 2004. 248p. An account of the North Korean crisis by a McCormack, which again is more sympathetic to the North's position.

Maretzki, Hans. *Kim-ismus in Nordkorea: Analyse des letzen DDR-Botschafters in Pjöngyang.* Böblingen: Anita Tykve Verlag, 1991. 206p. An insightful analysis (in German) of North Korea's political system by the last East German ambassador to Pyongyang.

Mazarr, Michael J. *North Korea and the Bomb: A Case Study in Nonproliferation.* Basingstoke and London: Macmillan, 1997. 290p. A study of North Korea's nuclear program by the Director of the International Security Strategies Project at the Center for Strategic and International Studies (CSIS) in Washington.

Moltz, James C., and Alexandre Y. Mansourov (eds.). *The North Korean Nuclear Program: Security, Strategy, and New Perspectives from Russia.* New York and London: Routledge, 2000. 276p. Drawing on previously unpublished Russian archival materials, this book is the first detailed history of the North Korean nuclear program by fifteen different authors.

Moon Chung-in (ed.). *Understanding Regime Dynamics in North Korea.* Seoul: Yonsei University Press, 1998. 317p. A collection of papers from a conference held in Seoul, August 1997.

Natsios, Andrew S. *The Great North Korean Famine: Famine, Politics and Foreign Policy.* Washington D.C.: United States Institute of Peace Press, 2001. 299p. A detailed account of the North Korean famine in the late 1990s and why it happened by an administrator of the U.S. Agency for International Development.

Noland, Marcus. *Avoiding the Apocalypse: The Future of the Two Koreas.* Washington D.C.: Institute for International Economics, 2000. 439p. The author, an American economist and Korea specialist, examines the cost of Korea's reunification.

————. (ed.). *Economic Integration of the Korean Peninsula.* Washing-ton: Institute of International Economics, 1998. 282p. A collection of conference papers on trade between the two Koreas, and the state of the North Korean economy.

Oberdorfer, Don. *The Two Koreas: A Contemporary History.* New York: Basic Books, 1997. 472p. An outstanding study of contem-porary South and North Korean politics by a resident scholar at the Foreign Policy Institute of Johns Hopkins University's Nitze School of Advanced International Studies in Washington DC.

Oh Kongdan, and Ralph C. Hassig. *North Korea Through the Looking Glass.* Washington D.C.: Brookings Institution Press, 2000. 256p. An overview of state, society, and politics in North Korea by a Korean-American staff member at the Institute for Defense Analyses (Oh) and a Washington-based consultant on Korean affairs (Hassig).

O'Hanlon, Michael, and Mike Mochizuki. *Crisis on the Korean Peninsula: How to Deal with a Nuclear North Korea*. New York: McGraw-Hill, 2003. 230p. A Brookings Institution Book which examines various policy options for North Korea's nuclear crisis.

Park Jae Kyu (ed.). *North Korea in Transition and Policy Choices: Domestic Structure and External Relations*. Seoul: Kyungnam University Press, 1999. 304p. A collection of papers from a conference held in Seoul, May 1998.

Ryang, Sonia. *North Koreans in Japan: Language, Ideology, and Identity*. Boulder, Colorado, and Oxford: Westview Press, 1997. 248p. An account of the pro-Pyongyang association of Korean residents in Japan by a former member of that community who now teaches at Johns Hopkins University, Baltimore.

Scalapino, Robert A., and Lee Chong-Sik. *Part 1: Communism in Korea: The Movement, Part 2: Communism in Korea: The Society*. Berkeley, California: University of California Press, 1972. 1533p. A very comprehensive account of Korea's Communist movement by a professor of political science at the University of California, Berkeley (Scalapino) and an associate professor of political science at the University of Pennsylvania (Lee).

Suh Dae-Sook. *Kim Il Sung: The North Korean Leader*. New York: Columbia University Press, 1988. 443p. One of the most detailed and authoritative biographies of Kim Il Sung by the director of the Center for Korean Studies at the University of Hawaii.

Suh Jaejean et. al. *White Paper on Human Rights in North Korea*. Seoul: Korea Institute for National Unification, 2001. 142p. A comprehensive report on the legal system and human rights in North Korea.

Vollertsen Norbert. *Inside North Korea: Diary of a Mad Place*. San Francisco: Encounter Books, 2004. 280p. By a German doctor who worked in hospitals in North Korea before he was expelled in 2000 for criticizing the government.

Yang Sung Chul. *The North and South Korean Political Systems: A Comparative Analysis*. Elizabeth, New Jersey, and Seoul: Hollym, 1999. 1013p. A comprehensive study of the political systems of the two Koreas by a member of South Korea's National Assembly and a former president of the Korean Association of International Studies.

Papers and Selected Articles

Babson, Bradley. "The North Korean Economy and Possibilities for Reform." Paper prepared for the Seventeenth Annual Conference on Korea-U.S. Security Studies, Seoul, Oct. 14–15, 2002.

Bartholet, Jeffrey. "Thank Heaven for Kim?" *Time* (Asia), Oct. 20, 1997.

Bermudez, Joseph. "Inside North Korea's Chemical Warfare Infrastructure." *Jane's Intelligence Review*, Aug. 1996.

———. "Ghauri Missile Cooperation." Paper outlining the history of North Korea's missile program, and North Korea's cooperation with Pakistan, May 21, 1998.

———. "Criminalization of the Democratic People's Republic of Korea." *Jane's Intelligence Review*, March 2001.

Bogert, Varroll. "Days of Hunger," *Newsweek* (Asia), May 5, 1997.

Browne, Andrew. "Korea: What Price Reunification?" *South China Morning Post*, July 11, 1996.

Chin Hee–gwan. "Divided by Fate: The Integration of Overseas Koreans in Japan." *East Asia Review*, vol. 13, no. 2, Summer 2001.

Cumings, Bruce. "North Korea: The Sequel." Paper for a Korea conference in Berlin, June 25, 2003.

Eberstadt, Nicholas. "Financial Transfers From Japan to the DPRK: Estimating the Unreported Flows." Paper, undated but written in the late 1990s.

Economist, The. "Greetings Earthlings!" June 15, 2000.

———. "Through a Glass, Darkly." March 13, 2004.

Foster-Carter, Aidan. "'North Koreans' in Japan: a Dying Breed?" *Asia Times* (online), March 17, 2001.

Foley, James. "Prospects for Rapprochement on the Korean Peninsula." *Jane's Intelligence Review*, March 2001.

Hawk, David. "The Hidden Gulag: Exposing North Korea's Prison Camps. Prisoners' Testimonies and Satellite Photographs." U.S. Committee for Human Rights in North Korea, Oct. 22, 2003. A detailed account of North Korea's labor camps based on interviews with refugees.

Hecker, Siegfried. "Senate Committee on Foreign Relations Hearing on 'Visit to the Yongbyon Nuclear Scientific Research Center in North Korea'." Testimony by a senior fellow at Los Alamos National Laboratory, Jan. 21, 2004.

Hiebert, Murray. "Putrid Penal System." *Far Eastern Economic Review*, Oct. 30, 2003.

Hwang Eui-Gak. "How will Unification Affect Korea's Participation in the World Economy?" Paper presented on June 28–29, 1996 at a conference on International Economic Implications of Korean Unification, Seoul.

Joint Interagency Task Force West (U.S. Department of Defense). "Assessment: North Korean Drug Trafficking, May 2000."

Kang Chul Hwan; Lee Sun Ok; Choi, Dong Chul; and Ahn Myung Chul. "Voices From the North Korean Gulag." *Journal of Democracy*, July 1998.

Kaplan, David. "The Wiseguy Regime." *U.S. News and World Report*, Feb. 17, 1999.

Kher, Unmesh. "Accounted for, at Last." *Time* (Asia), Sept. 30, 2002.

Lague, David. "Beijing's Tough Korea Call." *Far Eastern Economic Review*, March 6, 2003.

Larkin, John. "Quest for Secret Tunnels." *Far Eastern Economic Review*, Dec. 5, 2002.

———. "Exposed: Kim's Slave Camps." *Far Eastern Economic Review*, Dec. 12, 2002.

———., and Murray Hiebert. "Cost of Collapse." *Far Eastern Economic Review*, May 1, 2003.

Lee, Grace. "The Political Philosophy of *Juche*." *Stanford Journal of East Asian Affairs*, vol. 3, no.1, Spring, 2003.

Lintner, Bertil. "Another Menace: How The War on Terror Could Change North Korea: Coming In From the Cold?/The Macau Connection." Cover story, *Far Eastern Economic Review*, Oct. 25, 2001.

———. "Paper Trail Exposes Missile Merchants/Pyongyang's Banking Beachhead in Europe." *Far Eastern Economic Review*, Feb. 13, 2003.

———. "Tokyo Begins to Apply Pressure To the North Koreans in Japan." *Wall Street Journal*, March 25, 2003.

———. "It's Hard to Help Kim Jong Il/Japan's North Koreans." *Far Eastern Economic Review*, March 27, 2003.

———. "North Korea's Missile Trade Helps Fund Its Nuclear Program." *YaleGlobal Online*, May 5, 2003.

———. "Dynastic Lies and Secrets/Concealed History." *Far Eastern Economic Review*, July 10, 2003.

———. "Shop Till You Drop: Inside North Korea's New Market Economy." Cover story. *Far Eastern Economic Review*, May 13, 2004.

MacIntyre, Donald. "Northern Exposure/Twilight for Sunshine Policy." *Time* (Asia), Nov. 4, 2002.

———, and Sachiko Sakamaki. "Squeezing the Little Guy: Hungry, Surly and Nearly Broke, North Korea is Suspected of Plundering Japanese Credit Unions." *Time* (Asia), Dec. 6, 1999.

Mansouriv, Alexandre. "Giving Lip Service With an Attitude: North Korea's China Debate," in *Asia's China Debate*, Honolulu, Asia Pacific Center for Security Studies, Dec. 2003.

Moreau, Ron, and Watson, Russell. "Is Your Money Real?" *Newsweek* (Asia), June 10, 1996.

Niksch, Larry. "North Korea's Nuclear Program." Congressional Research Service, Library of Congress, Washington D.C., Jan. 22, 2003.

———. "Korea: U.S.-South Korean Relations—Issues for Congress." Congressional Research Service, Library of Congress, Washington D.C., March 5, 2002.

———. "Responding to Korean Shocks." Prepared for publication in *Sekai Shuho* (Japan), Feb. 6, 2003.

———. "Korea: U.S.-South Korean Relations—Issues for Congress." Congressional Research Service, Library of Congress, Washington D.C., Nov. 5, 2003.

Noland, Marcus. "Economic Integration and Cooperation on the Korean Peninsula." Paper prepared for a conference at Stanford University, California, Oct. 9–10, 2000.

———. "Famine and Reform in North Korea." Paper published by the Institute for International Economics, July 2003.

Perl, Raphael. "North Korean Drug Trafficking: Allegations and Issues for Congress." Congressional Research Service, Library of Congress, Washington D.C., Sept. 14, 1999.

———. "Drug Trafficking and North Korea: Issues for U.S. Policy." Congressional Research Service, Library of Congress, Washington D.C., Dec. 5, 2003.

Schuman, Michael. "Bizarre SAR." *Time* (Asia), Oct. 7, 2002.

Shim Jae Hoon. "No Turning Back." *Far Eastern Economic Review*, June 22, 2000.

———. "The Moral Cost of Engagement." *Far Eastern Economic Review*, Dec, 28, 2000.

Smith, Hazel. "Improving Intelligence on North Korea." *Jane's Intelligence Review*, March 2004.

Smith, Heather, and Huang Yiping. "What Caused North Korea's Agricultural Crisis?" Paper presented on Sept. 6/7, 2000 at a conference at the Australian National University, Canberra.

Solomon, Jay, and Jason Dean. "Heroin Bust Point to Source of Funds for North Korea." *Wall Street Journal*, April 23, 2003.

Solomon, Jay, and Chi Hae Won. "Mysterious Source of Kim's Power." *Wall Street Journal*, July 18, 2003.

Song Du Yul. "Eine verlorene Dekade? Nordkoreas Wirtschaftslage und die sozio-politische Folgen." Paper presented at a Korea conference in Berlin, June 25, 2003.

———. "From Nuclear Crisis to Peace Regime in Korea," Paper from a talk for the Asian Solidarity Network (Toronto, Canada), Aug. 22, 2003.

Song Ji Young. "The Invisible Refugees: North Korean Asylum Seekers in China." *China Rights Forum*, no. 3, 2002.

Speath, Anthony. "Kim's Rackets." *Time* (Asia), June 9, 2003.

Suh Dae-Sook. "Military-First Politics of Kim Jong Il." *Asian Perspective* (Kyungnam University, South Korea), vol. 26, no. 3, 2002.

Vatanka, Alex. "North Korea: Special Report." *Jane's Sentinel Security Assessment*, Feb. 20, 2003.

Wegner, Manfred. "Six Years After German Reunification: What are the Lessons for Korea?" Paper presented on June 28–29, 1996 at a conference on International Economic Implications of Korean Unification, Seoul.

Wolf, Charles. "How Much for One Korea?" *Asian Wall Street Journal*, Oct. 2, 2000.

Zellweger, Kähti. "Caritas in Nordkorea: für menschliche Würde und Gerechtigkeit." Paper presented at a Korea conference in Berlin, June 25, 2003.

North Korean Publications

The Criminal Procedures Act of the Democratic People's Republic of Korea. Pyongyang: Foreign Languages Publishing House, 1992. 56p. The complete text of the new law adopted on January 15, 1992.

The Juche Idea and Man's Destiny. Pyongyang: Foreign Languages Publishing House, 1989. 102p. The official explanation of the *Juche* Idea.

Kim Il Sung: Condensed Biography. Pyongyang: Foreign Languages Publishing House, 2001. 323p. An official biography of Kim Il Sung.

Kim Il Sung: Short Biography I. Pyongyang: Foreign Languages Publishing House, 1973. 444p. The official version of Kim Il Sung's life from 1912–1950.

Kim Il Sung: Short Biography II. Pyongyang: Foreign Languages Publishing House, 1973. 444p. The official version of Kim Il Sung's life from 1950–1972.

Kim Jong Il: Short Biography. Pyongyang: Foreign Languages Publishing House, 2001. 215p. An official biography of Kim Jong Il.

President Kim Il Sung: Interviews and Impressions. Pyongyang: Foreign Languages Publishing House, 1993. 232p. A collection of essays by Japanese writers and politicians.

Songun: Banner of Victory. Pyongyang: Korea Pictorial, 2003. 296p. A photo book depicting the army-first policy of Kim Jong Il.

Tangun: Founder-King of Korea (Collection of Treatises.) Pyongyang: Foreign Languages Publishing House, 1994. 154p.

Baeli, Carlo. *Kim Jong Il and the Democratic People's Republic of Korea.* Pyongyang: Foreign Languages Publishing House, 1996. 158p. An eulogy on Kim Jong Il by an Italian businessman.

Jo Am, and An Chol Gang (eds.). *Korea in the 20th Century: 100 Significant Events.* Pyongyang: Foreign Languages Publishing House, 2002. 212p. A North Korean account of the history of modern Korea.

Keskinen, L. Tapani. *Kim Jong Il: The Genuine People's Leader.* Pyongyang: Foreign Languages Publishing House, 1987. 123p. An eulogy on Kim Jong Il by the Finnish Director of the Board of the International Institute of the *Juche* Idea.

Kim Chang Ha. *The Immortal Juche Idea.* Pyongyang: Foreign Languages Publishing House, 1984. 371p.

Kim Chol U. *Army-Centered Politics of Kim Jong Il.* Pyongyang: Foreign Languages Publishing House, 2002. 98p.

Kim Gang Il. *The Leader Kim Jong Il.* Pyongyang: Foreign Languages Publishing House, 1990. 136p. One of several official biographies of Kim Jong Il.

Kim Jong Il. *On the Juche Idea.* Pyongyang: Foreign Languages Publishing House, 1989. 179p.

———. *On the Juche Philosophy.* Pyongyang: Foreign Languages Publishing House, 2002. 164p.

Kim Myong Chol. *Kim Jong Il: Day of Having Korea Reunified: North Korean Scenario for War and Peace.* Pyongyang: Foreign Languages Publishing House, 2001. 197p. By a pro-Pyongyang ethnic Korean writer from Japan.

Kim Ok Sun. *Kim Jong Suk: The Anti-Japanese Heroine.* Pyongyang: Foreign Languages Publishing House, 1997. 198p. The official account of the life of Kim Il Sung's first wife.

Li Il Bok, and Yun Sang Hyon. *The Great Man Kim Jong Il.* Pyongyang: Foreign Languages Publishing House, 1989. 167p. A collection of anecdotes about Kim Jong Il.

Takashi Nada. *Korea in Kim Jong Il's Era.* Pyongyang: Foreign Languages Publishing House, 2000. 163p. By a pro-Pyongyang Japanese freelance writer.

INDEX

Agreed Framework between the USA and the DPRK (nuclear), 24, 83, 120, 128
Air Koryo, 2, 143, 149
Albania, 44, 78
Albright, Madelaine, 18–19, 25–26
American Association of Jurists, 179
Arab Contractor Osman Ahmed Osman & Co, 115
Arab Organization for Industrialization (AOI), 112–113
Askikaga Bank, 164

Baader-Meinhof gang (Germany), 137
BBC documentary *Access to Evil*, 173
Bell, Peter, 51
Bermudez, Joseph, xii
Bhutto, Benazir, 117
Bhutto, Zulfikar Ali, 117
Boucher, Richard, 150
Brannikov, Victor, 122
Brezhnev, Leonid, 182
Bureau 39 *see* Korean Workers' Party
Burma: 1983 bombing, viii, 139–140; bombing of KAL flight 858, 140;
Bush, George W., viii, 25–26, 27, 93, 190, 195, 196

Buzo, Adrian, xii

Cambodia, 131–134
Cambodian Shipping Corporation, 134
Camp 22 (labor camp), 177
Carillo, Armando, 138
Carter, Jimmy, 25, 83
Ceaucescu, Nicolae, 193
Chang Song Kil, 104
Chang Song Taek: biodata 223; and Three Revolutions Teams, 88; 103; and smuggling operations, 143
Chang Song U: biodata 223; 103
Changgwang Sinyong Corporation *aka* the Korea Mining Development Trading Bureau, 118
Chemical and biological weapons, 126
Chiang Kai-shek, 66

Cho Myong Rok: biodata 223–4; visits Washington, 17; praises the Dear Leader, 95; 96, 100
Chollima movement, 75, 79, 199
Chochongryon *see* Chongryun
Choe Eun Hui, 90
Chongryun: x; 28; 103; 123; 152; Tokyo headquarters, 153–154; and death of Han Duk Su, 167;

and death of Kim Il Sung, 165; gift-sending campaign to DPRK, 161–162; and pachinko, 155–156, 162; schools in Japan, 155, 168; 201

Chosen Soren *see* Chongryun

Chun Doo Hwan, 139

Chun Ki Won, 183

Chung Ju Yung: biodata 224; and North Korean pay-off scandal, 21–22

Chung Moon Hun, 22, 24

Clinton, Bill, 25, 113

Confucianism: "Red Confucianism", xi; 41; 45–46; 79

Cornell, Erik, 46

Crocus Group, 114

Cumings, Bruce, xii, 27, 44, 86

Daesong Bank (Korea) & Trading, 112, 149, 165

Democratic People's Republic of Korea (DPRK): economic growth in the 1950s, 1960s and 1970s, 76; cost of reunification with the South, 2; Christian minority in, 181; collapse of heavy industry, 192–193; famine in, ix–x, 34–37, 48–51, 102; alleged involvement in counterfeiting & smuggling, 5, 148–149; alleged involvement in drug trafficking & production, 6, 144–148, 149, 151–152; missile sales to the Middle East, 7; origin of missile program, 116; new economic policies, 29; nuclear program, 120–125; refugees from, 33–34, 181–183, 185; and terrorism, vii-viii, 135–139;

Deng Xiaoping, 55

Eberstadt, Nicholas, xii

Egypt: missile business with, 111–116; DPRK support for war with Israel, 115

Eom Ho Sung, 20

"Farmers' markets" (jangmadang), 53

Foster-Carter, Aidan, xii

Gakushu-gumi, 163, 169

General Sherman (US ship), 77, 94

Golden Star Bank, 112, 149

Golden Star Trading, 114

Guyana: relations with DPRK, 136

Habbash, George, 135

Habib, Philip, 166

Hamhung Military Academy, 115

Han Duk Su: biodata 224; 157–158, 160, 167, 172

Han Myong Chol, 150

Hecker, Siegfried, 125, 191

Hegai, Aleksai Ivanovich *see* Ho Kai I

Helwan Factory, Egypt, 114

Ho Ka I (*aka* Aleksei Ivanovich Hegai): biodata 224; 69, 71

Ho, Stanley, 7

Honecker, Erich, 44

Hong Il Chun: biodata 225; 105

Hong Kong, eclipsing Macau, 149

Hong Sung Nam: biodata 225

Hossein Mantequei, Brig.-Gen., 116

Hunter, Alan, 138

Hunter, Helen-Louise, xii

Hwang Jang Yop: biodata 225; 80; 121; 180

Hwang Won Tak, 128

Hyon Chol Hae: biodata 225; 109

Hyundai, 15, 20–23, 143

International Atomic Energy Agency (IAEA), 122–123

International Federation for Human Rights, 51

Iran: missile business with, 116, 143

Japanese Communist Party, 157

Japanese Red Army Faction, 131, 135, 152

Jenkins, Charles Robert, 28

Jeung Se Hyun, 188

Johns Hopkins University's School of Public Health, 37

Jon In Chan, 125

Juche idea, 40–44, 45, 75, 76, 79, 82, 109, 163, 199

Kaba, Sidiki, 51

Kader Factory for Developed Industries, 111–114

Kang Chol Hwan, 172, 174

Kang Min Chul, 139–140

Kang Pan Suk, 63, 77

Kang Sok Ju: biodata 225; 26; 28

Kang Tae Gyu, 172

Kang Thae Yun, 118

Kato Hiroshi, 183

Kelly, James, 25, 124

Khan, Abdul Qadeer, Dr.: 118–119

Khan Research Laboratories (Pakistan), 118, 129

Khrushchev, Nikita: criticizes Stalin, 73; criticized by China's Red Guards, 82

Kil Jae Gyong, 150

Kim Bo Hyon, 77

Kim Chaek: biodata 226; 70

Kim Chaek Integrated Iron and Steel Works, 40

Kim Chi O, 139–140

Kim Chol Ju, 64

Kim Dae Jung: kidnapping of in Japan, 166; and sunshine policy, 2, 16, 31, 202; visit to Pyongyang, vii; 13–15; receives Nobel Peace Prize, 19–20; 27

Kim Du Nam: biodata 226; 96

Kim Hyong Jik, 63–64, 77

Kim Hyun Hee, 140

Kim Il Chol: biodata 226; 93, 96, 100

Kim Il Soo, 145

Kim Il Sung (*aka* Kim Song Ju) : biodata 226–7; childhood, 63–64; and Confucianism, 46–47; and Cambodia, 132–133; death of, 83–84, 165; joins the revolution, 65–66; and Han Duk Su, 158; personality cult of, xi, 47–48, 77–78, 98–99; in the Soviet Union, 40, 58–63; returns to Korea, 61;

Kim Jae Kyu, 196

Kim Jong Chul: biodata 227; 107

Kim Jong Il: biodata 227; real and alleged birthplace, 59, 61; alleged lavish lifestyle 88–89; childhood, 86–87; receives Kim Dae Jung in 2000, 13–14, 88; apologizes for abductions, 27, 154; and economic reforms, 197; and "farmers' markets", 54; on the Juche idea, 44; and Malta, 138; love of movies, 89–90; main support base, 100–101; and nuclear issue, 124; takes over, 85–86, 95, 105; youths arrested for criticizing, 176

Kim Jong Ju: biodata 227;

Kim Jong Nam; biodata 227; childhood of, 105–106; busted at Tokyo airport, 107; 108; in Macau 142–143

Kim Jong Oon: biodata 227; 108

Kim Jong Suk: biodata 227–8; in the Soviet Union, 59, 61; as a revolutionary heroine, 77; death of, 88; 107; 199

Kim Kum Jin, 111–113, 124, 165

Kim Kyong Hui: biodata 228; 87, 88

Kim Myong Chol, 194–195, 199

Kim Pyong Il (1): biodata 228; 59, 86

Kim Pyong Il (2): biodata 228;
    alleged rivalry with Kim Jong Il,
    104
Kim Sa Nae, 118
Kim Song Ae: biodata 228; becomes
    Kim Il Sung's common-law
    wife, 88; 97; 104
Kim Song Ju *see* Kim Il Sung
Kim Tu Bong: biodata 228; 68, 74
Kim Won Bong, 63
Kim Yong Chun: biodata 229
Kim Yong Gil, 159
Kim Yong Nam: biodata 229; 96;
    183
Kim Yong Suk: biodata 229; 107
Kim Yong Sun, 96
Kim Yong Yu, 64, 87
Kim Young Sam, 83
Kirpichenko, Tatiana, xiii
Koh Yong Hee: biodata 229; 107
Kohap Group, 16
Koizumi, Junichiro, 27, 153
Korean Development Bank, 20–21,
    23
Korean People's Army: involvement
    in business, 3; 70th anniversary
    of, 93;
Korean War, 70–71, 86
Korean Workers' Party: Bureau 39,
    5, 148–149; factionalism in the
    1950s, 67–73; purges in the
    1950s, 71–74; involvement in
    business, 3; "new" KWP, 98
Koryo Federation System, 197
Kröcher, Norbert, 137–138
Kosun Import-Export (Thailand), 4
Kovalnov, Sergei, 182

Lautze, Sue, 51
Lebedev, N. G., 69
Lee Chong Sik, xii
Lee, Grace; and the Juche idea, 43
Lee Keun Young, 23
Lee Nam Ok, 105–106
Lee Son Ok, 175

Lenin, Vladimir, 45
Li Bo Ik, 77
Libya: missile business with, 117
Lon Nol, Gen., 132–133
Loxley Pacific, 165, 189
Macau, x, 21, 108, 142, 149, 164
Malta, relations with DPRK, 138–
    139
McCormack, Gavan, xii
Manchukuo (Mangzhuguo),
    Japanese puppet state of, 65
Mangyongdae, 63, 78
Mangyongbong, 92, 155, 164
Mansourov, Alexandre, 184
Mao Zedong, 45, 55, 63, 66, 200
Maretzki, Hans, xi, 78, 179
Marx, Karl, 45
Médecins sans Frontieres (MSF), 51,
    185
Meishin *aka* Myongshin, 165
Mikoyan, Anastas, 74
Military First (songun) policy, 95–
    96, 109
Mindan, 158, 166, 169
Mintoff, Dom, 138
Missile Technology Control Regime
    (MTCR), p. 113
Missiles: Hwasong, 116; Shehab
    116; Ghauri, 117;
    Kwangmyongsong; Taepodong,
    126, 162; and threat perception
    in Japan, 128–129, 162
Moon Sun Myung, 16
Mount Paekdu, 60–61, 66, 78, 199
Mu Chong, 63
Mugabe, Robert, 135–136
Mun Se Kwang, 161
Musharraf, Pervez, Gen., 119

National Defense Commission, 95–
    96, 102, 104, 124
National Lawyers Guild (USA), 179
New World Trading Slovakia, 112,
    114
Noland, Marcus, xii, 55

Nonproliferation Treaty (nuclear), p. 122
North Korea *see* Democratic People's Republic of Korea (DPRK)

O Yong Jin, 62
Oberdorfer, Don, xii
Odusan Observatory, 1
Olympics, Seoul 1988, 141
Omar Fahmy, 114

Pak Chae Gyong: biodata 229; 101, 109
Pak Gi So: biodata 230; 100
Pak Hon Yong: biodata 230; 68, 72
Pak Ja Pyong, 21
Pakistan: missile business with, 117–120; nuclear tests, 119
Palestinian Liberation Organization (PLO), 135
Pang Hak Se: biodata 230; 70, 72–73
Park Chung Hee, 139, 161, 166, 196
Peng Duhai, 74
Popular Front for the Liberation of Palestine (PFLP), 135
Prichard, Charles (Jack), 125
Prisons and labor camps, 103
Pu Yi, 65
Pueblo (US ship), 94
Pulikovsky, Konstanstin, 89
Putin, Vladimir, 17

Rajin-Sonbong Free Economic and Trade Zone, 6, 167, 191
Ranard, Donald, 166
Rhee, Syngman, xv, 67, 156
Ri Do Sop, x, 149
Ri Hui Ho, 14
Ri Sun Hui, 111–113, 124, 165
Ri Sung Gi, 75
Rinnai Korea, 16
Roh Moo Hyun, 23, 81
Romanenko, Andrei Alekseevich, Maj-Gen., 69

Ryang, Sonia, xiv, 160
Ryongchon, explosion in 187–188, 200

Samsung, 15
Sandaechuii (or flunkeyism), 44
Scalapino, Robert, xii
Schultz, George, vii
Shim Jae Hoon, xiii
Shin Sang Ok, 90
Shtykon, Terentii Fomich, Col-Gen., 69
Sihanouk, prince and king, 132–133
Smith, Hazel, ix
Soga Hitomi, 28, 37
Song Du Yul *aka* Kim Chol Su: xiii, 55, 80–81
Sonh Hae Rang, 107
Song Hye Rim: biodata 230; 105, 107
Stalin, Josef, xi, 45, 66, 70, 72, 73
Suh Dea Sook, xii, 95, 109
Syria: missile business with, 117

Tanaka Yoshimi, 131–132
Tangun, king, 79
Three Revolutions Teams, 80, 88, 98
Tongjiang Foreign Trade Corporation (China), 3
Tunnels under the DMZ, 101

Ulbricht, Walter, 44
United Arab Emirates: missile business with, 117
United Wa State Army (Burma), 146

Vinalon (fiber), 75
Vollertsen, Norbert, 18–186, 188
Vyatskoye, 58, 59, 86, 199

Wassenaar Arrangement, 113
Wittgenstein, Ludwig, 81
Wolmyongsan Progress Joint Venture (Thailand), 3

Wong Sing-wa, 7
World Festival of Youth and
    Students, 1989, 141
World Food Program (WFP); gets
    involved in the DPRK, 49; and
    other UN agencies, 49–51;
    predicts new famine, 102

Yang Bin, 29–31
Yang Jingyu, 66
Yemen: missile business with, 7,
    134
Yeung, Albert *aka* Yeung Sau Shing,
    6
Yi Sung Yop, 72
Yi Kang Guk, 72
Yodok labor camp, 171–173, 174
Yongbyon Nuclear Facility, 25, 120–
    123
Yook Young Soo, 161
Yu Song Chol, 61

Zhou Baozhong, 59
Zimbabwe, 135–136
Zin Mo, 139
Zokwang Trading (Macau): x; 21;
    142; 150